European Commission

Employment in
EUROPE

1994

Directorate-General
for Employment, Industrial Relations and Social Affairs

Cataloguing data can be found at the end of this publication.

Luxembourg: Office for Official Publications of the European Communities, 1994

ISBN 92-826-8965-4

Printed in Belgium

Foreword

In December last year, the European Heads of State, meeting in the European Summit in Brussels, endorsed a new economic and social strategy for the Community — aimed at ridding it, once and for all, of the scourge of unemployment.

It was a highly ambitious strategy which, in great detail, expounded what needed to be done within the Community if we were to achieve the sort of goal that all of us feel to be necessary — at least halving the present level of unemployment by the end of the century.

That strategy was launched at a moment when Europe was at its lowest point for many years. Since 1990, unemployment had been climbing fast, wiping out virtually all those 10 million jobs we had created in the late 1980s. That was a disappointment, even a disillusionment, on a massive scale.

The scale of our losses galvanised us into action. From the summer of last year through to the early winter, the Commission services had mobilised their knowledge, and their energies, in the search for new solutions, new ways forward. It produced a strategy — simple in concept, but complex in implementation.

The simplicity lay in the view that growth alone was not sufficient to bring us full employment. The ex-perience of the high growth period of the late 1980s — at the end of which we still had 12 million unemployed, very low overall rates of employment compared with the rest of the developed World, and much hidden unemployment — drove us inexorably to that judgement.

We needed more than growth. We also needed to create a more employment intensive pattern of growth — using all the means and instruments available to us. We needed to negotiate the jobs at the level of the industry and workplace — using productivity gains to create more job possibilities, and not just to increase incomes of those already in employment. We needed to develop new labour market incentives — not to punish those struggling at the bottom, but to help them get into work and stay there.

Behind that simple phrase — a more employment intensive pattern of growth — we were laying the foundations for a revolution in the way in which we conduct our lives, we organise our work, and we share income and prosperity across our society.

This report is part of that continuing revolution. It provides further analytical depth to all that we said in the White Paper. In many cases it literally delves where no researcher has delved before, searching out the truth about the way our economies and labour markets work — pointing us in the direction of those actions and policies which could put us back on the path of rising employment.

Since the Brussels Summit, and the Corfu Summit in June, things have progressed. Governments have mobilised. They have posed many questions to themselves, and they have begun to take action. Obviously, we, in the Commission want more, and we want more fast. That is our role, that is what is expected of us. We are realistic, though, in knowing that we are in for the long haul. The White Paper is a medium term strategy for change, it is not a quick fix, overnight, solution.

The other crucial factor, driving us forward, has been the change in the general economic climate. Confidence has returned to the European economy. Money is being spent, money is being invested and we have, at last, halted the rising tide of unemployment. When we set our tack towards a more employment intensive pattern of growth, we all knew that it was built on the premise of growth. Now we have that growth, it makes our objectives more obtainable.

But we must not slacken in our efforts. we must not believe, against all the evidence of the last 20 years, that renewed growth means that we no longer need to address the structural issues which have bedeviled us for so long. President Jacques Delors has said that we must avoid 'conjunctural euphoria' — we must avoid getting carried away by the modest improvements in our economic situation. We must remember, as the White Paper said, that 'an end to recession will not bring an end to employment difficulties'.

We need to build on renewed growth, and extend and strengthen it. We need to use its power to enable us to carry through the structural changes in our employment systems that are so badly needed.

This report is the bedrock for that new process. On it, and its preceding volumes, we have built a sound house — a structure in which we have confidence, and which gives us conviction. It does not carry policy messages as such — although we are certainly considering whether we ought not to do more in that direction in the future. What it does do, however, is demonstrate to all those who read it with an open mind and a clear head, that there are facts and realities that we must take into account in developing policy — that there are ideas that need to be pursued and, most of all, that there are ways forward out of our difficulties.

In this report you will find chapters, not only describing recent and likely future developments in employment, but also those issues around which we have focused our attention in recent months — improving the competitive quality of our workforce, increasing the performance of our labour markets, ensuring better opportunities for those at the bottom end of the labour market, exploring where the new jobs are going to come from — all issues crucial to our continued success.

I recommend the report to you. And I encourage you, in whatever way you can, to join with us in achieving a lasting European, as well as national, solution to our employment difficulties.

Padraig Flynn

Table of contents

Summary and conclusions

After three years of recession, little net job creation and rising unemployment, the immediate outlook for the European economy looks more favourable. Output is recovering and the increase in unemployment seems to have come to an end in most parts of the Community. Favourable developments do not signify, however, that the problem of excessive levels of unemployment is about to be resolved, still less that the failure of the Community to generate enough jobs to employ all those who wish to work — whether recorded as unemployed or not — is a thing of the past.

Despite the short-term improvement in economic fortunes, unemployment remains the major economic problem facing the Community — both now and for the rest of the decade. While the outlook for the remainder of 1994 and for 1995 can be forecast with some degree of confidence, the prospects for the longer-term are highly uncertain.

Whether economic growth can be sustained, and whether this can successfully be translated into jobs, depends in part on whether growth of the global economy continues and spreads. It also depends, however, on what happens within the Community itself. In particular, it depends on how far the long-standing structural problems identified and analysed in the Commission White Paper on *Growth, competitiveness, employment* published towards the end of 1993 can be overcome.

These problems are:

- the lack of sufficient coordination of economic policy in Member States which has led to instability and inadequate rates of economic growth;

- the failure to achieve a sufficiently employment-intensive pattern of growth which has led not only to high levels of recorded unemployment but also to substantial hidden unemployment as people, especially women, have been discouraged by the lack of jobs even to look for work;

- insufficient flexibility of labour markets which has slowed down the structural change in economic activity necessary to maintain competitiveness and led to high levels of long-term unemployment;

- inadequate investment in education and training to improve the skills and capabilities of the Community labour force on which long-term competitiveness ultimately depends.

At the same time, these problems have been accompanied by — and have helped to create — widening disparities and growing social problems in terms of:

- increasing divergences in incomes and job opportunities between those in strong positions in the labour market — because of their skills, and their possibilities for determining and controlling their job prospects — and those in weak positions;

- limited progress in convergence of living standards and job opportunities between people living in different regions of the Union, despite the increasing economic integration of the Member States.

To tackle these problems effectively, the strategy proposed in the White Paper has two basic elements. One is a strengthening of economic growth through the better coordination of national economic policies. The other is a more employment-intensive pattern of production in order to generate more jobs from the economic growth which is attained.

The strategy outlined in the White Paper and the analysis underlying it were endorsed by Member State

Governments at the European Council meeting in Brussels in December 1993 and were confirmed at the meeting in Corfu in June 1994. In addition, the Council identified seven key areas for particular attention by the Member States. These were:

- improving flexibility within enterprises and in the labour market;

- the reorganisation of work at enterprise level;

- targeted reductions in the indirect costs of labour, especially statutory contributions and particularly of less skilled work;

- better use of public funds set aside for combating unemployment;

- developing employment in new areas of activity in connection with new requirements;

- specific measures aimed at young people without adequate training;

- improving education and training systems, especially continuing training.

These key areas for action define the themes of this report. Specifically, the report focuses on the first five of these issues, addressing particular aspects of each in the chapters in Part II. It also touches upon the sixth issue — young people without training — by examining the changing problem of youth unemployment (in Chapter 7).

In many respects, these areas for action do not lend themselves easily to the kind of quantitative analysis which has been the hallmark of the *Employment in Europe* report over the past five years. Indeed, for cases such as labour market flexibility, it is difficult even to define the concepts to be measured and monitored. Nevertheless, it is important to bring as much empirical evidence to bear in order to improve understanding of the way labour markets function and how employment systems — more broadly defined to encompass influences such as education and training and social protection — operate to create jobs and provide work and income for people.

Better understanding is critical to strengthening the basis for policy-making. While much policy action to improve the way employment systems function and to increase job creation is the responsibility of Member States, a major task for the Commission is to provide information and analysis about developments in key areas across the Community on a consistent basis.

This report contributes to fulfilling that task. Like its predecessors, it is deliberately quantitative in its approach, its major aim being to provide a stronger basis for policy-making, partly by reducing the scope for disagreements and disputes about matters of fact on problems to be overcome.

Before addressing the key areas for action in Part II, however, Part I sets out the scale of the employment challenge facing Community countries. It reviews the main employment and unemployment developments over the recent past and the prospects for the remainder of 1994 and for 1995. In addition, it examines why employment in the Community is much lower relative to working-age population than elsewhere and why the labour force could expand considerably in future years, despite the expected decline in the number of young people entering the labour market.

Part I also considers the relationship between output growth and employment growth over the long-term in the Community and other decelopped countries. This is to provide the basis for assessing the prospects for translating growth into more jobs in the future.

The main findings and major points to emerge from the analysis are summarised below.

Employment and unemployment trends

At the latest count, unemployment in the Community stood at more than 11%, significantly higher than in the US, Japan and the EFTA countries.

The employment difficulties of the Community since 1990 are however, reflected more comprehensively in the employment rate — the total numbers employed in relation to the population of working-age. This measure includes the effect of low labour force participation as well as high unemployment. In 1993, it fell to below 58% as employment declined by 2%, the largest fall in the numbers in work since the immediate post-war years. As a result, the average employment rate in the Community is now even further below levels in the US and Japan — in both cases over 70%. Moreover, despite the significant fall in employment in the EFTA countries since 1990, the rate remains some 10 percentage points higher than in the Community.

The rate of unemployment among women remains higher than for men in all Member States except the UK. However, the gap between the two rates narrowed over the recent recession as job losses among men were larger than for women, as is usual in such periods.

How many unemployed?

While harmonised figures for unemployment produced by the Community Statistical Office imply that there are some 18 million unemployed in the Community (including 1 million in the new Länder), monthly figures published in each Member State for those registered as unemployed show a somewhat different picture. This is an important source of confusion, since in some cases — Italy being a prime example — registered totals differ considerably from harmonised totals because of the different method of estimation. Whereas the harmonised totals are based on the Community Labour Force Survey of how many people out of work are both available for, and actively seeking, work — the standard internationally-accepted definition — registered figures for each country reflect a variety of rules and regulations about who should be included.

Not only do the totals differ, but there is only a limited degree of overlap between the people recorded in the two sets of figures. In 1992, some 22% of those counted as unemployed by the LFS were not registered as such by the respective national employment offices, while only 63% of those included in the national figures met the international standard conditions.

The difference between the two measures, moreover, is tending to increase over time, adding to the complexity of the policy debate since it makes it harder to track what is happening to unemployment and to define the target group for assistance.

Short-term economic prospects

Economic growth in the Community as a whole seems to have resumed in the first half of 1993 and, according to the May 1994 forecasts is likely to average $1^1/_2\%$ in 1994 and to increase to $2^1/_2\%$ in 1995. This is unlikely to be sufficient to prevent employment from falling across the Community in 1994 or to achieve more than a very modest increase in 1995.

In most Member States, the rise in the numbers employed is likely to remain below the level required to make any significant impact on unemployment. On the other hand, the depressing effect of a low rate of job creation on labour force growth could help to secure some reduction in the unemployment figures in 1995, though only in four Member States is this forecast to be more than marginal (Denmark, Ireland, Italy and the UK).

Labour force growth and participation

The inadequate rate of net job creation in the Community in relation to the people who want to work is associated not only with large numbers recorded as unemployed, but also with hidden unemployment — not only among women but also among older people persuaded to relinquish their jobs and retire early.

Increasing importance of women in the labour force

The number of women working or seeking employment has increased rapidly across the Community over the past two decades. The growth shows little sign of slowing, still less of coming to an end. As shown in Chapter 2, this has been the main source of labour force growth in the Community for many years. In all Member States, especially those in the South, women will continue to add to the labour supply in future years, representing as much of a challenge for employment creation as reducing present recorded levels of unemployment.

The growth in importance of women has been a feature of all Member States, especially those in the South, where all or almost all of the expansion of the labour force was due to increased numbers of women. The trend has been as pronounced since 1980 as before. Only in Germany, as a result of large-scale immigration, and in the Netherlands, has there been any significant increase in the number of men in the labour force.

While the share of women in the labour force has risen almost as much in the EFTA countries as in the Community, men accounted for some 40% of labour force growth in the US between 1960 and 1992 and in Japan for almost 60%.

The trend increase in the participation of women in the Community, especially among those of prime working age (25 to 49), has been accompanied by a decline in participation among men of the same age — from 97% to 94% — a trend also apparent in the EFTA countries and the US, where almost 10% of prime-age men are not recorded as being economically active at all.

The proportion of both men over 55 and under 25 in work, or looking for work, has declined even more markedly. These three trends have tended to offset the sharply increasing participation of women, so that the average activity rate has changed comparatively little over the past 30 years, giving a misleading impression of stability. Since the reduction in male participation seems largely to have come to an end, the overall activity rate in future years is likely to be dominated by the upward trend in female participation.

Participation of older people

Between 1960 and 1992, the numbers of men in the labour force in the Community over the age of 55 fell significantly as many Member States, faced with rising unemployment, introduced policies of early retirement to free up jobs. While there was also a marked decline in the participation of older men in the EFTA countries, in the US and Japan, participation only fell slightly.

Since the mid-1980s, however, the decline in participation in the Community has slowed down, indicating a possible end of the trend towards early retirement, in response to the escalating costs of the policy with the growing number of older people. Nevertheless, as a result of past reductions, only 6% of men aged 65 and over in the Community were still economically active in 1992, as opposed to 15% in the US and 40% in Japan.

For women, the trend increase in participation has tended to offset the trend towards earlier retirement. There has, therefore, been comparatively little change in the Community in the proportion of those over 55 who are part of the labour force. Nevertheless, the rate of participation among women in this age group is still much lower than in either the US or Japan.

Participation among the young

Since 1960, the proportion of young people of 15 to 19 in the labour force has fallen in the Community from 55% to 30%, as more have stayed longer in education. A similar fall has occurred in Japan and the EFTA countries while in the US, falling participation among men has been offset by increasing participation among women.

For young people aged 20 to 24, a tendency for men to stay longer in education has been coupled in recent years with a similar tendency for women. While, overall, the proportion of those under 25 who are economically active is still tending to decline in the Community, it is already lower than in the EFTA countries or the US.

Participation of women of prime working age

The growth in the participation of women of prime working age (25 to 49) has been the main reason for labour force growth in Western Europe for many years. In the Community, participation rose from 34% in 1960 to 67% in 1992, slightly less than in the EFTA countries and the US, in both of which it was over 75% in 1992. In Japan, the increase was much more modest, though the present rate is similar to that in the Community.

These comparisons suggest that the upward trend in the participation of women in this age group in the Community may still have some way to go, particularly in Member States where rates are relatively low — in Italy, Spain, Greece, Ireland and the Benelux countries.

In Spain, Ireland and Southern Italy, this continuing increase could result in labour force growth of over 3% a year over the remainder of the decade and beyond, posing a considerable challenge for job creation.

Participation and employment

Changes in labour force participation and, therefore, in labour supply are themselves significantly affected by the rate of job creation. Past Community experience clearly demonstrates that the more employment opportunities expand, the greater the increase in labour force participation is likely to be. The act of creating jobs, therefore, tends to encourage more people to join the labour market.

In the three years between 1990 and 1993, as net job creation declined, the labour force expanded only slightly, by under $1/2$% in total, as many people effectively disappeared from the labour force.

As recovery occurs, these people are likely to re-emerge in the labour force figures, taking up a significant proportion of the additional jobs created — as happened during the period 1985 to 1990 — and reducing the impact of employment growth on unemployment.

If, on the other hand, employment creation remains depressed, then these people are likely to stay hidden, neither adding to unemployment nor labour force totals, so continuing to disguise the true scale of the employment problem.

Economic growth and employment

The relationship between economic growth and the process of job creation is of key importance for employment policy in the Community, a strategic objective of which is to raise the employment-intensity of growth.

As shown in Chapter 3, all developed countries, without exception, experienced a marked decline in underlying productivity growth around the mid-1970s, coinciding with the reduced rate of output growth following the first oil crisis. Since then, a much lower growth of GDP has been required to achieve a given rate of employment increase than before.

The increase in employment which has occurred in the Community since the mid-1970s has, therefore, largely been accommodated by a slowdown in the rate of productivity growth per person employed. While this slowdown may seem beneficial from an employment perspective, it is potentially worrying so far as the Community's competitiveness on world markets is concerned.

However, it is in large measure productivity growth in manufacturing, rather than in the rest of the economy which is important, since manufactures still account for the major part of Community trade. To understand employment developments over the past and to assess the prospects for the future, it is essential to distinguish manufacturing from other sectors of the economy.

Changes in employment in manufacturing are even more closely related to output growth than in the economy as a whole. While some reduction in productivity growth in manufacturing has occurred since the mid-1970s, the fall has been relatively small.

In the non-manufacturing sector, on the other hand, annual productivity growth has halved. This slowdown has enabled more jobs to be created in non-manufacturing in the Community since the mid-1970s than in the 20 years before. Moreover, as labour force growth has risen — most notably in the 1985–1990 period — productivity growth has fallen even more. Nevertheless, the reduction has not been enough to compensate for almost continuous job losses in manufacturing and prevent unemployment from rising.

Unlike in earlier years, over the past decade productivity in manufacturing in the US has grown at a faster rate than in the Community. In contrast, average productivity growth in non-manufacturing in the US has barely been above zero since the 1970s — any increase in value-added thereby being directly translated into more jobs.

In Japan, productivity growth in manufacturing has halved from the rates of over 10% a year achieved in the 1960s as output growth has slowed. The decline has been even more pronounced in the rest of the economy giving rise to higher growth in employment over the past 20 years than before and securing a more stable level of employment than in the Community or the US.

A similar tendency is evident in the EFTA countries, at least up to 1990. In these countries and in Japan, the non-manufacturing sector has absorbed those coming onto the labour

market despite lower output growth and, until recently, succeeded in keeping down unemployment. While a similar tendency has occurred in the Community, it has not been strong enough to achieve the same result.

In the US, where underlying productivity growth has also accommodated to the fall in output growth, this has been associated with much more instability in employment — and unemployment. It has also been accompanied by a significant widening of wage differentials (with the average wages of the low-paid declining markedly in real terms over the 1980s).

Productivity, real wages and unit labour costs

Productivity growth affects cost competitiveness through its interaction with wages and the exchange rate. All three variables are, therefore, critical for inflation and trade performance and, through these, for economic growth and employment.

Over the past 20 years, real wages in manufacturing in the Community as a whole have risen in line with the growth of labour productivity and the share of profits in value-added has been broadly maintained. The same has been the case in the four largest Member States.

Since 1980, however, in all of these countries, wages adjusted for inflation have risen by less than productivity and profits have taken a greater share of value-added. This has also been the case in the US, while in Japan, real wages have gone up broadly in line with productivity.

In national currency terms, nominal unit labour costs in manufacturing in the Community increased by twice the rate in the US and Japan between 1970 and 1991, implying in itself a steady deterioration in cost competitiveness. To a major extent, however, exchange rates have compensated for the differences, especially so far as Japan is concerned. Indeed when measured in terms of ECU, unit labour costs in Japan rose at a faster pace than in the Community over the period.

In general, it is exchange rate movements rather than differentials in productivity or wage rises which have been the major determinant of the cost competitiveness of European producers relative to those in the rest of the world, as well as between producers in different European countries. Exchange rate movements have been far from smooth, however, and rates have fluctuated wildly over the past 10–15 years, causing equally wide swings in relative costs of production and almost certainly damaging world trade, economic growth and employment.

Labour market flexibility

The maintenance of the competitiveness of European producers depends on their ability to be able to hire people with the skills they require and to modify the composition and organisation of their workforce in line with their methods of production.

Although the extent to which such an ability exists is difficult to identify, it is important to understand better the way labour markets function across the Community. A key aspect of this concerns the ease with which it is possible to move into a job from being unemployed or inactive and the scale of mobility of labour between sectors. This is the focus of Chapter 4.

Flows into and out of employment

Change in the overall level of employment from one year to the next conceal large movements of people into and out of work. Both tend to vary in some degree with the net rate of job creation, though the rate of exit varies by more than the rate of entry.

Typically, therefore, years of low net job creation tend to be associated more with a high rate of job loss than a low rate of new recruitment.

Women are much more likely to both enter and leave employment than men. Between 1984 and 1992, an average of 9% of women in employment had been unemployed or inactive the year before, as compared with 6% men.

The typical size of movement into employment from unemployment or inactivity varies markedly between Member States. Between 1984 and 1992 the average size of flow was some 2–3 times higher in the UK, France, Denmark, Ireland and, above all, in Spain than in other Community countries.

The difference in rates bears little relationship, however, to employment growth and is only loosely related to levels of employment. In Germany and Greece, only some 4% of those in employment had been out of work the year before as compared with some 10% in the UK and 15% in Spain. The rate of exit shows a similarly large difference.

Entry into sectors from unemployment and inactivity

The rate of entry into services, at around 8% a year in the Community as a whole, was consistently higher than for industry (6%), reflecting differences in the relative rate of job creation. The rate of entry into agriculture was, perhaps unexpectedly, much the same as into industry, and in a number of Northern Member States — France and Germany in particular — was higher.

Within services, the distribution and catering sector stands out as having a high rate of new entrants, almost 10% of those employed in the sector not having had a job one year before.

Within industry, the other manufacturing sector — which includes basic products like textiles and clothing and food processing — had a higher rate of new entry than other areas such as engineering. For all sectors, the rate of entry of women was higher than for men.

Sectoral mobility

The data available only enable movements of labour between sectors of activity to be assessed at a relatively broad sectoral level (NACE 1-digit which is a division of the economy into 11 sectors). On this basis, an average of 4% of those in employment in the Community moved from one sector to another between 1985 and 1992. The proportion, however, was consistently higher in years of high employment growth than when employment rose relatively little or fell. In 1990, for example, 5% of those in employment moved between sectors whereas, in 1992, only $3^{1}/_{2}$% did so.

In this case, the rate of movement between sectors tended to be lower in Southern Member States plus Ireland and relatively high in the North. The main exceptions are Belgium and Germany, where only around $2^1/_2\%$ changed their jobs each year. This compares with a figure of about 6% in the UK — the highest in the Community — and around 5% in France and Denmark.

As might be expected, the rate of movement into agriculture from other sectors was relatively low over the period. Perhaps less expectedly, the rate of movement into industrial sectors was much the same as into services, despite the much lower rate of employment growth.

Within services, the sectors to show the highest rates of entry from other sectors were finance and business services rather than more basic services, while there was little difference between the figures for different industrial sectors.

While there was a tendency for inter-sectoral mobility to be higher for women than for men, the average Community difference was marginal and entirely accounted for by the UK, where an average of $6^1/_2\%$ of women in employment each year changed sectors as against 5% of men.

As might be expected the chances of someone moving from one sector to another decline with age. For young people under 25, an average of just over 7% of those in employment in the Community changed the sector in which they worked each year between 1984 and 1992. For those aged 25 to 49, an average of around 4% a year moved, while for those aged 50 and over, the proportion was only around 2% a year.

Labour turnover

The figures for inter-sectoral movements together with those for the movement from unemployment and inactivity into work provide an indication of the scale of labour turnover in the Community. Between 1984 and 1992, an average of $11^1/_2\%$ of those in employment — more than one person in 9 — had taken on a new job during the preceding year. On average around 60% of those entering a new job were previously unemployed or inactive while 40% had been employed in another sector.

The extent of labour turnover was highest in Spain, with an average of almost one in five of those employed in a particular sector between 1986 and 1992 not having worked in that sector the previous year, and in the UK, where the figure was one in six. Whereas in the former, however, the high turnover is due predominantly to a high flow from unemployment and inactivity into work, in the UK, a high rate of new entry into employment was combined with a high rate of inter-sector mobility. France and Denmark, the only two other countries with a rate of labour turnover above the Community average, were similar to the UK in this respect.

At the other extreme, in Germany and Greece, only an average of one in 15 of those in employment were newcomers to the sector in any year. At the sectoral level, the rate of labour turnover is lowest in agriculture, though even here, an average of 7% of those in employment in the Community during the period 1984 to 1992 had moved into the sector over the preceding year, while 10% had left.

In the industrial sectors, the rate of entry averaged around 10% over the period and in services, $11^1/_2\%$. In the latter, however, the rate of exit was also high, with the probability of someone leaving their job in a service sector being much the same as in agriculture.

Labour turnover among women is significantly greater than among men. Between 1984 and 1992, an average of 15% of women working in a sector had entered since the previous year, while the average figure for men was under 10%. This difference was true for all Member States, but especially for Ireland, the UK and Luxembourg.

In terms of both labour turnover and sectoral mobility, therefore, there are considerable differences between Member States. From this it would seem that the (external) labour market is used significantly more in the UK, France and Denmark than in Germany, Belgium and Greece.

Job turnover

The Community Labour Force Survey for 1992 provides, for the first time, evidence on the numbers of people changing their jobs in a particular year. For the Community as a whole, it indicates that 17% of those in work — one in six — had not been in the present job one year earlier. As with labour turnover, the figure was highest in Spain, Denmark and the UK as well as in the Netherlands, and lowest in Greece and Italy (for which no data are available on and over labour turnover) at under 13%, with Belgium, Germany and Luxembourg having figures only slightly above this (around 15%).

Changes in working time

There has been a long-term tendency for the average time worked by those in employment in the Community, to decline, so contributing to the growth of the number of people in work. Between 1983 and 1992, average hours worked per week in the Community declined by just under 4%, as shown in Chapter 5. However, the fall was only 1% or less in the UK and Italy. In Germany, Belgium and Denmark, it was around 5% and in the Netherlands 13%.

The distribution of working time

In 1992, 58% of male employees in industry and services in the Community worked between 38 and 40 hours a week, while a further 13% worked between 35 and 37 hours. Only 6% of men worked fewer hours than this, while 23% had a working week of over 40 hours. Indeed, 12% of men employed in industry and services in the Community — almost 7 million in total — had jobs which exceeded the maximum which will be allowed on average under the Community Working Time Directive.

Women tend to work fewer hours than men in all Member States, 41% of those with jobs in industry and services working between 38 and 40 hours in 1992 and 49% working less than this. A significant proportion of these — over 4% in total — had a normal working week of under 10 hours, over half of whom usually worked for 6 hours a week or less.

At the other end of the scale, 4% of women employees in industry and

services — 2 million in total — normally worked 48 hours a week or more. While there is very little difference between the distribution of hours worked by men in industry and by those in services, a much higher proportion of women worked less than 35 hours a week in services than industry, reflecting the greater incidence of part-time jobs.

For both men and women, there are marked differences in working arrangements across the Community. For men:

- in Greece, Spain, Italy and Luxembourg, the normal working week in 1992 was 40 hours;

- in France and Ireland, the normal week was either 39 or 40 hours;

- in Belgium, Germany and Denmark, between 37 and 38 hours;

- in the Netherlands, either 38 or 40 hours;

- in Portugal, between 40 and 44 hours, though a significant proportion worked 45 and more hours a week;

- in the UK, 55% of men, more than anywhere else in the Community, worked more than 40 hours a week.

The long hours worked by men in the UK is emphasised by the fact that 28% of those employed in industry and services had jobs involving working 48 hours a week or more, half as much again as in any other Member State in 1992, and three times higher than in all but Greece, Spain, Ireland and Portugal. Accordingly, 44% of male employees in the Community working 48 hours a week or more, outside agriculture, were in the UK.

For women, the pattern of working time varies between Member States in much the same way as for men. Countries can, therefore, be divided into the same groups as regards typical full-time working in 1992. In each case, however, the proportion of women working these hours was much less than for men, especially in the Northern Member States, reflecting the significant proportions working part-time.

Sizable numbers of women in three of these countries — the Netherlands (15%), the UK (8%) and Denmark (6%) — had jobs of less than 10 hours a week, suggesting that employment figures need to be adjusted downwards when making comparisons with other countries.

Changes in weekly hours

The main change in working time at the Community level over the past decade, for both men and women employees, has been a reduction in full-time working hours by one or two hours a week. In 1983, 51% of men employed in industry and services in the Community usually worked for 40 hours a week, and 16% for between 37 and 39 hours. In 1992, only 29% of men worked 40 hours, and 36% worked between 37 and 39 hours. The proportions working either more or less than this changed by relatively little. Nevertheless, the proportion of men working 48 hours or more increased from 10% to 12% over this period.

For women, the proportion with a working week of 40 hours fell from 33% to 17%, while the proportion working between 37 and 39 hours rose from 17% to 29%. There was little change in the relative number working more than 40 hours (10%), while those working under 30 hours a week rose only slightly from 27% to 29%.

Germany, Denmark and the Netherlands showed the largest reduction in full-time hours worked by men, typically from 40 to 37 or 38. In Greece and Portugal as well, there was a marked reduction in normal full-time hours, with the proportion of men with jobs of over 40 hours a week declining considerably.

In the UK, the proportion of jobs with long hours increased between 1983 and 1992. Those working 48 hours a week or more went up from 22% of the total to 28% over the period. Seven other Member States, however, also showed a significant rise in this proportion.

A similar pattern of change across the Community is also evident for women. In Germany, the Netherlands and Denmark, there were marked falls in normal full-time hours. In Belgium, Ireland and Italy, there was also a fall but on a smaller scale. In France, Spain and Luxembourg, full-time hours for women changed relatively little, while in Greece and Portugal, there was a significant reduction in the importance of jobs of over 40 hours a week.

In contrast, in the UK, there was some rise in the proportion of women working very long hours whereas the relative numbers working under 35 hours a week changed hardly at all.

Working hours of the self-employed

A high proportion of people working long hours in the Community are self-employed rather than employees. In 1992, 51% of self-employed men and 42% of self-employed women usually worked 48 hours a week or more,

and only 12% of men and under 35% of women worked less than 40 hours. This pattern is common to all Member States, though it was less marked for Spain, Ireland, Italy and Portugal, where under 50% of self-employed men worked at least 48 hours a week, and more pronounced in Germany and the Benelux countries, where over 60% did so.

For both men and women self-employed, changes in the pattern of working time changed by much less between 1983 and 1992 than for employees.

Part-time working and normal hours

Part-time working predominantly involves women, who fill 85% of all part-time jobs. What is meant by a part-time job seems to vary, however, across the Community. Figures for part-time employment derived from surveys of how people regard their job can differ substantially from those derived from information on hours worked.

In general, in the Northern Member States, there tend to be significantly more people, especially women, reported as working part-time than there are working part-time hours — especially in the Netherlands, the UK and Denmark — while in the Southern Member States, the reverse is the case, especially in Italy.

In 1992, 31% of women regarded themselves as being in part-time jobs in the Community. At the same time, 29% of women worked under 30 hours a week, 25% working what can be termed part-time hours of between 10 and 29 hours. Another 6% of women were employed for between 30 and 34 hours a week, most

of whom, therefore, seem to have regarded themselves as full-time rather than part-time.

In the Netherlands, whereas 59% of women employees were in part-time jobs in 1992, 36% worked part-time hours of between 10 and 29 a week. In the UK, 33% of women employees worked part-time hours, while 44% were in part-time jobs, in Denmark, 37% were classified as part-time, while 23% worked part-time hours.

By contrast, in Italy, Greece and Portugal, the numbers of women classified as working part-time amounted to less than half those working part-time hours. In these countries, therefore, considerable numbers of women working in jobs of under 30 hours regarded themselves as full-time employees. This was also the case in Belgium and Luxembourg.

Thus, while a higher proportion of women employees were classified as part-time in France than in Italy, the proportion working part-time hours was much the same in the two countries in 1992. Similarly, Belgium had almost the same proportion of women working part-time hours as in the UK, and a significantly higher proportion than in Denmark, yet a much lower proportion of women classified to part-time jobs than either.

Much the same is true of men working part-time in these countries, the difference between Member States in the relative numbers working part-time hours being considerably smaller then the difference in the numbers regarded as having part-time jobs.

The rise in the proportion of women working part-time hours between 1983 and 1992 was substantially less than the increase in those with part-time jobs. In only five Member States was the rise in the former more than two percentage points over this period. The implication is that the recorded growth in part-time working since 1983 is due not so much to a reduction in hours as to an increase in jobs for women classified as part-time, relative to ones classified as full-time. even though the hours worked might be only slightly — if any — less.

Second jobs

Only a small proportion of men and women in the Community have more than one job — about 3% in each case. Though there is a greater chance of women having second jobs the fewer hours they work in their main job, in all Member States, apart from France and Portugal, less than 10% of women working under 20 hours a week in their first jobs have a second one.

Unsocial or flexible hours

The great majority of people in the Community work between 8 in the morning and 7 in the evening from Monday to Friday. Jobs which involve working outside this normal time, from one perspective, can be viewed as unsocial, from another, as a sign of flexibility. The 1992 Community Labour Force Survey, which contains estimates of this for the first time, shows that around 5 million men in the Community — 7% — and 2 million women — 3% — normally worked nights, while a further 11% of men and 5% of women sometimes did so.

The variation in Member States in the proportion usually working at night is wide and bears little relationship to the level of prosperity or stage of economic development. It is higher in Germany and Denmark — for both men and women — than

anywhere else in the Community and lowest in the Netherlands. At the same time, the proportion *occasionally* working at night is much higher in the UK than in other Member States, suggesting more flexible working time arrangements.

Half the men and just over 40% of women employed in the Community in 1992 had jobs which involved them working at least sometimes on a Saturday. Unlike night working, Saturday working seems more prevalent in the South of the Community than the North — in Spain and Italy, especially. Again, the relative number sometimes working on a Saturday was higher in the UK than elsewhere (over 40% of men), though it was also high in Denmark and France (over 30%) whereas in Spain and Portugal, under 10% of men and women had jobs which involved occasional Saturday working.

This suggests relatively inflexible working arrangements in the latter two countries. Moreover, the much lower proportion of women sometimes working on a Saturday, in all Member States, also suggests that women generally have less flexible working arrangements than men.

Less than half as many employees in the Community work Sundays as work Saturdays (8% of both men and women usually do so, 15% sometimes).

The pattern of Sunday working across the Community, however, is different from Saturday working, showing little tendency to be more prevalent in the South than in the North. In Italy, where Saturday working is important, the proportion of men and women working Sundays is among the lowest in the

Community, whereas the reverse is the case for the Netherlands. In France, Belgium and Luxembourg, the relative numbers working Sundays were also much lower than elsewhere, while in Denmark, for women in particular, they were the highest in the Community.

The evidence on Saturday and Sunday working seems to demonstrate the importance of social, cultural and religious factors as influences on working arrangements. These affect the pattern of consumer demand for services, and, therefore, the incentive for business to employ people to work weekends. The evidence also indicates that working arrangements are more flexible in some countries than others — the Southern Member States appearing to have relatively inflexible arrangements — and seemingly more flexible for men than for women.

Labour costs, social contributions and taxes

A distinguishing feature of the European economies is the high level of social protection provided through the State or State-supported systems. The financing of extensive social welfare systems has become an increasing matter of concern as regards the possible consequence for competitiveness and the process of job creation.

As discussed in Chapter 6, three interrelated questions are of central importance:

- the extent to which the means of financing social protection systems adds to labour costs and discourages firms from taking on more workers;

- whether a different method of financing would have less effect on labour and production costs and so provide an inducement to increase employment;

- whether a less extensive and costly system of social protection would reduce labour costs.

The impact of employment taxes

The effects in terms of output and employment of increased costs to businesses from the imposition of social contributions and taxes cannot be judged simply on the basis of their initial incidence. It is important to consider how far they are passed on by businesses in higher prices or lead to the wages paid to employees being lower, as opposed to being absorbed in lower profits. This will tend to vary between economic sectors of activity and between individual firms.

It is also important to recognise, when making comparisons between Europe and the US and Japan, that large companies in particular often contribute significant amounts to private schemes of social protection for their employees. Moreover, these may not always show up as social contributions — or non-wage labour costs — but may be consolidated in pay schedules.

The effects of any reduction in social contributions on labour and productivity costs are not easy to assess once account is taken of the effect of compensating for revenue lost by raising other forms of tax or by reducing social expenditure.

Nevertheless, whatever the effects over the long-term once economic forces have fully worked themselves out, in the short and medium-term, any substantial reduction in social contributions may provide a significant incentive for job creation. This is particularly so because of the scale of the tax "wedge" between what employees receive in net earnings and what employers pay to employ people, implying both a possible deterrent to employment and an incentive to avoid, or evade, paying taxes and contributions. This may apply especially to workers at the lower end of the pay scale. (For this reason, the Commission has suggested reducing the combined rate of tax and contributions on employment, especially that of less skilled workers, by 1–2% of GDP.)

Rates of taxes and contributions

The rate of social contribution paid by employers — including both statutory and voluntary contributions — averaged 22% of total labour costs in 1991 for an employee receiving the average wage paid to male workers in manufacturing. It varied, however from close to 30% of labour costs in France, Italy and Belgium to under 15% in the UK and under 5% in Denmark. This variation is largely due to differences in the statutory element of contributions, though this itself varies from 60% in the UK and Ireland to over 95% in Belgium and Italy.

In the US, social contributions amounted to 21% of labour costs in 1991 and in Japan, to 15%.

While the rate of social contribution has risen in some Member States in recent years, it has fallen in others. Only in Belgium did it rise by more than 1% of labour costs (for someone on average male earnings). In the UK and Denmark, the rate was reduced significantly. In Japan, the rate increased over the same period, but only by around 1% of labour costs.

The relative stability in the Community in respect of someone on average male earnings may, however, conceal changes at different earnings levels. In particular, since 1991, and since mid-1993 especially, a number of Member States have reduced contributions on young employees in an attempt to increase the incentive to businesses to employ them.

Differences between the Community and the US and Japan seem more pronounced in respect of employees' contributions and taxes on wages. These amounted to around 10–15% of labour costs in 1991 in the latter two cases and over 20% in the Community. With employers' contributions, they averaged 45% of labour costs in the latter in 1991 in respect of the average wage of a male worker in manufacturing. This represents a significant wedge between the cost of employing labour to companies and the net earnings which workers receive.

The size of the wedge for someone on average male earnings varied broadly with GDP per head, from over 50% of labour costs in Belgium, Germany and the Netherlands in 1991 and only slightly below this in Denmark and France to under 40% in the UK, Spain, Portugal and Greece. In Luxembourg, however, it was the smallest in the Community at little more than 30% of labour costs.

In the Community as a whole, the wedge was reduced somewhat between 1985 and 1991 — by almost 2% of labour costs. Only in France, Belgium and Portugal was there an increase — in each case by less than 2% of labour costs — while in Luxembourg, the UK and the Netherlands, there were significant reductions.

Labour costs and earnings

The average monthly cost of employing a male manual worker in manufacturing in the Community in 1991 varied from around 2,750 ECU in Germany, and just over 2,500 ECU in Belgium, to under 1,000 in Greece and under 600 in Portugal. These differences broadly correspond with differences in value-added. In terms of net earnings, however, the differences are narrower because of the high taxes and contributions in the high income countries.

In most Member States, both employers' and employees' social contributions are proportional to earnings up to a certain level and then become regressive, in the sense that the rate declines as earnings increase. This generally happens, however, only at relatively high earnings levels.

This contrasts with taxes on wages which are mainly progressive at most income levels, the major exception being Greece where rates are proportional over a wide range of earnings. The UK is the only country in the Community with progressive contribution rates, while Belgium and Portugal, where rates are proportional to earnings, are the only other Member States where rates are not regressive at some level of earnings. In 9 of the Member States, therefore, non-wage labour costs imposed by governments bear proportionately more in respect of workers at the bottom scale than at the upper end of the earnings scale.

Tax and contribution rates for men and women

Single women are treated the same as single men for tax and contribution purposes in all Member States, though tax rates for women are generally below those for men because their earnings are significantly less. The relative cost of employing a woman on average earnings in manufacturing was 28% less than a man in 1991, though in Denmark, it was only 15% less and in France 20% less, as compared with around 40% less in the UK and Ireland.

Between 1985 and 1991, the gap between the average labour costs for men, and those for women, remained virtually unchanged across the Community, declining only in France and widening in Germany and the Benelux countries. The incentive to employ women as opposed to men, therefore, remained much the same over this period.

In four countries, Belgium, France, Ireland and Portugal — especially the latter two — women who are married effectively paid more tax in 1991 than single women, which may represent some disincentive for married women to seek work.

Marginal tax rates

Progression in the combined tax and contribution rate means that marginal rates are above average rates in most countries. As employers increase the wages paid to their workers, progressively less of the increase goes to the employee and more to the State, so potentially affecting the incentive to work and the inducement to reward higher levels of productivity.

This potential effect was greatest in 1991 in Belgium, where the combined marginal rate was 63% on earnings between 80% of average earnings and the average level. This means that twice as much of any increase in earnings goes to the State as to the employee. The marginal rate was almost as high in Ireland and Germany (both above 60%). Only in five Member States — Luxembourg, and the UK as well as Spain, Greece and Portugal — was the marginal rate below 50%.

With the exception of Belgium and France, the combined marginal rate declined between 1985 and 1991, though the fall was small in Spain, Portugal and Ireland, with the largest fall — over 5 percentage points — occurring in the Netherlands and Greece.

Marginal rates in the Community are higher than in the US (around 40%) and Japan (30%). For lower paid workers, it was lower still in the US, because of the low level of statutory social contributions, with employers able to take on workers at costs not much greater than the net earnings they receive.

Given that a high proportion of the unemployed are low skilled, labour costs at the bottom end of the scale are particularly relevant. The challenge for policy is to bring about a reduction in the costs of employing low skilled workers such as to encourage employers to take on such people, while avoiding any significant reduction in their already low take-home pay.

Low pay and poverty

The importance of safeguarding the most disadvantaged on the labour market — many of whom are women — is emphasised by the fact that low pay seems to be associated with poverty in many Member States. Towards the end of the 1980s, almost 10% of households with at least one member working had a level of expenditure below 50% the average for households in the country concerned — which can be taken as a very approximate indicator of poverty in a relative sense. Moreover, 30% of these households had at least two members in work.

Whereas low pay is not the primary source of poverty in any Member State except Portugal, in a third of households with expenditure below 50% of the national average in 1988, the head was in paid employment. Of these, 30% were households where the head was self-employed, significantly greater than the proportion of self-employed in total employment.

Low pay tends to be a more important source of poverty in the Southern Member States than in those in the North, over 40% of the households with low expenditure in Greece, Spain and Italy and over 50% in Portugal having the head of the household in paid employment — in many cases in self-employment.

Unemployment and labour market policies

Labour market policies can help bring down unemployment across the Community. However, in order to be effective, they need to be adapted to the characteristics of the unemployed in different parts of the Community.

Youth unemployment

In the 1980s, youth unemployment was an acute problem. However, the combined effect of the measures introduced to combat the problem, coupled with high employment growth and a fall in the numbers of young people aged under 25, reduced the unemployment rate between 1985 and 1990 by over 5% of the youth labour force, much more than the fall in the rate of adult employment. Since 1990, the gap between the youth and adult unemployment rate has changed little. Whereas the rate among young women has risen only slowly since 1990, however, that for young men has increased sharply — more than for any other section of the labour force.

The average rate of youth unemployment in the Community — of 21% in May 1994 — remains double that of those over 25. In Italy, at 33%, and in Greece, at 23%, it was more than four times the adult rate. Although the gap between youth and adult unemployment was much less than this in Spain, the rate of youth unemployment was nevertheless some 38%, with some regions having rates well over 40%.

Changes in youth unemployment need to be judged, however, in terms of the number of young people under 25, whose numbers declined by 1% in the Community between 1985 and 1992. At the same time, rates of participation in the age group also fell (as detailed in Chapter 2), so that the youth labour force declined by 2%. The fall in participation more than offset the growth in the number of young people in the Member States where this occurred — Italy and Portugal, in particular. Only in the Netherlands did the number of people under 25 in the labour force expand.

To the extent that falling youth participation rates reflect more people staying longer in education and training, this can be seen as a potential benefit. It is difficult to judge how far this is in fact the case, however, because of differences between Member States in what is meant by education and training and, conversely, in how far young people are counted as being part of the labour force. The large variations in participation rates which exist across the Community may, therefore, reflect differences in classification rather than genuine differences.

Because of this, youth unemployment may be better measured by relating the numbers of young unemployed to the total numbers of those under 25, rather than in terms of the number that happen to be included as part of the labour force. On this measure, the unemployment rate in Spain is reduced to 20% and that in Italy to 17%, with Ireland having a rate of 15% and Greece, France, the Netherlands and the UK, rates of around 10%.

Whereas youth unemployment rates as conventionally measured were higher in May 1994 in France and Belgium than in the Netherlands and the UK, this largely reflects the much smaller numbers recorded as part of the youth labour force in the former two countries. In relation to population, youth unemployment was much the same in the four countries.

The overall effect of these changes is that, while young people under 25 accounted for 43% of the total unemployed in 1985, by May 1994 they represented only 32%.

Long-term unemployment

Long-term unemployment, which rose significantly during the first half of the 1980s, has also tended to decline since 1985, though it remains substantial. The proportion of the unemployed who had been out of work for a year or more fell from 52% to 43% between 1985 and 1992 — though it may well have risen somewhat since then. The fall was especially marked in Spain (60% to 45%) and Portugal (53% to 30%), reflecting their strong employment growth. In Greece, where there was little rise in employment, long-term unemployment increased (from 43% to 50%).

The proportion of long-term unemployed who are under 25 declined from 37% to 26% between 1985 and 1992 in the Community as a whole. In all Northern Member States except the UK and Ireland, the proportion was 15% or less in 1992 and in Germany, Denmark and Luxembourg, under 10%. In the North, therefore, the problem of long-term unemployment now predominantly affects older age groups, while in the South — where the share of long-term unemployed under 25 was still 30% or more — the problem of long-term and youth unemployment are still closely associated.

Methods of job search

The methods used by the unemployed to find work vary markedly across the Community. In many Member States, a high proportion of the unemployed, as defined by international conventions, are not registered at labour offices. They, therefore, have no contact with public employment services and rely on other methods of finding jobs. Even in countries where most of the unemployed are registered, they do not necessarily use these services as the primary means of finding employment.

In Germany and Spain, around 90% of the unemployed — both men and women — relied on a public employment services to find work in 1992, while in France over 80% did so. Elsewhere, only in the Netherlands did a significant majority of the unemployed use these services as their main method of job search. In Belgium, the figure was under 40%, in the UK and Portugal 30%, in Ireland under 20% and in Greece under 10%, the figures being much the same for women as for men.

Looking at newspaper advertisements or placing an advert was the most widely used method in most countries other than using the employment services (40% relied on this in the UK and Ireland). In Portugal and Greece asking friends, relatives and other acquaintances was also widely used.

In general, therefore, less formal and less organised methods of job search are more important than the use of public employment services in most Member States. Moreover, use of the latter seems to have declined in importance since 1985, possibly reflecting in part the tightening of regulations governing who can register as unemployed.

Labour market expenditure

Public expenditure on labour market measures in the Member States aimed at assisting the unemployed find work, or maintain their income levels, amounted to around 3% of Community GDP in 1992. Of this, over half went to income support and another 10% to funding early retirement schemes.

Little more than 1% of Community GDP was devoted to active measures aimed at getting the unemployed into work, half of which went on training and youth programmes, with job subsidies, payment to the disabled and the public employment services accounting for most of the remainder.

The last item accounted for 15% of active expenditure — under 0.2% of GDP. Only in Germany and Belgium did employment services account for more than this. In the four Southern Member States, as well as Denmark, spending amounted to only around 0.1% of GDP or less, and not much more in France and Ireland.

Between 1985 and 1992, public expenditure on labour market measures in the Community changed by little, though there was some shift to active measures — partly reflecting the fall in employment between these two years — especially on training, youth programmes and job subsidies.

The scale of expenditure on active measures varied substantially between Member States, ranging from 1.8% of GDP in Denmark and over 1% in Ireland and Germany (mainly reflecting the scale of support given in the new Länder) to under $1/2$% of GDP in the UK, Luxembourg, Spain and Greece. While expenditure on active measures increased relative to GDP in 8 Member States between 1985 and 1992 — especially in Germany where it doubled — it fell in the UK, Ireland and Luxembourg and, in Belgium, it remained unchanged.

In terms of expenditure per unemployed person, spending on passive measures varied between Member States in line with GDP per head. Between 1985 and 1992, it changed by little in real terms.

Active expenditure per unemployed person in 1992 varied between Member States in a similar way to passive expenditure, with the level in Luxembourg, Denmark and the Netherlands being much higher than the Community average and the level in Southern Member States much lower, with spending in the UK and Ireland (where expenditure relative to GDP is relatively high reflecting the high rate of unemployment), also being below the average.

Between 1985 and 1992, real expenditure per unemployed person on active measures increased in real terms in the Community as a whole, the rise being most pronounced in Germany, Spain and Portugal.

Between 1985 and 1990, expenditure on active measures per unemployed person rose in real terms in most countries. Between 1990 and 1992, however, as unemployment began to rise again, it fell in all countries apart from Germany, the Netherlands and Portugal, the decline being especially marked in the UK, where real spending on training per person unemployed halved.

In sum, therefore, there are pronounced differences between Member States in expenditure on active measures per person unemployed, which do not just reflect differences in GDP per head, but partly differing policies and approaches. Overall, however, in most countries in the early 1990s, the real value of the support to the unemployed to find work declined.

The structure of employment across the Community

Although it is well known that services in the Community now account for most jobs, there is a dearth of information on the precise activities in which these jobs are located. Some indication, however, can be obtained from the Community Labour Force Survey, even though the small sample on which this is based means that the details are only approximate.

This shows that, in 1992, there were more people employed in construction in the Community than in agriculture; business services employed almost as many people as agriculture, while as many were employed in leisure, arts and cultural activities as in the motor vehicle industry. Half as many again were employed in personal services, such as hairdressing or dry cleaning, as in iron and steel production.

There are marked variations in the structure of employment between Member States, reflecting cultural and other differences, which emphasise the difficulties of generalising about potential areas of job creation.

In Germany, for example, 50% more of the workforce are employed in engineering and motor vehicles than elsewhere, whereas in the less developed Southern Member States, these industries account for a very minor proportion of employment. On the other hand, the proportion employed in textiles, clothing and footwear in the latter countries, especially in Greece and Portugal, is some way above that in the rest of the Community.

Within services, the importance of retailing tends to be inversely related to income per head — the proportion employed being particularly small in France and Denmark.

Employment in domestic services follows a similar pattern, being much higher in Spain and Portugal than anywhere else, though it is also significant in France. Social services show an opposite tendency (accounting for 7–8% of total employment in Denmark and the Netherlands, but only 1% in Spain and Greece and $1/2$% in Portugal). Health care is similar but with less extreme variations, as is education, while employment in business services also tends to vary with income per head. By contrast, there is no clear pattern in respect of leisure, arts and culture, where the proportion employed was high in Denmark, the Netherlands and, especially, the UK, and low in Belgium and Germany, as well as Portugal.

Areas of job growth, 1985 to 1992

Most of the increase in employment in the period of high net job creation between 1985 and 1990 occurred in services, though unlike in years of low net job creation, industry also accounted for a significant part of the employment growth in a number of countries.

Over the Community as a whole, business services made the largest contribution to employment growth, accounting for almost one in five of the net addition to jobs. Employment in social and sanitary services, leisure, arts and cultural activities and travel and estate agents also increased markedly (by over 5% a year). On the other hand, the sector with the largest decline in jobs (6% a year), sea and inland water transport, was also in services, while employment in railways also declined significantly (by 3% a year).

Within industry, 14 of the 22 separately defined industrial sectors showed an increase in employment at the Community level over this period, with net job creation in office machinery, mechanical engineering, rubber and plastics and construction averaging 3% a year — more than in many services. These 14 industries accounted for 25% of total employment growth in the Community over this period (over 40% in Germany and Spain).

Changes in employment 1990 to 1992

Employment in industry fell significantly in the Community during the recession years between 1990 and 1992, reinforcing the continuing decline in agriculture and offsetting all the net job creation in services. Only five of the 22 industrial sectors showed an increase in employment. All the high growth sectors between 1985 and 1990 experienced substantial losses between 1990 and 1992, apart from mechanical engineering.

Unlike in industry, employment in services continued to expand between 1990 and 1992, with only 9 out of 25 sectors experiencing a decline in jobs, though some of these (estate and travel agents and research and development institutes) had been among the fastest growing sectors before 1990.

As in industry, the difference in the rise in employment between the high growth and recession period was most pronounced in what had been the fastest expanding sectors.

Recession, therefore, seems to hit employment in growth sectors disproportionately hard.

Long-term employment growth in the Community and elsewhere

Available data suggest that the areas of job growth in the Community over the past 20 years have been much the same as in US, Japan and the EFTA countries.

The most striking difference is not the areas where employment has risen but the scale of job losses which have occurred in declining sectors. This seems largely responsible for the lower overall rate of employment growth in the Community than elsewhere. The contribution to job growth made by services was almost identical in the Community to that in Japan and the EFTA countries. Half these jobs in the Community were in communal and personal services, as was the case elsewhere.

On the other hand, the reduction in jobs in agriculture was much greater in the Community than in the US, while there were also substantial job losses in industry in which employment rose in the US and Japan. Since these job losses were predominantly in the private sector, they partly offset the expansion of jobs in private services. As a direct result, a much higher proportion of net job creation in the Community was in the public sector than was the case in the US and Japan.

Comparing the high job creation period in the Community between 1985 and 1990 with other years demonstrates that the main dif-

ference was the fact that employment in industry rose between 1985 and 1990 and fell markedly in other years. This factor, rather than the faster growth of employment in services, accounts for two-thirds of the difference in the overall rate of net job creation between the first and second halves of the 1980s. This applies equally to individual Member States. While industry is unlikely to be a major source of job growth in future years, the extent of any changes in this sector are likely to have a major impact on the extent to which employment as a whole increases.

Changing skill needs in the Community

Not only is the structure of employment changing across the Community but so also is the nature of work. While the growth of services is leading to an expansion in the demand for highly-skilled labour, it is also creating a significant number of low-skilled jobs.

Overall, however, there seems to be a shift in occupational structure towards more skilled jobs. Between 1983 and 1991, the numbers classified as professional and technical workers in the Community expanded by over $2^1/2\%$ a year, as compared with a growth of total employment of just over 1% a year. At the same time, there was a decline of $2^1/2\%$ a year in the number of agricultural workers and $^1/2\%$ a year in production and transport workers. Professional and technical jobs, which accounted for only 15% of the total in 1983, were responsible for 40% of the overall rise in employment.

The shift in occupational structure was much more marked in periods of low employment growth than in high growth years. Indeed, in the low growth years (1983 to 1985 and in 1991), the increase in numbers in professional and technical jobs was only slightly less than between 1985 and 1990, and accounted for most of the small rise in employment. By contrast, production and transport jobs declined significantly in low growth years, but rose between 1985 and 1990. Much the same was true of clerical and related jobs, which were responsible for as much of the net job creation during these years as professional and technical jobs (30%).

This evidence implies that in periods of recession, it is the lower grade jobs which tend to be reduced, whereas in periods of expansion, such jobs account for a relatively high proportion of overall employment growth. The pace of change in occupational structure and the shift towards higher skilled occupations seem to depend, therefore, on the prevailing economic climate.

Occupations of men and women

Over the Community as a whole in 1992, a much higher proportion of men than women were classified as managers and legislators ($9^1/_2$% as against 6%). This holds true for all Member States, the difference being relatively uniform if the self-employed are excluded. For professional jobs, the proportions of men and women were broadly the same, while, in the case of technicians, the proportion of women was in most cases higher than that of men. Much the same proportion of women as men were, therefore, employed in these three relatively high grade occupational groups in 1992.

Employment in small and medium-sized firms

Most of the people employed in the Community work in small firms. In 1991, firms of less than 100 employees accounted for 55% of those employed in the private sector in the Community and firms of under 10 employees for about 30%. This is much the same as in Japan.

Small firms, however, are much more important in the Southern Member States than in the North of the Community, though Denmark is an exception. In Spain, firms of under 100 employees were responsible for 74% of private sector employment in 1991, in Italy, 69% and in Portugal, over 60%. In Belgium and Germany, however, they accounted for only 46% of the total and in the UK and Luxembourg, less than half.

Small firms are much less important in the Community in manufacturing than in services. In 1991, under 40% of those employed in manufacturing worked in firms of under 100, as against 60% in the case of services. In Japan, though the same phenomenon is evident, small firms account for a higher proportion of employment in manufacturing than in the Community (providing 45% of jobs), reflecting the prevalence of sub-contracting by large corporations. Similarly, in the South of the Community, small firms provide proportionally more jobs in manufacturing than in the North (60% in Italy and Spain as opposed to under a third in the UK and 28% in Germany).

In private sector services, over half of employment was in firms of under 100 in all Member States, except Belgium (where the data exclude the self-employed), and in Spain and Italy, over 75%. Within services, small firms account for over half of jobs in the two main growth sectors — other services (mainly personal services in this case) and business services.

Part I   Employment developments

Chapter 1   Employment trends and prospects in the Community

Economic recovery is now underway in the Community. Though unemployment is levelling off, it is likely to remain a major problem for some time to come. In the longer-term, it is uncertain whether the rate of job creation will be sufficient to increase employment to adequate levels.

Introduction

After a period of high employment growth in the second half of the 1980s, the Community has experienced a period of three years since 1990 when the numbers in work have progressively declined and unemployment has increased sharply. Although the decline in employment seems to have slowed significantly in 1994 and the outlook is gradually improving, there remains an important question-mark over the pace of recovery and how long it will last. In particular, the key issue is whether the rate of employment growth will return to the levels achieved before the onset of the present recession for long enough to have a major impact on the present rate of unemployment.

The failure of the Community to create jobs since 1990 is reflected in the employment rate — the ratio of the numbers employed to the population of working age, taken as 15 to 64 — which in 1993 declined to 58% from 60% three years earlier (Graph 1). While employment has fallen — by an estimate of almost 2% in 1993, the largest reduction in a single year since the 1950s —

working-age population has continued to grow, even if slowly. At the same time, the trend towards an increasing proportion of women of working-age to want to work has been held back by lack of jobs (see Box, p 28, for details of the employment rate).

As a result, the employment rate in the Community is now even further than ever below that in the US and Japan, which in both cases is over 70%. In the US, the rate increased again in 1993 as the economy recovered from recession while the rate of job creation rose sharply and

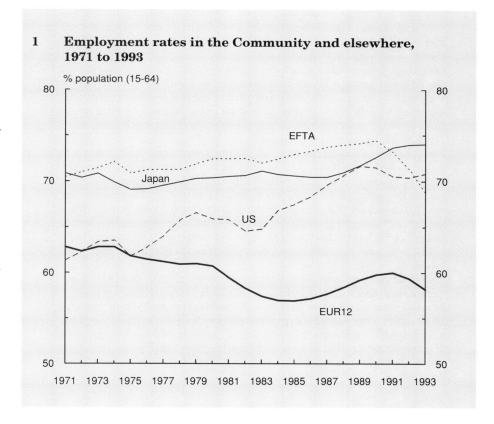

1   Employment rates in the Community and elsewhere, 1971 to 1993

% population (15-64)

The employment rate

The employment rate is a measure of an economy's success in creating jobs, taking its working-age population as a benchmark. Like any aggregate measure, however, it is inevitably relatively crude and needs to be interpreted with caution. In particular, it is important to know the underlying reasons for any change in employment rates over time, or for any differences between economies, before comparative performance can be unambiguously assessed.

Employment rates, being simple ratios of total employment to working-age population, are affected, in the first place, by differences in the importance of part-time working and in average working-time. Secondly, they are affected by differences in the number of people above working age who are in work. Since these people are included in the employment figures but not in the working-age population figures, an economy with high numbers of people above retirement age still in work may have a high employment rate but not necessarily a high proportion of its working-age population in work. As shown in Chapter 2, comparisons of the Community with Japan, in particular, are significantly affected by this.

Even if the comparison is confined to people between the ages of 15 and 64, perceived differences between economies can still be misleading. This is particularly the case for the lower age groups, where a low rate of employment, and of labour force participation, may reflect a high rate of participation in education or training. Such a configuration would generally be regarded as favourable rather than as a sign of failure to create adequate numbers of jobs. On the other hand, a high proportion of young people may be in education or training because the economy is unable to provide employment. The proliferation of training schemes for young people during the 1980s as youth unemployment rose and the encouragement given to stay longer in education were motivated by a desire to increase skills and qualifications for work, but they also reflected the lack of jobs.

Older age groups also pose potential problems, in the sense that if the effective age of retirement is below 65, this will also tend to reduce the employment rate as measured. From one perspective, this can be regarded as a favourable feature rather than as a weakness, since it can signify that an economy is capable of supporting a relatively high proportion of people in retirement.

From another perspective, however, it might imply that the economy is failing to create sufficient jobs to keep such people in employment. The early retirement schemes introduced in many Member States since the mid-1970s were motivated largely by a desire to free up jobs for other age groups, especially the young, rather than to benefit older people. What matters in this regard is that older people should have a choice of whether to work or not and that, on the other side, their skills and experience should not be lost to an economy simply because there is not enough work to go round.

These difficulties do not mean that the employment rate should be disregarded as a labour market indicator. On the contrary, in many respects, it is a more useful measure than the unemployment rate which excludes what can be a considerable number of people who are not actively seeking a job, but who would work if there was an opportunity to do so. Comparisons of employment rates are an essential starting-point in any analysis of the success or failure of an economy to create jobs for the people who live there.

is set to continue rising in 1994. In Japan, where the economy remains in recession, the employment rate has been maintained despite very little growth in output.

The EFTA countries, on the other hand, for the first time for several decades have not been able to maintain employment levels since 1990 as recession has taken hold. The employment rate has, therefore, fallen even more sharply than in the Community. Nevertheless, despite this, the average rate in these countries remains considerably higher than in the Community, at around 68%. At the same time, it should be emphasised that there are significant differences in the employment rate within both the Community and the EFTA countries. In 1993, in the Community, this was as high as 73% in Denmark, but as low as 45% in Spain, while in the EFTA countries, it varied from 73% in Switzerland to only 59% in Finland. On the other hand, with the exception of Denmark, all countries in the Community had lower employment rates than the US, Japan and the EFTA countries apart from Finland.

These respective changes in the employment rate are mirrored to a large extent in unemployment. In the Community, the average rate in 1993 increased to 10% from a low of under 8% in 1990. The gap with the US, which had narrowed when the US economy went into recession in 1990, has widened again (Graph 2).

The rise in unemployment in the Community, however, has been dwarfed by the increase in the EFTA countries, where the average rate rose from just 2.5% in 1990 to almost 8% in 1993, a rise even steeper than that experienced by the Community in the early 1980s.

This, however, was due to a large extent to the substantial increase in Finland, where the rate rose from 3½% to 18% between these two years. In Austria, on the other hand, the increase was only from 3% to 5%.

Although unemployment has also increased in Japan since 1990, the rise has so far been extremely small and the rate remains at around 2.5%, reflecting the extensive policy of job preservation practised by Japanese companies. How long this can be maintained in the face of very low output growth is open to question.

The rise in unemployment seems to have moderated in the Community during the first few months of 1994. At the latest count, the rate averaged 11% for the Member States taken together (excluding the new German Länder), which is only marginally above its level at the end of 1993 (Graph 3). Only in Germany, Spain, Portugal and Luxembourg, did the rate rise by more than 0.2% over the first five months of 1994 and in two countries, Ireland and the UK, it declined.

Unemployment of men and women

As has been the case for many years, though there were slightly fewer women included in the Community total than men, the unemployment rate for women was higher than that for men — 13% in May 1994 as opposed to 10% (Graph 4). This remains the case for all Member States, the only exception being the UK, where unemployment among men is sig-

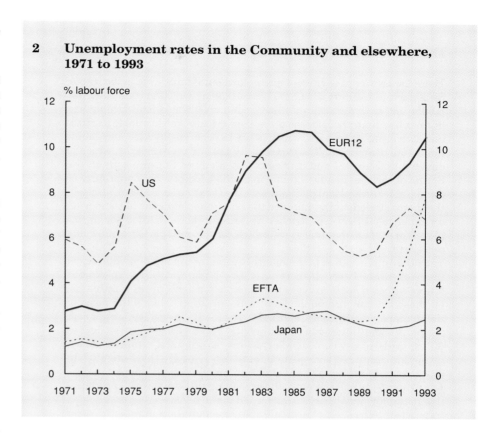

2 Unemployment rates in the Community and elsewhere, 1971 to 1993

% labour force

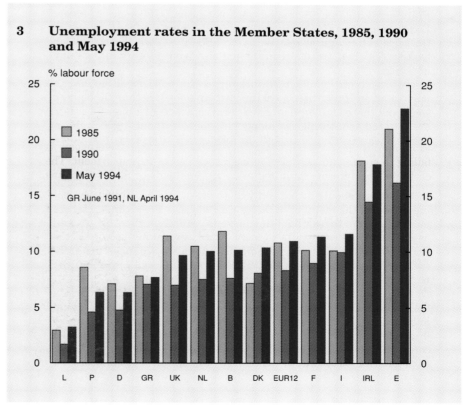

3 Unemployment rates in the Member States, 1985, 1990 and May 1994

% labour force

1985
1990
May 1994

GR June 1991, NL April 1994

L   P   D   GR   UK   NL   B   DK   EUR12   F   I   IRL   E

Data on unemployment

There are two main sources of unemployment figures. One is the labour force survey based on a sample of households which is conducted annually, and in some cases quarterly, in Member States. This attempts to find out how many people who are out of work are both available for work and actively seeking work, which is the internationally accepted definition of unemployment. The Community Labour Force Survey, which is directed by Eurostat and carried out by Member States mostly in the Spring of each year using a common methodology, is the main source of comparable unemployment figures for the Community as whole. Indeed, the figures based on the LFS are the only reliable means of comparing unemployment between Member States and the only totals for unemployment at the Community level which, for the most part, are internally consistent.

The other main source is the monthly count of unemployment in each Member State based largely on those registering in employment offices as being without work and looking for a job, or, in some cases, on those claiming unemployment compensation. This is the basis of the unemployment totals reported in the media in each country which are most widely quoted in public debate. The coverage of these figures differs widely between Member States, so that the totals produced cannot be compared across the Community. Nor are they intended, in most cases, to relate to the ILO definition of unemployment.

For example, in the UK, only those seeking full-time work and claiming unemployment benefit are counted in the registered figures, which in practice leaves out of account many women. In a number of other countries, the registered figures are confined to those seeking work for more than a given number of hours a week (full-time work in France and Ireland, 18 hours a week in Germany, 20 hours in Spain, Luxembourg and the Netherlands). Such limitations tend to reduce the registration figures relative to the LFS figures which cover all job seekers. The registration requirement also tends to work in the same direction.

There are, however, factors working in the opposite direction. In particular, in Italy, those working part-time for less than 20 hours a week and those employed on fixed-term contracts of 4 months or less are counted as unemployed along with those without a job at all. In the LFS people falling into both the former two categories are counted as employed.

More generally, although the registered figures in all countries should exclude those already with jobs, whether in the formal or informal economy, and should include only those available and actively searching for work, the methods of discerning whether these conditions are met differ from the confidential survey approach of the LFS, as well as varying from country to country. Moreover, taking people off the register once they have found work does not always happen instantaneously in all Member States. These are all possible reasons why registration figures can be higher than the LFS figures.

Despite the definitional differences and the occasional changes in definitions in individual countries, the monthly count is used to adjust and update the LFS figures to produce harmonised estimates of unemployment rates each month in the Community which are broadly comparable between Member States. (These are the figures published each month by Eurostat in the monthly unemployment bulletin.)

nificantly higher than among women.

Nevertheless, there has been some narrowing of the gap in recent years as unemployment has gone up. The rise in 7 of the 12 countries — especially Germany, France, Portugal and the UK — has affected men more than women. This was particularly so during the initial stages of the recession. As unemployment has begun to stabilise, however, female unemployment has being rising slightly faster than that of men. This might presage a repetition of what happened in the mid-1980s, when the unemployment rate for women went on increasing for over two years after the rate for men had stopped going up — partly because of the increased number of women attracted into the labour force — though it is too soon to be sure.

What is unemployment?

The above figures for unemployment relate to the harmonised series produced by Eurostat, which are intended to be comparable between Member States as well as to give a consistent picture of unemployment over time. These, however, differ from the figures most familiar in individual Member States, which is a source of some confusion and misunderstanding.

It should be emphasised that there is no single set of figures which provides an unambiguous measure of the scale of unemployment. This is partly because there are different ways of defining unemployment, partly because unemployment in itself is not a precise concept. In particular, the dividing line between unemployment and inactivity — between someone who is searching for work but cannot find it and someone who has decided that the lack of jobs makes it pointless to search but who would still like to work — can be extremely blurred.

Not only are there different figures published ostensibly measuring unemployment, but also there is an understandable tendency to regard the unemployment totals as a reliable measure of employment deficiency, whereas in reality it is a very partial measure of this (see Chapter 2).

The two main sources of unemployment figures are the Labour Force Survey of households, which attempts to find out from people themselves whether they are unemployed by applying the internationally accepted criteria for judging this, and the monthly count of unemployment in each Member State which is based on those registering at employment offices (or, in the case of the UK, those making a claim for unemployment-related benefits). It is the second measure which is the best known in Member States. It is the first which conforms to international standard definitions, specifically that recomended by ILO, and which is most comparable across countries (see Box).

In order to combine the advantages of these two measures, to provide up-to-date estimates of unemployment whilst retaining the maximum degree of international comparability, it is necessary to reconcile the two sets of figures to produce a "harmonised" rate. This tends to show a higher total for the Community as a whole than the LFS figures, but a lower total than the national administrative figures. In 1993, the difference

4   Unemployment rates of men and women in the Member States, 1990 and May 1994

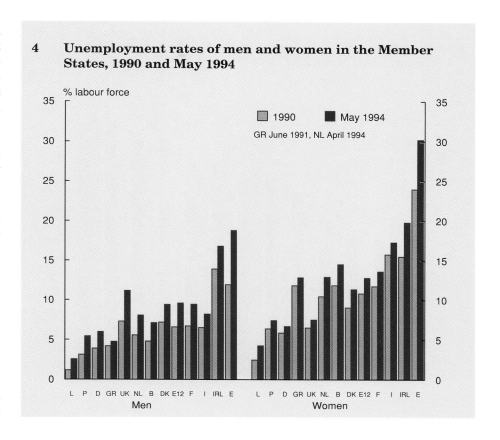

5   Unemployment rates in the Member States on alternative definitions, 1986 and 1993

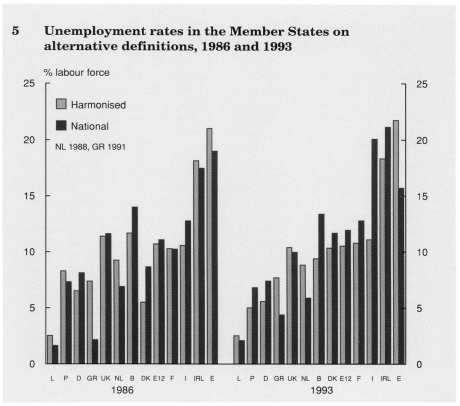

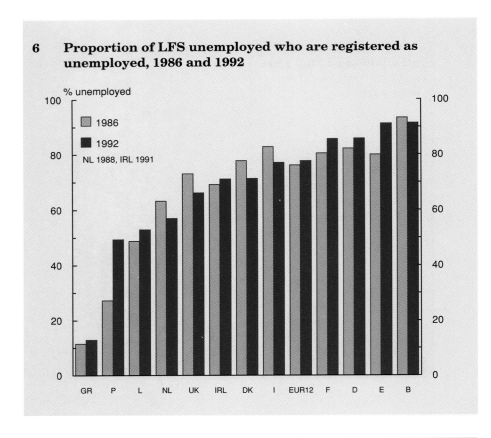

6   Proportion of LFS unemployed who are registered as unemployed, 1986 and 1992

% unemployed

- 1986
- 1992

NL 1988, IRL 1991

GR   P   L   NL   UK   IRL   DK   I   EUR12   F   D   E   B

Comparisons of LFS and registered unemployed

To make valid comparisons of those registered as unemployed who are also counted in the Community Labour Force Survey as being unemployed, a certain amount of manipulation is necessary. This is because the LFS is carried out at different times in different Member States, which means that, in most cases, it is not possible to compare directly the LFS figures with the registration figures for a particular month.

In some countries, the comparison is straightforward. In Germany, for example, the LFS for 1992, as previous surveys, relates to a particular week at the end of April, so that the LFS figures can be directly compared with the registration figures for the same month (the unseasonally adjusted figures, since, of course, the LFS figures are not seasonally adjusted). For most countries, however, the LFS is conducted over a number of weeks — in the Netherlands, in the extreme, over 24 weeks from January to June — mostly between March and May. In order to make the monthly registration figures comparable with the LFS estimates, therefore, they need to be weighted according to the proportion of LFS respondents in each country covered in each month. In the case of Spain, for example, where some 16% of LFS respondents were covered in March and 42% in both April and May, these percentages need to be applied to the registration figures in each of these three months to obtain a weighted average figure comparable with the LFS totals.

between the national administrative figures and the harmonised figures amounted to over 2 million over the Community as a whole, 18 million as against 16 million, or an implied rate of 11.9% as opposed to one of 10.5% (Graph 5).

One country, Italy, however — where, as noted above, the national administrative figures are based on a particularly liberal interpretation of unemployment — accounted for all of this difference. In Belgium, Germany, France and Portugal, the national figure also exceeded the harmonised figure significantly, in each case by some 20% or more, while the former figure was also some way above the latter in Denmark and Ireland.

On the other hand, in Greece, Spain and the Netherlands, the Community harmonised total exceeded the national administrative one by some 40% or more, while in the UK and Luxembourg, the difference was in the same direction but much smaller.

Comparisons with earlier years indicate that the overall gap between the harmonised and administrative registration figures has tended to widen over time. Though Italy is responsible for most of the increase in respect of the Community totals, the difference between the two sets of figures has also widened for a few other countries. In a number of other cases, however, it has narrowed. Between 1986 — a year of similarly high unemployment — and 1993, the difference widened significantly in Greece, Spain and the Netherlands, narrowed in Belgium, Denmark and Luxembourg and was reversed in France, Ireland, Portugal and the UK. Not only, therefore, are the two sets of figures different at any point in time, but for most countries, they also change in different ways over time.

Unemployed or not unemployed?

Even the above comparisons, however, do not reveal the full extent of the difference between the two sets of figures. A significant proportion of those counted by the Community LFS as being unemployed are not registered as so in the national totals, while an even larger proportion of those registered in individual Member States are not included in the LFS totals as being genuinely unemployed, as internationally understood. To a significant degree, therefore, the two sources relate to two different, if overlapping, groups of people.

Of the 13 million or so recorded as unemployed by the Community LFS in 1992, only just over 10 million, or 78%, were registered in the Member States (Graph 6). (These figures relate to the estimates calculated from the 1992 LFS for the period during the year to which the survey relates — see Box for further details.) The proportion registered was lower for women than for men — 73% as opposed to 82%.

The variation in this proportion between Member States, however, was extreme. Whereas in Belgium and Spain, it was over 91% and in Germany and France, over 85%, in the Netherlands, it was only 57%, in Luxembourg, 53%, in Portugal, 49% and in Greece, as low as 13%. In half the Member States, therefore — the last four listed plus the UK and Ireland — some 30% or more of those counted as unemployed in the Community statistics were not included in national totals. Moreover in each of these countries, except

Portugal where the proportion was just over half, under half of the women counted as unemployed do not appear as such in the national figures.

At the same time, only 63% of those included in the national totals of unemployment were counted by the LFS as being unemployed in 1992 (Graph 7 — in which for Spain, it should be noted, that there is some inconsistency between the numbers registered as unemployed and those who stated that they were registered in the LFS, the latter being greater than the former). This implies that in 1992 some 19 million altogether were counted as unemployed in the Community on either the Community or national definitions of unemployment — 6 million higher than the LFS total (equivalent to 4% of the labour force), 4 million higher than the registered total. To put this into perspective,

it implies that, on the latest count, instead of 17 million being unemployed in the Community (excluding the new German Länder), which is the harmonised total for May 1994, some 23 million are counted as unemployed on either of the two definitions. In no Member State, apart from Spain — where all those registered were also included in the LFS unemployment totals — were more than 75% of those included in registration figures treated as unemployed by the LFS in 1992 and in half the countries, the figure was under 60%.

In most countries — the only exceptions being France, Italy and the Netherlands — the proportion of women registered and counted as unemployed by the LFS was less than for men, and below 40% in three of the four Southern Member States — the only exception being Spain — as well as in Ireland. In

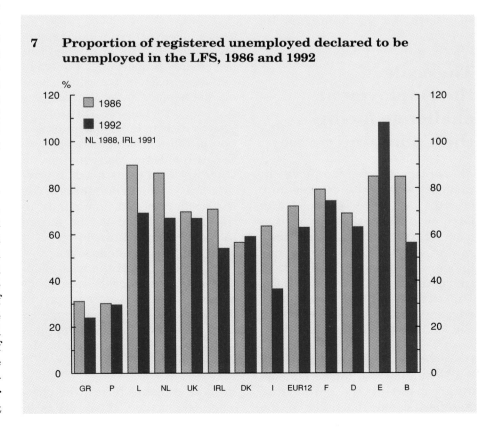

7   Proportion of registered unemployed declared to be unemployed in the LFS, 1986 and 1992

these countries, therefore, the large majority of women included in national unemployment registers did not appear in the LFS unemployment total.

While the proportion of the LFS unemployed who were registered as such in national statistics was much the same in 1992 as in 1986, the proportion of those registered who were also counted in the LFS total went down significantly between these two years in virtually all Member States (from 72% to 63% in the Community as a whole). A growing number of the people included in national unemployment registers, therefore, do not appear in Community totals as being unemployed. Consequently, in some sense, discussions of the unemployment problem in a number of Member States do not relate to the same group of people as discussions at the Community level, which does not make the policy debate any easier, let alone the formulation of policies.

The scale of the employment challenge facing the Community

The prospects of unemployment coming down across the Community over the next few years depend in large measure on the pace of economic recovery and the longer-term rate of growth which can be sustained, as well as on the success in translating growth into new jobs. The outlook for the Community economy for the remainder of 1994 and for 1995 is summarised below.

However, the challenge confronting the Community so far as employment creation is concerned is reflected only partially in the

prevailing level of unemployment. A major part of the problem to be addressed lies in the low level of labour force participation of people of working-age. These together are responsible for the low rate of employment in the Community as compared with other countries described above.

As is indicated in Chapter 2, the low level of labour force participation, especially among women, together with the clear trend towards increasing numbers of those who are at present inactive — and not counted as part of the labour force — to want to work, means that efforts at reducing unemployment are akin to aiming at a moving target. The more success is achieved in creating jobs, the more people, especially women but also men in older age groups, will be encouraged to look for work and, therefore, the more they will tend to expand labour supply.

This hidden potential labour supply, which emerges only when jobs are created, undermines the traditional approach of assessing labour market balance in terms of comparing the prospective rate of job growth with an independent projection of those seeking employment. The two sides of the equation, in other words, are very much interrelated. By the same token, the performance of the Community in this regard should not be judged solely, or even mainly, in terms of what happens to unemployment — even though this is the most palpable indicator of policy success or failure — but at least as much in terms of the rise in participation rates to a level more comparable with that in other parts of the developed world.

In more concrete terms, the challenge facing the Community is to

raise its *employment* rate, both by reducing unemployment and by increasing participation, by around 10% or more over the coming years. Given the likely, if small, growth in people of working-age who will be swelling the numbers coming onto the labour market independently of what happens to participation, this translates into an increase in employment of around $1\frac{1}{2}$% a year sustained for the next 10 years achieve an employment rate similar to that in the US by the year 2005.

The economic prospects described below, and their likely implications for job growth, need to be assessed in these terms.

Economic and employment prospects for 1994 and 1995

The economic situation and outlook for the Community economy have improved considerably over the past year. The recession which has plagued the economy during most of 1992 and 1993 has receded and recent evidence suggests that economic recovery is

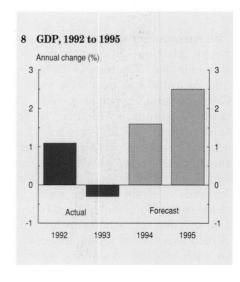

8   GDP, 1992 to 1995

Annual change (%)

Actual — 1992, 1993
Forecast — 1994, 1995

strengthening and that the foundations are being laid for sustained, non-inflationary-growth of output and employment over the medium term.

Gradual recovery of the Community economy seems to have begun in Spring 1993, GDP growth averaging 1–1½% during the remainder of the year (Graph 8). Nevertheless, for the Community as a whole growth was not sufficient to prevent a decline in GDP of 0.3% between 1992 and 1993. Preliminary quarterly data suggest that the recovery strengthened during the first half of 1994.

According to the May 1994 forecasts, Community GDP is expected to expand by 1½% in 1994 and by 2½% in 1995, with the projected recovery being widespread throughout the Community. All Member States which experienced a fall in output or no increase in 1993 are expected to record growth in 1994. Higher than average rates of growth are expected in Ireland, Denmark and the UK. The prospects are for a further increase in growth in 1995 with the rate in most Member States averaging around 2½%.

The factors underlying the probability of increased growth are:

- the growth of the global economy is set to gather momentum, so benefiting Community exporters, as a result of the successful conclusion of the Uruguay round, the much improved performance of the US economy and the buoyant Asian markets;

- short-term interest rates in the Community could come down further because of declining inflation and the fact that budgetary and wage developments seem to be increasingly consistent with monetary stability;

- business and consumer confidence is improving because of recovery, the fading of uncertainties about European integration and the enlargement to include Austria, Finland, Norway and Sweden; this improvement in confidence is likely to strengthen company and household spending;

- consumers' expenditure stands to expand in response not only

to lower interest rates and improving confidence, but also to the moderation of the rise in unemployment which will improve perceptions about job security and lead to less need for precautionary savings.

On the other hand, as a corollary of wage moderation and fiscal consolidation, there will be little or no growth in real disposable income which could restrain growth in the short-term.

The recovery is initially being driven by exports. Following an estimated fall of almost 1% in 1993, export volumes are projected to expand at an annual rate of around 6% in 1994 and 1995. This should progressively spill over into domestic expenditure and induce an increase in investment. Following a decline of almost 5% in 1993 (Graph 9), fixed investment is likely to increase slightly in 1994 and more substantially in 1995 (to around 5%).

Because of the depressed growth in real disposable income, however, private consumption is expected to lag behind output growth in both years (Graph 10), though improved

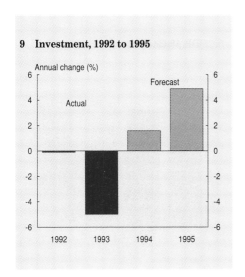

9 Investment, 1992 to 1995

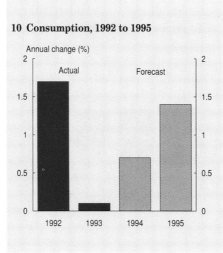

10 Consumption, 1992 to 1995

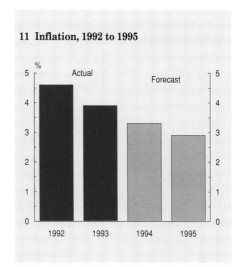

11 Inflation, 1992 to 1995

confidence should gradually bring a revival in expenditure. The projected export and investment driven recovery is in line with the strategy underlying the Commission's White Paper on *Growth, Competitiveness, Employment* and if growth forecasts for 1994 and 1995 are realised, output growth in the Community could accelerate further to 3% or more in 1996.

Inflation

After falling in 1992 (Graph 11), the rate of inflation is likely to decline further in the short-term, despite indirect tax increases, to an average of just below 3% in 1995. Inflation remains high in Greece as well as in Spain and Portugal, though in both latter cases it is falling. A major underlying factor is the strong moderation in wage cost pressures. Real wages are not expected to increase at all in 1994 and 1995 and labour costs per unit of output in real terms are likely to decline by almost 2% a year, so contributing to a rise in profitability.

Public finances

Recovery of output is combining with lower interest rates and fiscal restraint to reduce budget deficits in the Community — by a projected 1% of GDP between 1993 and 1995 — reducing the aggregate deficit of Member States to around 5% of GDP. Significant reductions in structural deficits are expected in a large number of Member States but especially in Belgium, Germany, Spain, Portugal and the UK. Because of output continuing to be below trend, however, actual budget deficits are likely to come down by less. Over the next two years, the largest adjustment is projected in the UK where the deficit is expected to decline by some 3% of GDP between 1993 and 1995. Considerable but less pronounced cuts in budget deficits are also expected in Belgium and Portugal. Conversely, in Greece and Italy, where the budgetary situation is most problematic, little reduction is expected.

External balances

As a result of weak domestic expenditure growth relative to other countries and improved export performance, the Community's trade surplus is set to increase significantly in 1994 and 1995 to reach 90 billion ECUs or 1½% of GDP in the latter year (Graph 12), which would imply an overall current account surplus of ½% of GDP.

Risk and uncertainties

With the upswing now underway, the major uncertainty in the short-term relates to the future strength of the recovery. There are number of reasons why growth could turn out higher than expected. In particular, investment could rebound more strongly if businesses react more vigorously to improved demand and profitability, while consumers expenditure could increase more markedly if confidence were to improve by more than is expected as unemployment stabilises.

On the other hand, growth might be weaker if monetary conditions, and long-term interest rates in particular, were to develop unfavourably. At the same time, there is some uncertainty about the growth of Community exports, both because expansion of global markets could turn out to be less buoyant than expected and because the recent weakening of the US dollar could make it more difficult for European producers to compete.

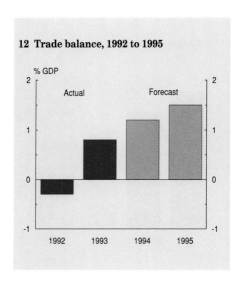

12 Trade balance, 1992 to 1995

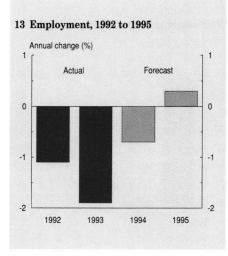

13 Employment, 1992 to 1995

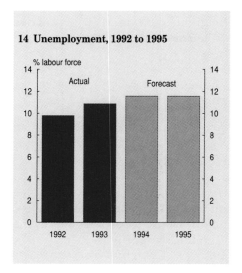

14 Unemployment, 1992 to 1995

Employment

The expected growth of output is unlikely to prove sufficient, given the probable growth in productivity, to prevent employment from falling in the Community as a whole in 1994 for the third year in succession. In 1994, the number employed is likely to be some $3\frac{1}{2}\%$ less than in 1991. It is only during 1995 that the growth of output is likely to reach a rate high enough to bring the decline in employment to an end and enable a renewed increase to take place. However, it will take two to three years of high rates of net job creation similar to those experienced in the 1985 to 1990 period for the number in employment to return to the level reached before the recession began (Graph 13).

Indeed, only in Denmark, Ireland, Luxembourg and the UK is employment expected to increase in 1994, and only in Ireland, is the rise likely to be more than 1%. In Germany, Spain, Italy and Portugal, by contrast, the numbers employed are expected to decline by over 1% between 1993 and 1994.

In 1995, although some recovery in employment is anticipated in all Member States, apart from Belgium, only in three countries — Denmark, Luxembourg and Ireland — is growth of more than 1% projected. In most countries, therefore, the rate of net job creation is likely to remain below the level required to make any appreciable impact on unemployment.

Unemployment

Given the continuing depressed rate of employment growth, there might be little expansion in the Community labour force in 1994 or 1995 as participation, especially among women, is discouraged. On this basis, the rise in unemployment, which was already showing signs of moderating significantly in the first part of 1994, could come to an end in the first half of 1995 (Graph 14). At that time, however, unemployment is likely to be over $11\frac{1}{2}\%$ of the Community labour force.

In only three Member States — three of the four in which employment is expected to rise, Denmark, Ireland and the UK — is the average rate of unemployment in 1994 likely to be lower than in 1993. In Italy, where employment is also forecast to rise, no change in unemployment is expevted. Moreover, in 1995, despite the general improvement in employment conditions, unemployment is expected to be higher than in 1994 in five of the 12 Member States — Belgium, Germany, Greece, Spain and the Netherlands — and in another three — Portugal, Luxembourg and France — the decline is expected to be marginal.

As shown in the next chapter, however, these unemployment figures conceal the fact that significant numbers of the Community's potential workforce remain outside the labour market primarily because of the inadequate rate of job creation. It is their presence, and their likely entry into the labour market if the recovery in employment were to accelerate significantly, which makes it difficult to reduce unemployment substantially over the medium-term. It is their presence, moreover, which, as noted above and elaborated in the next chapter, makes the employment rate rather than the unemployment rate a more meaningful indicator of progress in tackling the employment problem in the Community.

Key employment indicators in the Member States, 1985

Units : 1000s
Unless otherwise specified

	B	DK	D	GR	E	F
Total						
Total population	9805	5064	59859	9656	37549	52929
Population of working age (15–64)	6610	3357	42002	6259	24306	34825
Total employment	3512	2539	26167	3589	10834	21297
Ratio of employment to working-age population (%)	53.1	75.6	62.3	57.3	44.6	61.2
Total unemployment	449	215	1932	304	2925	2436
Unemployment rate (%)	11.3	7.8	6.9	7.8	21.3	10.3
Youth (<25) unemployment rate (%)	23.6	11.5	9.8	23.9	46.5	25.8
Employment in agriculture	127	170	1349	1037	1752	1734
Employment in industry	1119	706	10728	921	3445	6871
Employment in services	2266	1657	14090	1629	5619	12610
Share of employment in agriculture (%)	3.6	6.7	5.2	28.9	16.2	8.1
Share of employment in industry (%)	31.9	27.8	41.0	25.7	31.8	32.3
Share of employment in services (%)	64.5	65.5	53.8	45.4	51.9	59.2
Men						
Total population	4779	2501	28430	4662	18235	25556
Population of working age (15–64)	3301	1689	20672	3002	11930	17088
Total employment	2280	1400	15958	2371	7658	12439
Ratio of employment to working-age population (%)	69.1	82.9	77.2	79.0	64.2	72.8
Total unemployment	181	95	987	142	1866	1155
Unemployment rate (%)	7.4	6.4	5.8	5.6	19.6	8.5
Youth (<25) unemployment rate (%)	17.7	10.0	9.0	17.5	44.2	22.9
Employment in agriculture	89	131	711	576	1314	1108
Employment in industry	914	526	8114	720	2913	5167
Employment in services	1278	738	7133	1074	3422	6116
Share of employment in agriculture (%)	3.9	9.3	4.5	24.3	17.2	8.9
Share of employment in industry (%)	40.1	37.6	50.8	30.4	38.0	41.5
Share of employment in services (%)	56.0	52.7	44.7	45.3	44.7	49.2
Women						
Total population	5026	2562	31429	4994	19314	27373
Population of working age (15–64)	3309	1668	21330	3257	12376	17736
Total employment	1231	1139	10209	1218	3175	8858
Ratio of employment to working-age population (%)	37.2	68.3	47.9	37.4	25.7	49.9
Total unemployment	267	119	945	162	1059	1281
Unemployment rate (%)	17.8	9.5	8.5	11.7	25.0	12.6
Youth (<25) unemployment rate (%)	29.8	13.2	10.7	31.7	49.6	28.8
Employment in agriculture	38	39	639	461	439	626
Employment in industry	205	180	2614	201	532	1704
Employment in services	988	918	6956	555	2197	6495
Share of employment in agriculture (%)	3.1	3.4	6.3	37.9	13.8	7.1
Share of employment in industry (%)	16.7	15.8	25.6	16.5	16.8	19.2
Share of employment in services (%)	80.2	80.6	68.1	45.6	69.2	73.3

Note: All figures for Germany exclude the new Länder
Source: Eurostat, Labour Force Survey, 1985; E 1986

Key employment indicators in the Member States, 1992

Units : 1000s
Unless otherwise specified

	B	DK	D	GR	E	F
Total						
Total population	9963	5112	63748	9943	38624	55478
Population of working age (15–64)	6635	3467	43859	6640	25540	36386
Total employment	3770	2637	29715	3680	12458	22021
Ratio of employment to working-age population (%)	56.8	76.1	67.8	55.4	48.8	60.5
Total unemployment	*271*	*262*	1286	*313*	2684	2514
Unemployment rate (%)	*6.7*	*9.0*	4.1	*7.8*	17.7	10.2
Youth (<25) unemployment rate (%)	*13.2*	*12.3*	7.3	*25.0*	33.3	21.7
Employment in agriculture	109	136	1044	804	1257	1301
Employment in industry	1164	715	11719	933	4075	6497
Employment in services	2498	1780	16952	1942	7126	14187
Share of employment in agriculture (%)	2.9	5.2	3.5	21.9	10.1	5.9
Share of employment in industry (%)	30.9	27.1	39.4	25.4	32.7	29.5
Share of employment in services (%)	66.2	67.5	57.0	52.8	57.2	64.4
Men						
Total population	4859	2521	30938	4817	18745	26817
Population of working age (15–64)	3324	1752	22173	3202	12604	17884
Total employment	2286	1414	17538	2400	8360	12489
Ratio of employment to working-age population (%)	68.8	80.7	79.1	74.9	66.3	69.8
Total unemployment	*115*	*128*	681	*124*	1313	1105
Unemployment rate (%)	*4.8*	*8.3*	3.7	*4.9*	13.6	8.1
Youth (<25) unemployment rate (%)	*11.3*	*12.1*	4.2	*17.2*	28.0	18.6
Employment in agriculture	72	103	612	467	910	835
Employment in industry	932	524	8771	713	3403	4884
Employment in services	1281	784	8155	1220	4047	6750
Share of employment in agriculture (%)	3.2	7.3	3.5	19.5	10.9	6.7
Share of employment in industry (%)	40.8	37.1	50.0	29.7	40.7	39.1
Share of employment in services (%)	56.1	55.6	46.5	50.8	48.4	54.0
Women						
Total population	5104	2592	32810	5125	19878	28661
Population of working age (15–64)	3311	1714	21687	3438	12936	18501
Total employment	1484	1222	12177	1280	4098	9532
Ratio of employment to working-age population (%)	44.8	71.3	56.2	37.2	31.7	51.5
Total unemployment	*156*	*134*	605	*189*	1371	1409
Unemployment rate (%)	*9.5*	*9.9*	4.7	*12.9*	25.1	12.9
Youth (<25) unemployment rate (%)	*15.2*	*12.6*	4.3	*34.2*	39.8	25.0
Employment in agriculture	37	32	432	337	347	466
Employment in industry	231	190	2947	221	672	1613
Employment in services	1216	996	8797	722	3079	7437
Share of employment in agriculture (%)	2.5	2.7	3.6	26.3	8.5	4.9
Share of employment in industry (%)	15.6	15.6	24.2	17.2	16.4	16.9
Share of employment in services (%)	81.9	81.5	72.2	56.4	75.1	78.0

Note: All figures for Germany exclude the new Länder
Source: Eurostat, Labour Force Survey, 1992; figures in italic are not comparable with earlier years.

Key employment indicators in the Member States, 1985

Units : 1000s
Unless otherwise specified

	IRL	I	L	NL	P	UK
Total						
Total population	3472	56267	356	14103	10167	55769
Population of working age (15–64)	2079	38048	250	9744	6562	36706
Total employment	1069	20583	148	5124	4225	24282
Ratio of employment to working-age population (%)	51.4	54.1	59.0	52.6	64.4	66.2
Total unemployment	234	2154	4	601	408	3151
Unemployment rate (%)	18.0	9.5	3.0	10.5	8.8	11.5
Youth (<25) unemployment rate (%)	25.1	32.2	6.5	17.7	20.3	18.2
Employment in agriculture	175	2258	7	269	909	563
Employment in industry	319	6902	47	1436	1431	8274
Employment in services	571	11422	93	3378	1878	15040
Share of employment in agriculture (%)	16.4	11.0	4.6	5.2	21.5	2.3
Share of employment in industry (%)	29.8	33.5	31.7	28.0	33.9	34.1
Share of employment in services (%)	53.4	55.5	62.9	65.9	44.5	61.9
Men						
Total population	1748	27267	175	6989	4879	27176
Population of working age (15–64)	1053	18601	124	4907	3152	18333
Total employment	739	13955	97	3375	2541	14173
Ratio of employment to working-age population (%)	70.2	75.0	78.2	68.8	80.6	77.3
Total unemployment	155	947	2	353	186	1903
Unemployment rate (%)	17.4	6.4	2.2	9.5	6.8	11.8
Youth (<25) unemployment rate (%)	26.4	26.5	6.4	18.7	16.5	19.6
Employment in agriculture	152	1496	5	215	472	438
Employment in industry	256	5278	42	1229	1019	6327
Employment in services	329	7180	50	1904	1044	7145
Share of employment in agriculture (%)	20.5	10.7	4.9	6.4	18.6	3.1
Share of employment in industry (%)	34.6	37.8	42.8	36.4	40.1	44.6
Share of employment in services (%)	44.4	51.5	51.0	56.4	41.1	50.4
Women						
Total population	1725	28999	181	7114	5288	28593
Population of working age (15–64)	1026	19447	126	4837	3410	18372
Total employment	330	6628	50	1749	1684	10110
Ratio of employment to working-age population (%)	32.1	34.1	40.1	36.2	49.4	55.0
Total unemployment	79	1207	2	247	222	1248
Unemployment rate (%)	19.3	15.4	4.3	12.4	11.6	11.0
Youth (<25) unemployment rate (%)	23.5	39.3	6.5	16.7	25.3	16.6
Employment in agriculture	23	762	2	54	436	125
Employment in industry	63	1624	5	206	412	1946
Employment in services	242	4242	43	1473	834	7895
Share of employment in agriculture (%)	7.0	11.5	3.8	3.1	25.9	1.2
Share of employment in industry (%)	19.0	24.5	10.0	11.8	24.5	19.2
Share of employment in services (%)	73.3	64.0	86.7	84.2	49.5	78.1

Source: Eurostat, Labour Force Survey, 1985; P 1986

Key employment indicators in the Member States, 1992

Units : 1000s
Unless otherwise specified

	IRL	I	L	NL	P	UK
Total						
Total population	3494	56947	382	14822	*9736*	56772
Population of working age (15–64)	2191	39189	266	10294	*6591*	36941
Total employment	1149	21015	165	6614	*4509*	25630
Ratio of employment to working-age population (%)	52.4	53.6	62.0	64.2	*68.4*	69.4
Total unemployment	*203*	*2191*	*3*	*389*	*187*	2755
Unemployment rate (%)	*15.0*	*9.4*	*2.0*	*5.6*	*4.0*	9.7
Youth (<25) unemployment rate (%)	*22.7*	*28.2*	*3.7*	*8.1*	*9.7*	15.6
Employment in agriculture	157	1657	5	247	*517*	569
Employment in industry	322	6962	47	1571	*1468*	7715
Employment in services	667	12396	107	4503	*2523*	17237
Share of employment in agriculture (%)	13.7	7.9	3.2	3.7	*11.5*	2.2
Share of employment in industry (%)	28.0	33.1	28.6	23.8	*32.6*	30.1
Share of employment in services (%)	58.1	59.0	65.1	68.1	*56.0*	67.3
Men						
Total population	1744	27587	188	7341	*4620*	27768
Population of working age (15–64)	1104	19368	135	5201	*3131*	18497
Total employment	743	13642	104	4006	*2522*	14229
Ratio of employment to working-age population (%)	67.3	70.4	76.9	77.0	*80.5*	76.9
Total unemployment	*130*	*1014*	*2*	*169*	*88*	1857
Unemployment rate (%)	*14.9*	*6.9*	*1.6*	*4.0*	*3.4*	11.5
Youth (<25) unemployment rate (%)	*24.3*	*24.4*	*4.2*	*7.7*	*8.7*	18.9
Employment in agriculture	143	1050	4	189	*261*	440
Employment in industry	247	5283	41	1310	*984*	5872
Employment in services	351	7309	56	2384	*1276*	7853
Share of employment in agriculture (%)	19.2	7.7	3.6	4.7	*10.4*	3.1
Share of employment in industry (%)	33.3	38.7	39.5	32.7	*39.0*	41.3
Share of employment in services (%)	47.3	53.6	53.9	59.5	*50.6*	55.2
Women						
Total population	1750	29359	193	7481	*5117*	29003
Population of working age (15–64)	1088	19821	131	5094	*3460*	18444
Total employment	406	7373	61	2608	*1987*	11400
Ratio of employment to working-age population (%)	37.3	37.2	46.6	51.2	*57.4*	61.8
Total unemployment	*73*	*1176*	*2*	*220*	*99*	898
Unemployment rate (%)	*15.6*	*13.8*	*2.8*	*7.8*	*4.8*	7.3
Youth (<25) unemployment rate (%)	*20.8*	*32.9*	*3.1*	*8.5*	*10.8*	11.7
Employment in agriculture	14	606	2	58	*256*	129
Employment in industry	75	1679	6	262	*484*	1843
Employment in services	316	5087	51	2118	*1247*	9384
Share of employment in agriculture (%)	3.5	8.2	2.5	2.2	*12.9*	1.1
Share of employment in industry (%)	18.4	22.8	10.1	10.0	*24.4*	16.2
Share of employment in services (%)	77.8	69.0	84.2	81.2	*62.8*	82.3

Source: Eurostat, Labour Force Survey, 1992; figures in italic are not comparable with earlier years.

Key employment indicators in the Community

Units : Millions

Unless otherwise specified

	1965	1975	1985	1990	1992	1993
Total						
Total population	293.2	312.4	322.0	327.7	331.0	331.6
Population of working age (15–64)	188.0	197.9	215.2	219.7	221.7	222.3
Total employment	122.6	124.3	122.7	132.8	132.0	128.8
Ratio of employment to working-age population (%)	65.2	62.8	57.0	60.5	59.5	58.0
Total unemployment	2.6	5.3	15.0	12.2	13.9	15.8
Unemployment rate (%)	2.1	4.1	10.8	8.3	9.4	10.5
Youth (<25) unemployment rate (%)			23.3	16.8	18.4	20.1
Employment in agriculture	20.1	13.9	10.4	8.6	7.6	7.1
Employment in industry	49.5	48.3	41.3	43.0	41.0	39.3
Employment in services	53.1	62.2	71.1	81.2	85.0	82.3
Share of employment in agriculture (%)	16.4	11.2	8.4	6.5	5.8	5.5
Share of employment in industry (%)	40.4	38.8	33.6	32.4	31.1	30.5
Share of employment in services (%)	43.3	50.0	57.9	61.2	62.9	63.9
Men						
Total population	142.3	152.0	156.6	159.7	161.3	161.8
Population of working age (15–64)			107.3	109.5	110.7	111.0
Total employment	83.0	81.9	75.8	79.6	77.8	76.0
Ratio of employment to working-age population (%)			70.6	72.7	70.3	68.4
Total unemployment		3.3	8.0	5.8	7.2	8.3
Unemployment rate (%)		3.9	9.4	6.6	8.1	9.3
Youth (<25) unemployment rate (%)			21.6	14.7	17.4	19.5
Employment in agriculture	13.3	9.1	6.7	5.6	5.0	4.8
Employment in industry	38.0	37.1	31.7	32.8	31.3	29.7
Employment in services	31.6	35.7	37.3	41.2	41.5	41.4
Share of employment in agriculture (%)	16.0	11.1	8.9	7.0	6.4	6.3
Share of employment in industry (%)	45.8	45.3	41.9	41.2	40.2	39.2
Share of employment in services (%)	38.0	43.6	49.2	51.8	53.2	54.5
Women						
Total population	150.9	160.4	165.4	168.0	169.7	169.8
Population of working age (15–64)			107.9	110.2	111.0	111.2
Total employment	39.6	42.5	46.9	53.2	53.9	53.5
Ratio of employment to working-age population (%)			43.5	48.3	48.5	48.1
Total unemployment		2.3	7.0	6.4	6.8	7.5
Unemployment rate (%)		5.1	13.0	10.8	11.3	12.3
Youth (<25) unemployment rate (%)			25.0	19.1	19.5	21.0
Employment in agriculture	6.8	4.8	3.6	3.0	2.6	2.4
Employment in industry	11.5	11.2	9.6	10.2	9.7	9.4
Employment in services	21.5	26.5	33.8	40.0	41.5	41.7
Share of employment in agriculture (%)	17.2	11.3	7.7	5.7	4.8	4.6
Share of employment in industry (%)	29.0	26.4	20.4	19.1	18.1	17.5
Share of employment in services (%)	54.2	62.4	71.9	75.2	77.1	78.0

Note: Figures for all years exclude the German new Länder.
Source: Eurostat National estimates of population and employment and unemployment rates for comparison between
*   Member States; 1993 figures are provisional; 1965 figures from OECD.*

Chapter 2   Labour force growth and participation

The low rate of employment in the Community reflects not only high unemployment but low levels of activity. Too few women have the opportunity of working and too many older people are forced to retire early. Participation of women, however, is rising strongly and the labour supply is set to expand as and when job creation increases.

Introduction

A distinguishing feature of the Community in relation to other comparable parts of the world is its low rate of employment. As noted in Chapter 1 above, this results not only from a high rate of unemployment, a rate which has risen significantly over the past 20 years, but also from a low rate of labour market participation among people of working-age. Unlike unemployment, this has shown only a small tendency to change over the past 20 years and more, at least so far as the *aggregate* rate is concerned. Indeed the average proportion of people of working-age who are recorded as being economically active and part of the labour force is only slightly higher now than in 1960. This relative stability, however, conceals markedly divergent trends for men and women, as well as for people of different age-groups.

In consequence, the aggregate rate represents a highly misleading basis for assessing future labour force developments. In particular, it is liable to lead to gross underesti-

mates of the growth in labour supply over the coming years and, correspondingly, over-optimistic assessments of the prospective path of unemployment.

The concern of this chapter is to examine in detail rates of labour market participation in the Community and Member States for men and women in different age groups, and how these are tending to change over time. This is intended to identify the groups for which the gap in participation rates between the Community and other comparable parts of the world is widest and which, therefore, represent a major part of the explanation for the relatively low employment rate. It also, however, provides essential background analysis for judging the prospective growth in the Community labour force over the coming years.

More specifically, labour force growth in the Community over the past three decades is, first, compared with that in the US, Japan and the EFTA countries, distinguishing between the contribution of the growth of population of working age and that of changes in

participation and between the different trends for men and women.

Secondly, the changes which have occurred for people in different age groups are examined in the four regions, focusing on older people of 55 and over, younger people under 25 and women of prime working age, since it is these groups which have shown the most significant changes during this period.

Thirdly, rates of participation and the trends which are evident are compared between Member States within the Community.

Fourthly, the implications of these trends for future labour force participation and the growth in labour supply in the Community over the coming years are examined, drawing attention to the interrelationship between these and the growth of employment opportunities.

Labour force growth since 1960

Over the past 30 years, the labour force in Community countries has

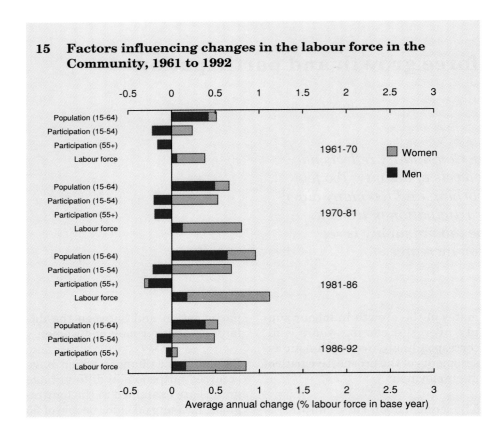

15   Factors influencing changes in the labour force in the Community, 1961 to 1992

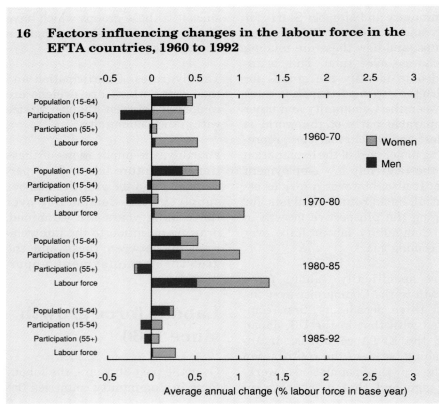

16   Factors influencing changes in the labour force in the EFTA countries, 1960 to 1992

grown by around 30 million. Around half of this growth has been matched by an increase in employment, half by a rise in unemployment. Of this 30 million, over 25 million have been women, (Graph 15) a disparity which is mirrored in the EFTA countries, where over 2 million of the 2½ million or so who came into the labour force over the same period were women (Graph 16).

This pronounced feature of labour force growth in the Community is true of all Member States, to varying degrees. It is most marked, perhaps surprisingly, in the South of the Community where the proportion of women in paid employment in the 1960s and 1970s was, in most cases, low. In Italy and Portugal, there has been no growth at all in the number of men in the labour force over the past 30 years, while in Spain and Greece, there has been only a small increase. All, or virtually all, the expansion of the workforce in these four countries has come from more women working. This is also true of Belgium and the UK where the male labour force has fallen since 1960.

These differences in relative rates of growth of men and women have shown little sign of narrowing in recent years. Since 1980, the Community's labour force has grown by almost 15 million, the number of women in the labour force by over 12 million.

All Member States experienced a substantial growth of the female workforce over this period — of over 50% in Spain, Greece and the Netherlands and almost 50% in Portugal. Only in Germany — because of immigration — and the Netherlands was there any significant expansion in the number of men in the labour force.

The overall effect has been to increase the importance of women in the European labour force. In 1960, women accounted for under 30% of the Community's workforce. By 1992, they accounted for over 40%. In the US and Japan, labour force growth has been much more evenly divided between the sexes. Indeed, in Japan, of the increase of 21 million in the labour force over these 30 years, 12 million were men and only 9 million were women (Graph 17), while in the US, men accounted for some 40% of the additional 57 million people who entered the labour force during this period (Graph 18).

These differences in the relative growth of working men and women do not reflect differences in the relative increase of men and women of working age (defined as 15 to 64). In fact, in the Community as in all developed parts of the world, there has been a larger rise in the number of working-age men than working-age women over the past 30 years. Rather they are a reflection of a marked decline in the participation of working-age men in the labour force in Europe and the even more pronounced growth in the participation of women. Both trends are apparent in the US and Japan over this period, though much less so in the latter.

Changing participation of older people

In Europe, however, there has been a significant decline in the numbers of men over the age of 65 who remain in the labour force, a decline which has occurred to a much smaller extent in the US and not at all in Japan (see Box, p 46, for details of the data used in this analysis).

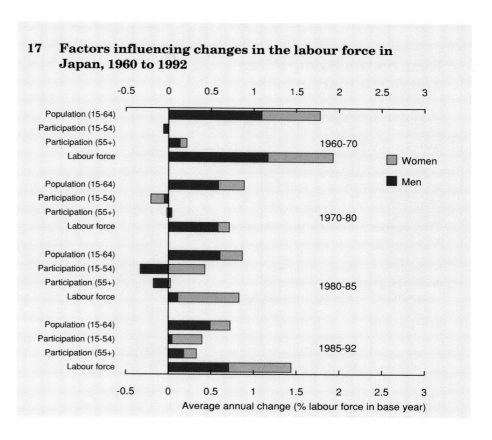

17   Factors influencing changes in the labour force in Japan, 1960 to 1992

Average annual change (% labour force in base year)

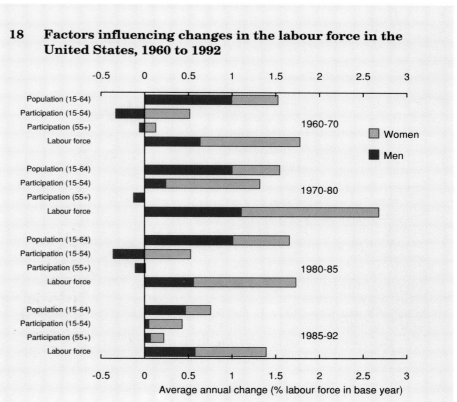

18   Factors influencing changes in the labour force in the United States, 1960 to 1992

Average annual change (% labour force in base year)

Data on the labour force and participation rates

The figures for the labour force and rates of participation by age group for the period 1960 to 1980 are taken from the ILO *Retrospective Year Book,* which in turn is based mainly on Censuses of Population for each of the countries. Although the Censuses were conducted at approximately the same time in each country — around the first year of the decade — in a few countries, they were a year earlier or later than this. This ought not to affect the changes in activity rates shown more than marginally.

Since data for Switzerland are not available for the same age groups as the other countries, Switzerland has been excluded from the analysis. The EFTA figures therefore relate to Austria, Finland, Norway and Sweden only.

For 1985 and 1992, the figures are taken from the ILO *Yearbook of Labour Statistics* in respect of the US, Japan and the EFTA countries. For the Community and Member States, the figures for 1986 and 1992 are based on the Community Labour Force Survey. Figures for earlier years from ILO sources have been approximately adjusted to an LFS basis by applying the ratio of the latter figures to the former in a year for which both sets of data exist. In practice, this adjustment is in almost all cases very small since the ILO and LFS figures for the labour force and, most especially, participation rates are very close for the different age groups distinguished here.

Although the data are from a common source and are based on a standard set of definitions, differences may still exist between the precise methods chosen by countries to collect and compile the data. Two areas in particular where discrepancies may be significant are in the definition of activity, where much depends on the number of hours a person needs to be working to be counted as employed and how actively they need to be searching for work in order to be counted as unemployed, and in the treatment of groups such as the armed forces, people engaged in part-time work and students.

Observed changes in activity rates, of women especially, may, therefore, in some cases partly reflect changes in the way activity is defined in practice as well as genuine changes. There is little way of knowing how important this factor is likely to be in practice, but over a time span of 30 years, it may be significant in some cases.

Between 1961 and 1992, in the Community, the number of men older than working age who were part of the labour force fell by 2 million. The number of women above this age fell by some 700 thousand. Together they effectively reduced the Community's workforce by almost 3 million. While there was also a marked decline in the number of this age group in the EFTA countries, in the US, the number of men over the age of 65 in the labour force went down only slightly and the number of women increased. In Japan, the number of both men and women of 65 and over rose significantly (by over 2 million) — though this was coupled with some decline in the rate of participation.

At the same time, the participation of older men of working age also fell considerably in Europe but declined only to a small extent in the US and Japan. Between 1960 and 1992, the rate of participation of men aged 55 to 64 in the Community fell from over 75% to below 55%, so reducing the workforce by a further 3 million or so, while in the EFTA countries it fell to a very similar extent (Graphs 19 and 20).

Virtually all the decline in participation of older men both above and below 65 occurred, however, between 1960 and the mid-1980s. Since then, the proportion of men aged 55 and over in the labour force has fallen only slightly. The trend towards earlier retirement, which was so pronounced in the years before 1980 seems to have come to an end. Nevertheless, it has left Europe with a much lower rate of participation among older men than in either the US and Japan.

Whereas only just over 35% of men aged 60 to 64 were still in the labour force in the Community in 1992, in the US, the figure was around 55%

Participation rates of men by age group
in the Community and elsewhere, 1960 to 1992

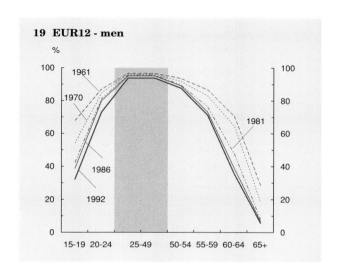

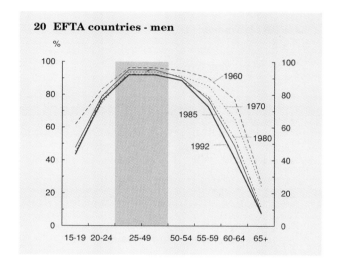

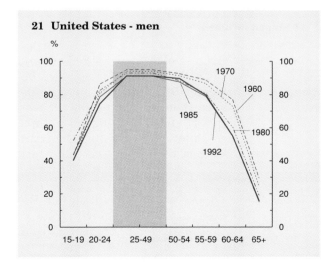

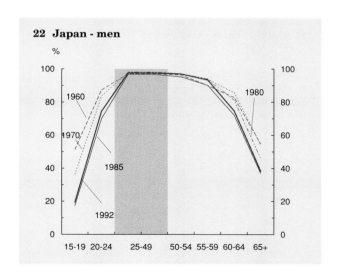

Participation rates of women by age group
in the Community and elsewhere, 1960 to 1992

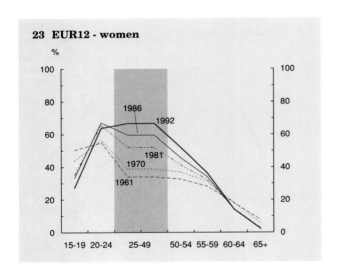

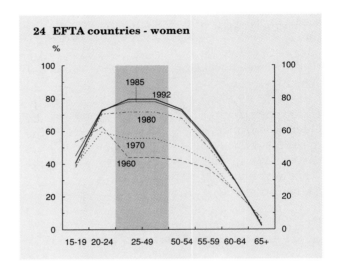

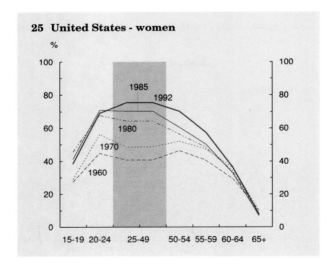

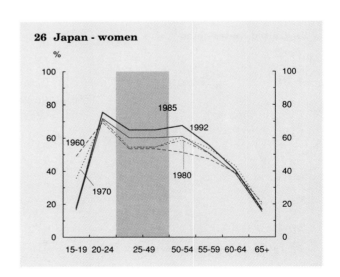

and in Japan, almost 75% (Graphs 21 and 22). Moreover, while only around 6% of men of 65 and over were still economically active in the Community, in the US, the figure was over 15% and in Japan, almost 40%. Furthermore, in the US, as in Europe, the trend decline in rates of participation among men of this age which was evident before 1980 seems to have come to an end during the 1980s and, especially, over the past 5–6 years. This seems to be true for most Member States (as shown below).

Differences in the participation of older men contribute significantly to the low overall rate of activity in the Community as compared with other advanced countries. Low participation rates of older women, however, are also a factor. Though the average proportion of women aged 55 and over who are in the labour force has not changed much since 1960, it has increased for women aged 55 to 59, reflecting the trend among younger age groups for more women to work, and fallen for those over 60, reflecting the trend towards earlier retirement. In the EFTA countries and the US, however, it has increased and in Japan, it has remained at a relatively high level (Graphs 23, 24, 25 and 26).

In the Community, just over 5% of women of 60 and over were still economically active in 1992, as compared with 9% in the EFTA countries, 14% in the US and almost 25% in Japan.

Participation among the young

Since 1960, the proportion of young people over 15 but under 20 who are either in work or actively looking for a job has fallen markedly in the Community, from around 55% to 30%, reflecting the growing tendency for men and women in this age group to stay longer in education or embark on a training course. Although this fall in participation was more pronounced up to 1980 than since, the downward trend has, nevertheless, continued. There are, however, differences between Member States, as described below.

This trend is also evident in Japan, where the rate of participation of 15 to 19 year olds has declined from 50% to under 20% since 1960, though it seems to have stabilised during the 1980s. Similarly, in the EFTA countries, participation of young people has also fallen over the past 30 years, though the rate in 1992 was still over 40%, significantly higher than in either the Community or Japan. In the US, however, where the rate is also around 40%, a decline in participation among men has been offset since 1960 by higher participation among women, resulting in little overall change.

For young people aged 20 to 24, in the Community as elsewhere, there have been opposing trends for men and women since 1960. While labour force participation of men of this age group has declined as participation in education and training has risen — with no sign of this trend coming to an end over the past few years — that of women has increased, the tendency for more women to work offsetting the tendency for more to stay longer in education. Over the past few years, however, the latter tendency seems to have outweighed the former and the proportion of women of this age who are economically active has fallen slightly. This also seems to have occurred to a marginal extent in the EFTA countries and the US.

Participation of prime age men

One of the most significant trends of the past 30 years has been the tendency for the participation of men of prime working age — between 25 and 49 — to decline. In the Community, the rate fell from 97% to 94%, which may not seem much of a change, but implies that some 3 million men in this age group in 1992 were neither working nor actively seeking work (which is equivalent to almost half the total number of men recorded as being unemployed). Moreover half of this reduction occurred in the six years between 1986 and 1992, when almost 2 million men effectively disappeared from the workforce with no obvious reason, except a lack of employment opportunities.

A similar tendency is evident in the EFTA countries and the US. In the former, the rate of participation of prime age men in 1992 was down to 92% (from 96% in 1960), and in the US to only 91% (from 95% in 1960), significantly below the rate in the Community. In Japan, on the other hand, the rate for prime age men has declined only marginally over the past 30 years and in 1992 was still almost 98%.

Participation of women

The rate of participation of prime age women in the labour force has shown the most radical change since 1960 in both Europe and the US. In the Community, it has risen from 34% in 1960, and from 39% in 1970, to 67% in 1992, with little sign of any slowdown. Indeed, it rose by much the same rate between 1980 and 1992 as in the 1970s and by the same in the second half of this period as in the first half.

This growth in the participation of women of prime working age has been the main factor behind the growth of the labour force in the Community over the past 30 years. Between 1980 and 1992, for example, it was responsible for 10 million of the 15 million increase in the workforce. Given the continued upward trend, there remains significant scope for further increases in most parts of the Community. As shown below, the average rate is still well below that in the EFTA countries or the US and it is likely to continue to be the main factor for some time to come.

In the EFTA countries, the growth of participation of women in this age group has been even more pronounced, the rate rising from 44% in 1960 to 80% in 1992. Here, however, a marked slowdown in the rate of increase is evident since the mid-1980s, with the rate going up by only 2 percentage points between 1985 and 1992. Further increases of any significance may, therefore, be unlikely.

In the US, the proportion of women of prime working age in the labour force has risen over the past 30 years by only slightly less than in the EFTA countries but by more than in the Community, and in 1992, it stood at 76%.

In Japan, on the other hand, the rate of participation of prime age women has risen by much less over the past 30 years, from 54% in 1960 to 65% in 1992, almost the same level as in the Community. Virtually all of this increase, however, has been concentrated into the period since 1980. Between 1980 and 1992, participation of women in the labour force went up by

almost the same rate as in the Community.

Prospects for labour force growth in the next 10 years

Trends in participation over the past 30 years are marked by:

- a declining rate of participation of young people under the age of 25 as more stay longer in education and basic training;

- a declining rate of participation of older people, particularly men, partly in response to policies to encourage people to retire early to free up jobs for younger people;

- a growing rate of participation of women, especially those within the prime working-age group of 25 to 49.

These trends have been evident in other countries. However, the decline in the participation of older people has proceeded much further in the Community than in the US or Japan, while the growth in participation of women has been less rapid and remains much lower than in the US or the EFTA countries. The low participation of prime-age women and older people are the two main explanations for the low overall proportion of working-age population in the workforce. Together with higher rates of unemployment than elsewhere, they also explain the low employment rate of the Community relative to other economies.

At the same time, while the growing participation of women in the labour force shows no sign of coming to an end, there are clear signs that the falling participation of older

people is slowing considerably as Member States reassess the costs of supporting high numbers of people in retirement. Indeed in a number of Community countries, as shown below, there are signs of the fall being reversed. This suggests that the future trend in participation in the Community is likely to be dominated by a continuing increase in the proportion of prime-age women joining the workforce, whereas in the past this has tended to be offset by earlier retirement.

It has also been offset in the past, as in other economies, by declining participation among younger people reflecting the growth of further and higher education. However, the decline has been relatively small in recent years, largely because participation rates in most Member States have already fallen to comparatively low levels. While some further fall in the future might be expected in those parts of the Community where the proportion of young people staying in education beyond the official school-leaving age is still relatively small, the overall decline in this age group for the Community as a whole is unlikely to be very large. It should, therefore, represent a relatively minor offset to the trend rise in the participation of women over the coming years.

The implication is that, if participation rates in the younger and older age groups change little over the remainder of the decade, and if the participation of women continues to rise at the same rate as over the past 10 years, then the Community labour force would grow by around $\frac{1}{2}$% a year *over and above* the growth of working-age population.

Current (Eurostat) projections of working-age population, suggest a rate of increase of around 0.2–0.3% a year up to the year 2000. Increasing participation could, therefore, be twice as important as the growth of working-age population as a source of labour force growth over this period. Overall, therefore, the Community labour force can be expected to grow by 0.7–0.8% a year over the remainder of the decade, which would mean an additional 7 million or so joining the workforce between 1993 and the year 2000. Most of these, as in the past, would be women.

Moreover, since most of the women would also be of prime working age, this — together with young people entering the labour market for the first time — is likely to result in some reduction in the average age of the workforce, or at least prevent an increase. Thus, though some concern has been expressed about the prospect of an ageing labour force in the Community in future years as a consequence of declining birth rates, this is something which is unlikely to occur to any significant extent within the next 10 or 20 years, at least in the Community as a whole. A few Member States, however, particularly those where female participation is already high, could experience some ageing.

The challenge to Community countries is to ensure that the rate of job creation is sufficient not only to provide employment for these new entrants to the labour market but also to reduce the numbers in the workforce who are unemployed.

Participation and labour force growth in Member States

The future rate of job creation required, however, differs widely between Member States not only in terms of levels of unemployment but also in terms of the prospective labour force growth. Thus although the trends in participation noted above have, for the most part, been common to all Member States, they have differed significantly in scale (see Graphs 27 to 38 for activity rates of men over the period 1960 to 1992 and Graphs 39 to 50 for activity rates of women).

Present rates of participation, especially of women, vary substantially between countries. Therefore, the prospective growth in participation in the coming years also varies markedly — quite apart from differences in the likely expansion of working-age population.

In terms of labour force participation among older men, the slowdown in the rate of decline over the 1980s as compared with earlier years has been common to all Member States. It has been particularly pronounced in Germany, Italy, Portugal and the UK, where the downward trend in participation among this age group seems to have slowed down considerably in recent years. In the case of Germany and Italy, it has even started to be reversed. Significantly perhaps, these are both countries where the indigenous population has ceased to grow because of a reduction in the birth rate. The growth of working-age population in future years, in the absence of significant immigration, is, therefore, likely to be negative or very small. Both are countries where a policy of encouraging earlier retirement has largely been abandoned.

Nevertheless, the steep fall in participation has left the activity rate of men of 55 and over at 30% or below in half the Member States and only in Ireland and Portugal was the rate in 1992 above that in the US at close to 40% (Graph 51).

For men of 65 and over, participation was below 5% in Belgium, Germany, Spain, France and Luxembourg and over 15% only in Ireland and Portugal.

A similar tendency is apparent for older women as well. In most countries, any downward trend in participation rates of women of 60 and over seems to have come to an end. Moreover, in half the Member States, participation of women of between 55 and 59 has tended to increase in recent years — in Denmark, Germany, Spain, the Netherlands, Portugal (where it is also true of older age groups) and the UK. As a result the average rate of participation for women of 55 and over was under 10% in 1992 in half the Member States and above 15% only in the UK, Denmark and Portugal (Graph 52). Even in these three countries, however, the rate was below that in the US (just over 25%). Nowhere except Portugal was the participation rate of women of 65 and over more than 5%.

There is very little possibility, therefore, of any significant reduction in rates of participation of older people, men or women, in any Member State in the coming years. Indeed, on the contrary, there is some chance of an increase as policies for earlier retirement are reversed.

Among younger age groups, the pattern is more mixed. In most Member States, participation of men younger than 25 has fallen markedly over the past 30 years and by almost 10 percentage points between 1980 and 1992 over the Community as a whole (Graph 53). In the Netherlands, Denmark and the UK, however — the three countries where the rate was highest in 1992 and the only three where it was higher than in the US or Japan

Participation rates of men by age group in the Member States, 1960 to 1992

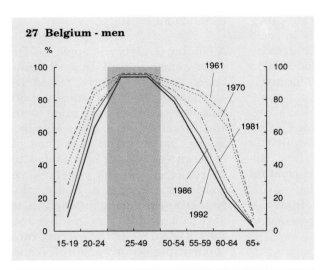

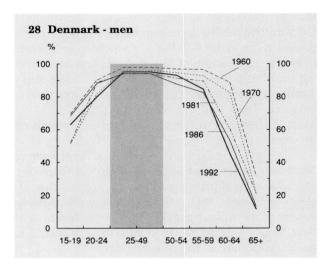

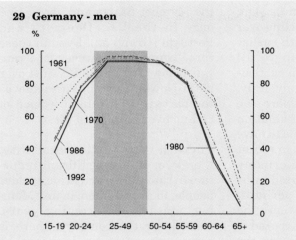

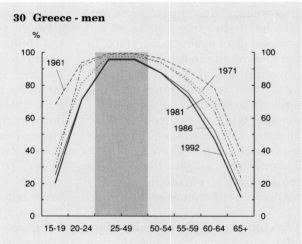

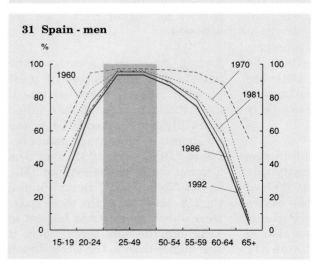

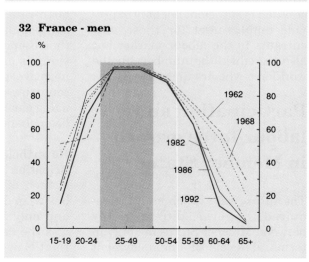

Participation rates of men by age group in the Member States, 1960 to 1992

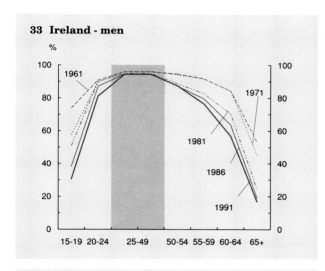

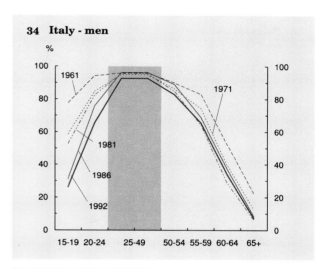

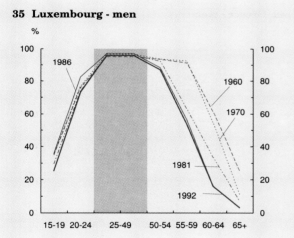

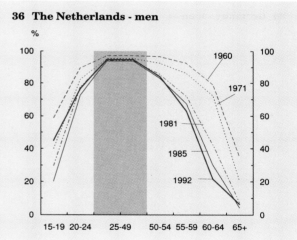

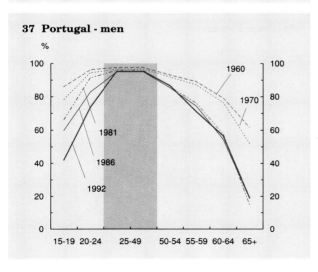

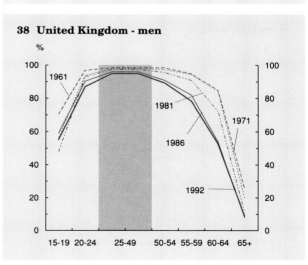

Participation rates of women by age group in the Member States, 1960 to 1992

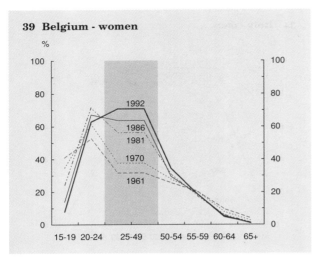

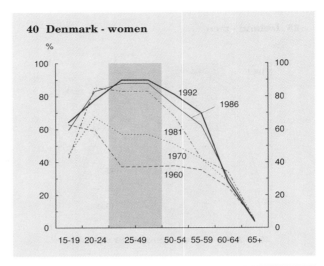

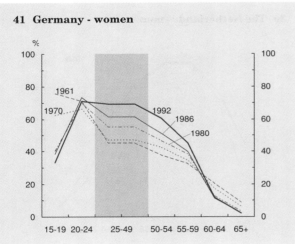

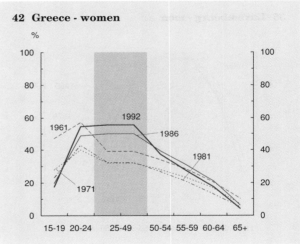

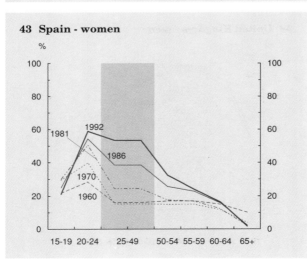

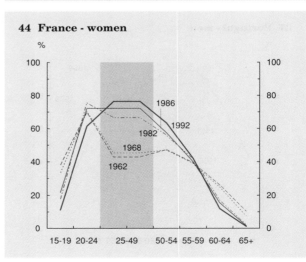

Participation rates of women by age group in the Member States, 1960 to 1992

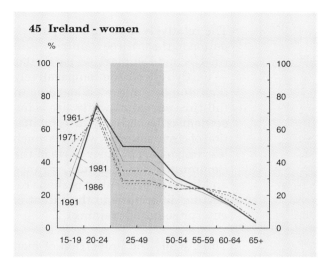

45 Ireland - women

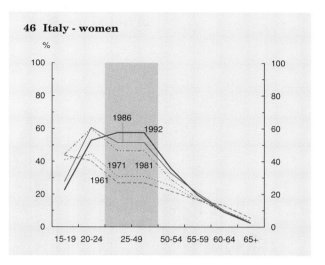

46 Italy - women

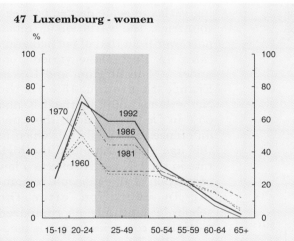

47 Luxembourg - women

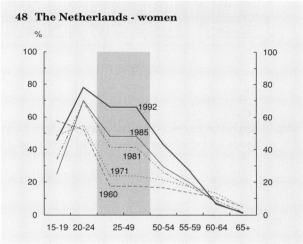

48 The Netherlands - women

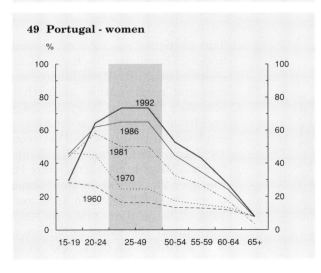

49 Portugal - women

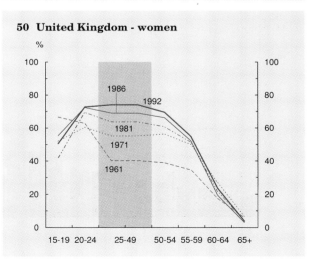

50 United Kingdom - women

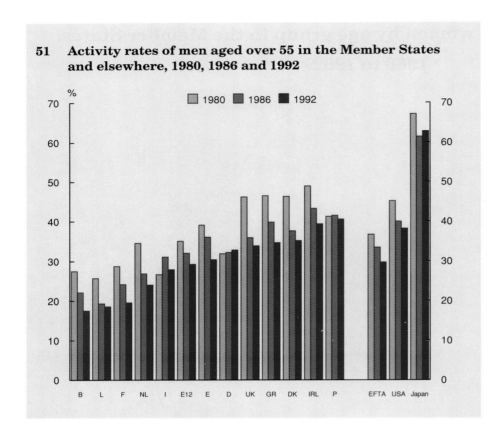

51   Activity rates of men aged over 55 in the Member States and elsewhere, 1980, 1986 and 1992

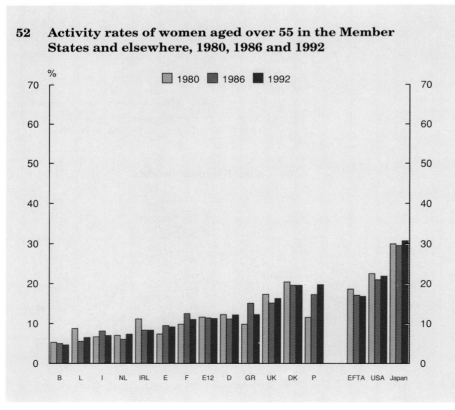

52   Activity rates of women aged over 55 in the Member States and elsewhere, 1980, 1986 and 1992

— the rate of participation rose slightly during the 1980s, though in the latter two cases it has declined since 1986.

The relatively high rates of participation in these three countries — in the UK and Denmark, in particular — partly reflects the comparatively high numbers recorded as being in full-time education while also being economically active — a combination of circumstances which is much less important in other parts of the Community (in Belgium, France and Italy, in particular, perhaps reflecting differences in the extent of enterprise-based training).

Thus, while the proportion of men aged 15 to 19 in education or training varies in some degree between countries, the variation is much narrower than that of participation rates. In 1992, these varied from under 10% in Belgium and 15% in France to around 45% in the Netherlands, 55% in the UK and 65% in Denmark. Much the same differences also apply to women in this age group. Although the high rate in the UK partly reflects a low proportion of young people remaining in education after the school-leaving age as compared with other countries (which is tending to change over time), this is not the case in Denmark.

The participation rate of women under 25 has generally changed less — increasing activity balancing increasing participation in further education. Only in Belgium, Italy and Ireland was there a consistent tendency for the rate to fall between 1980 and 1992 (Graph 54). While half the Member States registered a rise over this period, in all of these there was a fall between 1986 and 1992. The relative rates in 1992 were much the same as for men, with participation being highest in

Denmark, the UK and the Netherlands — with Germany, the only Member States where the rate was higher than in the US — and lowest in Belgium, France and Greece.

Overall, there seems little reason to expect a marked reduction in activity rates of younger people in future years in most Member States, though Denmark and the UK, where rates of 15–19 year-olds are much higher than elsewhere, might be exceptions. Even in the Southern Member States, rates of participation for this age group are already low in most cases. In Spain and Greece, rates for young men are below 30% and for young women below 25%, while the same is true in Southern Italy. Only in Portugal, where the rate for men in this age group is just above 40% and for women around 30%, does there seem much scope for further reduction.

This leaves participation among people of prime working age, as at the Community level, as the major determinant of future changes. While there has been a tendency in all Member States for the proportion of prime-age men in the labour force to decline, especially over the 1980s, the main trend in this age group has been the increase in participation among prime-age women. This is common to all countries and in the 1980s has been most marked in those parts of the Community — Spain, Ireland, Germany and the Netherlands — where it was comparatively low initially. Even in Denmark, however, where the rate is significantly higher than elsewhere — and almost on a par with that of men — it has continued to rise in recent years, even though at a much slower rate than before. (See *Employment in Europe, 1993*, Chapter 6, for a detailed break down of the long-term change in

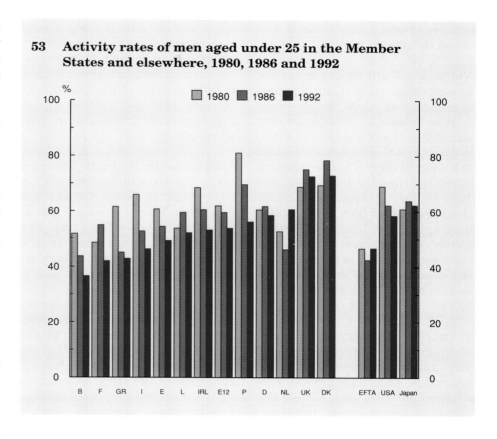

53   Activity rates of men aged under 25 in the Member States and elsewhere, 1980, 1986 and 1992

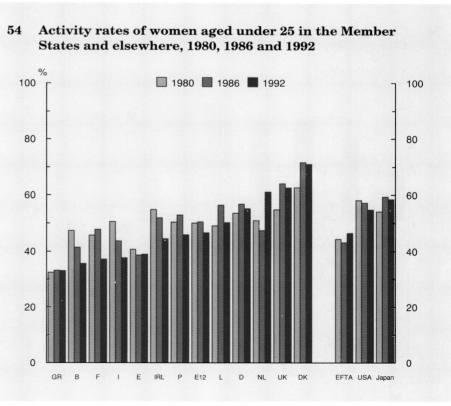

54   Activity rates of women aged under 25 in the Member States and elsewhere, 1980, 1986 and 1992

participation rates of women between the ages of 24 and 49.)

Nevertheless, differences across the Community in rates of participation of women in this age group remain extremely wide. In Ireland, the rate was still only around 50% in 1992, in Spain and Greece below 55% and in Italy only slightly above, whereas in Portugal and the UK, it was over 70%, in France over 75% and in Denmark almost 90%. This implies that, apart from Denmark, further increases in participation are likely, but most especially in those parts of the Community where rates for women are still significantly below 60%.

These to a large extent are areas which are still developing economically and where there is scope for high rates of economic growth — as occurred in the latter part of the 1980s in many cases. However,

growth in the past has not always been accompanied by large-scale job creation — in Ireland, for example, employment increased by much less than in the rest of the Community between 1986 and 1990 despite a higher rate of growth than anywhere else.

Such areas also tend to be, however, areas where unemployment is relatively high. In Spain, Ireland and Southern Italy — where participation rates of women are significantly lower than in the North of the country — unemployment is around 20%.

Moreover, these are also areas where growth of working-age population over the remainder of the decade is projected to be well above the Community average. Indeed, according to the latest forecast, in Spain and Ireland, working-age population will increase by more be-

tween 1995 and 2000 than anywhere else in the Community – by over 10% on the mean projection. Combined with the increasing participation of women, this could mean a labour force growth of around 3% a year or more. In other words, without significant emigration, employment would need to increase at this rate merely in order to keep unemployment from rising. In this respect, it can be noted that Spain has achieved growth of employment of 3% or more only three times in the past 30 years — but all three since 1986 — and Ireland only twice.

In the rest of the Community, growth of working-age population of over ½% a year is projected in six other Member States as well as in Spain and Ireland — in Denmark, Greece, France, Luxembourg, the Netherlands and Portugal. Given the prospective increase in participation, the growth of the labour force could, therefore, be around 1% or more in 8 of the 12 Community countries, and not much less than this, if any, in Italy and the UK.

The only exceptions are Denmark, where participation rates are already very high and may not rise much further, and Germany, where without immigration on a substantial scale, working-age population is set to decline by over 1% a year. Although a continuing increase in the participation of women may offset this fall, it is unlikely to give rise to any substantial growth in the labour force.

The outlook for Germany depends critically on the scale of inward migration, however. In recent years, this has been large enough more than to offset the natural decline in working-age population and to cause the latter to expand by more than in most other countries in the

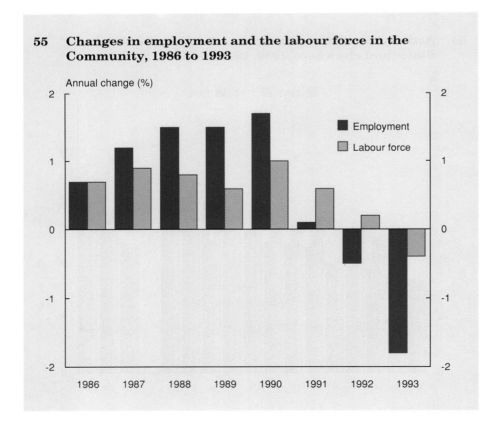

55   Changes in employment and the labour force in the Community, 1986 to 1993

Community (by almost 1% a year between 1986 and 1991). If immigration from Central and Eastern Europe were to continue on a similar scale as in the past, then any fall in working-age population would be relatively small and labour force growth would be closer to that in other Member States. To other Member States, however, immigration is unlikely to be a major cause of labour force growth.

Changes in participation and employment

Matching job growth to labour force growth is not a simple equation. The rate at which the latter occurs is likely itself to be related to the former, in the sense that the more employment opportunities expand the greater the increase in labour force participation is likely to be. In other words, creating more jobs will, on past evidence, encourage more people who are at present economically inactive, to join the labour force.

As noted in previous *Employment in Europe* reports, the high growth in employment which occurred between 1985 and 1990 was associated more with increased numbers of people entering the labour force than with a reduction in unemployment. Of the net additional jobs created over this period, some 70% were filled by new entrants to the labour market rather than by those who were officially recorded as being unemployed. While population of working age increased by just over 2% over these five years, boosted by significant immigration from Central and Eastern Europe in the later part of the period, the labour force expanded by 4% as a result of

increasing participation (Graph 55).

Since 1990, however, as net job creation has declined, the labour force has expanded only slightly. Between 1990 and 1993, it increased by under $\frac{1}{2}$% in total, less than the rise in working-age population, which was around 1% over these three years. Indeed in 1993, the labour force as measured actually seems to have contracted significantly (though it should be borne in mind that the 1993 figures for employment in particular involve a significant amount of estimation and so are subject to revision). Instead of increasing, therefore, labour force participation has fallen since 1990. The rise in unemployment, therefore, large though it has been, has not revealed the true extent of the employment problem.

The implication is that the contraction in employment opportunities over the past few years has deterred many people from actively looking for a job and they have disappeared from the labour force. This is unlikely to be a permanent state of affairs. If and when employment opportunities begin to be created in significant numbers, it is probable that these people will re-emerge as job seekers to swell the size of the Community labour force once again.

On the other hand, if recovery of employment on any substantial scale fails to occur, then labour force growth is likely to remain depressed, so tending to moderate the rise in unemployment. This would not mean, however, that the employment problem is any less serious, simply that it has been disguised to a greater extent.

Chapter 3   Economic growth and employment

Employment growth in the Community as elsewhere is closely related to output growth, but productivity growth has slowed down markedly since the mid-1970s which has boosted the rate of job creation. This has been especially the case in non-manufacturing sectors.

Introduction

The relationship between economic growth and the process of job creation is of key importance for employment in the Community. On the one hand, it indicates how much employment is likely to rise as recovery takes place, on the other, what rate of growth might be required to achieve any given rate of job creation. Moreover, the stability or otherwise of the relationship over time, as well as the variation between Member States, gives some guide to how far it is likely to be susceptible to the influence of policy.

In practice, the historical evidence demonstrates that the relationship between the growth of output and employment tends to be very close for individual countries as well as for the Community as a whole. However, the form of the relationship has changed markedly over the long-term. It also varies significantly between Member States as well as between the Community and other advanced economies.

Thus some countries, like the US have experienced a significant increase in employment with a relatively low rate of output growth, while others, like Ireland, have had very little rise in employment despite a much higher rate of growth.

The fact that these variations exist suggests that it may be possible, through policy, to influence the nature of the relationship in future years and achieve a more employment-intensive pattern of output growth.

A key aspect underlying the relationship between output and employment is technology, the advance of which is a major factor determining the growth of productivity. The use made of technology, and, in particular, information technology, is likely to have a major influence on the development of both the economy and society in future years, and, therefore, on the process of job creation. This issue is considered only indirectly in the analysis below.

GDP and employment growth in the Community since the 1960s

The numbers in employment in the Community have varied closely with the rate of growth of GDP over the past 30 years. Upturns in output growth have on every occasion been followed, within the space of six months or so, by an increase in employment growth, while downturns have, equally consistently, led to a reduction in growth, and on occasions to an absolute decline — notably in 1967, 1975, 1981 and, most strikingly, during the present recession (Graph 56, where GDP growth is lagged two quarters to adjust for the delayed response of employment to changes in output). Indeed the pattern of employment growth since the early 1960s has been almost an exact image of that of GDP growth.

What has changed, however, is the gap between the two or, in other words, the rate of increase in output per person employed, which is an indicator of productivity growth (though it leaves out of account changes in average working time). In the 1960s, the trend rise in productivity in the Community was over 4% a year, so that in 1967, for example a fall in GDP growth to a little under 4% led to a decline in employment of almost 1%. By the early 1970s, the trend rise in productivity had fallen to about 4% a year, but after the oil crisis of 1973–74 — when output growth fell

Growth of employment and GDP
in the Community, US, Japan and EFTA countries, 1962 to 1993

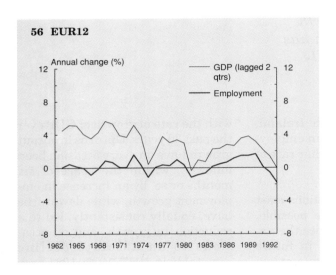

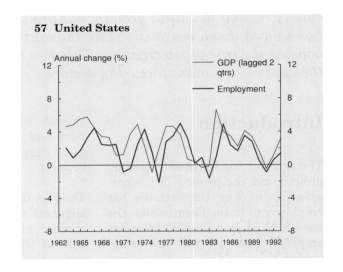

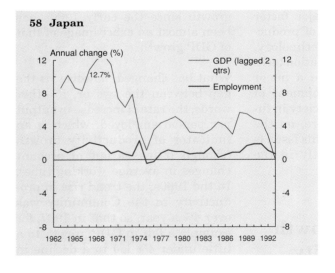

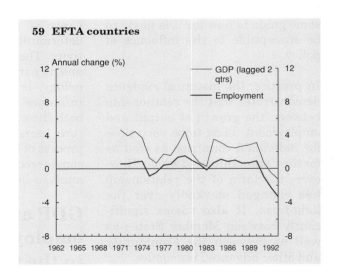

sharply — it slowed further to around 3% a year.

Since the second oil crisis in 1979–80, there has been another apparent slowdown in trend productivity growth to not much more than 2% a year. As a result, the GDP growth which occurred in the latter part of the 1980s, which was modest by the standards of the 1960s, was accompanied by a larger increase in employment than at any time since 1960.

This apparent reduction in underlying productivity growth can be regarded as being favourable from an employment perspective. It suggests that the rate of output recovery which could be expected to generate the size of increase in employment required to have any significant impact on unemployment in the Community over the remainder of the 1990s is much lower than it used to be.

At the same time, however, it might be regarded as unfavourable to the extent that, especially through weakening competitiveness, it reduces the attainable growth of output and so the capacity of the economy to create employment. In this regard, the sectors where the slowdown in productivity occurred assume some importance.

As indicated below, the fact that there was a decline in aggregate productivity growth does not mean that there was a similar reduction in all sectors. It is perfectly compatible with continued high productivity growth in key areas of the economy — in manufacturing, in particular — where the international competitiveness of production is critical for trade performance and long-term economic growth. Indeed the shift of labour from high productivity growth

sectors to those with lower growth has been an important part of the employment creation process, while at the same time providing part of the explanation for the slowdown in overall productivity growth itself.

A further part of the apparent fall in underlying productivity growth seems to be due to a reduction in the average amount of time those in employment work. Since 1988, the evidence of the Community Labour Force Survey is that the average number of hours worked per week (both actual and usual) have gradually fallen. This seems to have been as significant in 1989 and 1990 at the peak of the economic upturn as in 1991 and 1992 when recession set in. In practice, this means that a given amount of work has been shared among more people, so adding appreciably to the numbers in employment and reducing apparent productivity.

Between 1988 and 1992, the reduction in average working time could be interpreted to mean that the numbers in employment in 1992 were almost 3 million higher than if there had been no change in hours worked. This almost certainly overstates the effect of reducing working time on the numbers employed. Thus in certain sectors of activity the nature of the production process may limit the extent to which numbers can be reduced when the volume of work declines — ie even if working time had not fallen the same number of people would have needed to have been employed. Moreover, in a number of cases, the reduction in working-time may have been accompanied by an increase in productivity which would not have occurred if average hours had not fallen. In this case, the number of people employed would have been the same, but their productivity lower. Nevertheless, it is

indicative of the significance of this factor.

Unfortunately, it is not possible with the data available to distinguish between the numbers employed and the volume of work performed in earlier years, nor, therefore, to examine the change in productivity growth on a more meaningful basis than in terms of the numbers in employment.

In seeking an explanation for the slowdown in productivity growth in the Community, it is important to be aware that not only is it a common feature of all Member States, but that it also occurred at around the same time in other developed parts of the world.

GDP and employment growth in other developed countries

The relationship between GDP and employment growth in the US has been just as close as in the Community (Graph 57, where, it should be noted, the data for GDP growth for the years before 1978 are based on annual rather than quarterly figures and where the two-quarter lag is, therefore, only very approximate, which affects the timing of changes in GDP growth and which may explain why the two series are less in synchrony than for the Community). Nevertheless, there are three major differences in the pattern of growth rates. In the first place, both output and, especially, employment growth have fluctuated far more than in the Community since 1960. Much larger increases in employment have been recorded — 4% or more in a single year on at least four occasions, while the Community has never achieved an annual rise of even 2% — coupled with larger downward variations.

Secondly, the rate of GDP growth has slowed by less over these 30 years than in the Community. Peak rates of GDP growth attained in the 1970s and 1980s were on a par with those achieved in the 1960s. The main difference in the later period was that these were interspersed with much larger downturns — and lower cyclical troughs — than in the earlier post-war years.

Thirdly, the gap between output growth and employment growth — ie the growth in productivity — has been consistently smaller than in the Community, averaging under 1% a year since the early 1970s. Like the Community, this represents a reduction in the underlying rate compared with that which was evident in the years before then, by around 2% a year. The US, there-fore, has been able to achieve considerably larger increases in em-ployment with a given rate of GDP growth over the past 30 years than the Community, though equally it has had a much faster growing la-bour force requiring more jobs to be created.

The evidence suggests that, unlike the Community, none of this low rate of apparent productivity growth has been due, over the past decade at least, to a reduction in the average time worked per person in employment. Indeed between 1983 and 1992, both average hours worked per week and average hours worked per year increased slightly in the US (according to the US La-bour Force Survey).

The relationship between GDP and employment growth in Japan has been similar in a number of ways to

that in the Community. Economic growth has slowed down markedly since the 1960s — when rates of 10% a year or more were common. This slowdown has been accompa-nied, as in the Community, by a significant reduction in productiv-ity growth — from around 9% a year in the 1960s to not much more than 3% a year since the mid-1970s (Graph 58). As a result, the average rate of employment growth attained in recent years, at around 1% a year, has been similar to the growth in the 1960s.

As compared with the Community, however, employment growth in Japan has varied much less from year to year. The contrast has been most marked since 1990 when the present recession began. Though the fall in output growth has been even more pronounced in Japan than in the Community, declining from 5% to zero, the numbers in employment have continued to go up, while in the Community they have declined sharply.

Moreover, unlike in the Com-munity, average hours worked by those in employment in Japan seem to have remained broadly unchanged during most of the 1980s (at a level at least a third higher than the average in the Community). Since 1989, however, there is evidence of a reduction in working time as output growth slowed down, average hours worked per week falling by around 5% between then and 1992 (accord-ing to the Japanese Labour Force Survey).

Finally, the EFTA countries have also shown a similar pattern to the Community as regards GDP and employment change over the past 20 years. The rate of both output and productivity growth has slowed since the mid-1970s — the latter to

much the same level, just over 2% a year, as in the Community — while up until the present recession, growth of employment was main-tained at around 1% a year (Graph 59). Since 1990 and the onset of recession, however, em-ployment has fallen considerably, declining by 2% in 1992 and by an estimated 4% in 1993.

One common feature which emerges from this comparative analysis is that productivity growth — measured by output per person employed — has been signi-ficantly lower in all the developed economies since the mid-1970s than before. In the US, Japan and, until recently, in the EFTA coun-tries, this decline in productivity growth has been on the scale which was necessary to maintain employ-ment at the level required to keep unemployment down to reasonable levels.

Japan and the EFTA countries, in other words, succeeded in offsetting the adverse effects of the decline in GDP growth which, on earlier ex-perience, would have been expected to result in a substantial increase in unemployment. For the EFTA coun-tries, however, this success has faltered since 1990, while in Japan, the costs of maintaining levels of employment when production re-mains depressed are becoming increasingly difficult for enterprises to sustain.

In the Community, on the other hand, though productivity growth has also fallen appreciably since the mid-1970s, and though this has en-abled employment to be maintained at higher levels than would have been expected previously in the face of the slowdown of GDP growth, the fall has not been enough to prevent unemployment from increasing con-siderably.

Growth of employment and GDP
in Germany, France, UK and Italy, 1962 to 1993

60 Germany

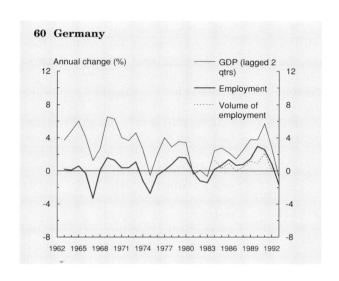

61 France

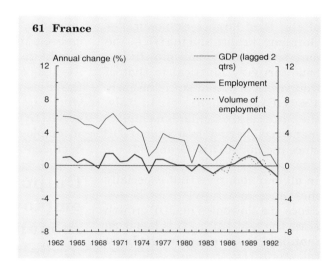

62 United Kingdom

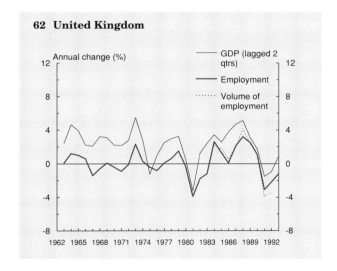

63 Italy

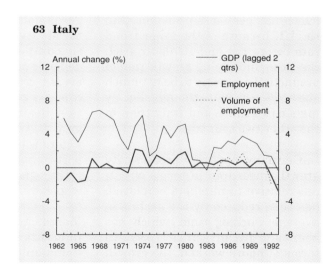

GDP and employment growth in Member States

The close relationship between GDP growth and changes in employment is also evident in individual Member States. In three of the four largest economies — Germany, France and the UK — the pattern of employment growth has been virtually identical to that of the growth of output since the early 1960s (Graphs 60, 61, 62). In Italy, the patterns are similar but employment has varied less than GDP since the mid-1970s (Graph 63).

In all four countries (but especially in France and Italy) there is evidence of a slowdown in GDP growth since the mid-1970s. This has been disguised in Germany by the boost to output from the process of unification and in the UK by the greater amplitude of cyclical fluctuations than elsewhere over this period. The slowdown in output growth has been accompanied by a significant decline in productivity growth, which has been less pronounced in the UK because of the lower trend rate before the mid-1970s. In each case, the underlying growth rate of productivity appears to be not much above 2% a year — though slightly higher in France and Italy than in the other two countries.

In Germany, apparent productivity growth, measured in terms of output relative to numbers employed, has been reduced by the decline in average working time, which has been significant since 1989. In terms of hours worked, the growth of productivity over this period has been around 3% a year rather than 2%. Sharing available work among more people has, therefore, been a major factor over the past 3–4 years

in increasing the numbers in work, even if by not enough to prevent unemployment from rising.

In Italy and the UK, in contrast, changes in working time have served to exaggerate apparent productivity growth. In both countries, average hours worked per person went up in years of high output growth to meet the demand for increased production. On the other hand, in both cases also, hours worked per person declined during the present recession. Reductions in working-time have, therefore, served to maintain higher numbers in employment as production has been depressed.

Output and employment growth in manufacturing and elsewhere

The apparent slowdown in productivity growth in the Community, though seemingly beneficial from an employment perspective, is a potential cause for concern as regards competitiveness. Insofar as the ability of Community producers to compete on world markets depends on their efficiency, productivity growth underpins the capacity of the Community to sustain desirable rates of economic growth. What matters most in this regard is productivity in export, import-competing and related sectors rather than over the economy as a whole.

Manufactured goods still dominate international trade. Over 70% of Community export earnings come from manufactures rather than primary production or services. Though trade in services has grown significantly in recent years, the rate of increase has been no higher

than for manufactures. It is in large measure productivity growth in manufacturing rather than in the rest of the economy which is of importance in assessing the implications for competitiveness. Moreover, the measurement of productivity growth is more meaningful for manufacturing than the rest of the economy since the difficulties of measuring changes in output are much less serious, both in principle and practice, than in the case of services where output tends to be less tangible.

Changes in employment in manufacturing in the Community are even more closely related to output growth than for the economy as a whole. Since the late 1960s — data problems make it difficult to go back much further than this for a representative number of Member States — the numbers employed in the sector, with a lag of some six months, have followed variations in production almost exactly (Graph 64).

Although the relationship between output and employment in the rest of the economy is less close than in manufacturing, growth in the numbers employed has, nevertheless, varied systematically with output growth over the past 25 years (Graph 65). There is, however, a difference in productivity growth between the two parts of the economy. In particular, the gap between output and employment growth in manufacturing has remained more stable than for the rest of the economy. While there has been some reduction in productivity growth in manufacturing since the mid-1970s, the underlying rate in the early 1990s, at around 3% a year, was only slightly lower than in the early 1970s, when it was some 4% a year, even if significantly lower than in the 1960s.

Growth of manufacturing and non-manufacturing value-added and employment in the Community, US and Japan, 1962 to 1993

64 EUR7 - manufacturing

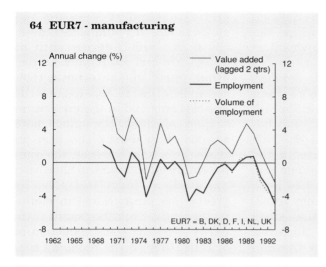

65 EUR7 - non-manufacturing

66 United States - manufacturing

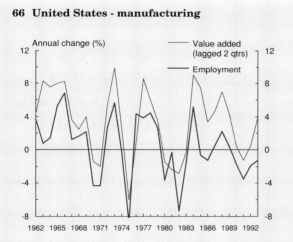

67 United States - non-manufacturing

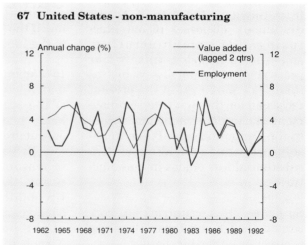

68 Japan - manufacturing

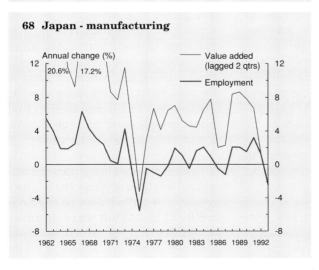

69 Japan - non-manufacturing

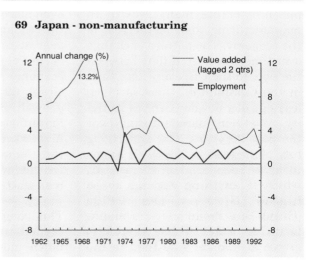

In other sectors, there are clearer signs of a narrowing of the gap between value-added and employment growth. In the 1980s, productivity growth in non-manufacturing seems to have fallen to 2% a year or below, as compared with $2^1/_2$% or so in the late 1970s and 4% or more in the 1960s. As a result, employment has tended to rise at a faster rate after the mid-1970s than before, despite the slower growth of output.

Nevertheless, though the slowdown in productivity since the mid-1970s has increased the rate of job creation significantly, it has not done so by enough in most years to maintain employment at the level required to prevent unemployment from rising in the face of almost continuous job losses in manufacturing. (In manufacturing, employment has risen in only four years since 1974 and always by less than 1%.) Moreover, in the present recession for the first time, employment in non-manufacturing sectors in the Community has fallen in absolute terms, coinciding with a substantial loss of jobs in manufacturing.

So far as other countries are concerned, the US and Japan also show a closer relationship between output and employment growth in manufacturing than in the rest of the economy. The pattern of change over time, however, differs between the two. In the US, even more than in the Community, there is much less sign of a slowdown in productivity growth in manufacturing over the past 20 years. The underlying rate of increase in the 1980s seems to have been around 4% a year, which if anything appears to be higher than in the 1960s (Graph 66). Productivity in manufacturing in the US has, therefore, grown at a faster rate than in the

Community over the past decade, whereas before 1974, the reverse was the case.

In other sectors of the US economy, in contrast, the relationship between output and employment is much less systematic than for manufacturing. Indeed, employment has fluctuated more than value-added and in number of years, implied productivity has fallen significantly (Graph 67). This was particularly the case in the 1970s. Since then, the average rate of productivity growth has been barely above zero — thereby translating any increase in value-added directly into more jobs. Moreover, average hours worked by those in employment in non-manufacturing activities seem to have remained much the same over this period and in the 1980s even increased slightly.

In Japan, productivity growth in manufacturing as well as in the rest of the economy has declined markedly over the past 20 years as output growth has slowed. Since the mid-1970s, the underlying rate of increase of productivity in manufacturing, though higher than in the US and the Community at around 5% a year, seems to have been only about half that in the 1960s (Graph 68). The decline has been even more pronounced in the rest of the economy, falling to around 3% a year as compared with rates of 8% or more in the 1960s (when the economy was growing rapidly — Graph 69). As a result, the rate of growth in employment in non-manufacturing has tended to be higher since 1973 than before, as in the Community, so compensating for the lower rate of job creation in manufacturing.

This compensatory effect has succeeded in achieving in Japan a much more stable growth in the

overall numbers employed in the economy as a whole than in the Community and, more especially, than in the US. The effect was especially marked in years when employment in manufacturing declined in absolute terms, such as 1975, 1978 and 1987, when jobs in other parts of the economy increased by more than average. It has also occurred in the present recession, which has been much more serious than during the first oil crisis. This time however, the compensatory effect seems to have been assisted, at least initially, by greater job preservation in manufacturing than was the case in 1975, partly aided by some reduction in working time. If the recession continues, however, it will clearly become more difficult to maintain employment levels in the economy as a whole.

The slowdown of productivity growth in the Community

The separation of manufacturing from the rest of the economy provides some insight into the proximate causes of the slowdown in GDP per person employed observed in the Community. In the first place, this slowdown is more marked in non-manufacturing sectors than in manufacturing. Since the former consist predominantly of service activities, which, at least in the past, have had less scope for the introduction of mechanisation and other labour-saving techniques, this is perhaps to be expected.

Secondly, since value-added in non-manufacturing sectors has invariably increased since the mid-1970s at a higher rate than in manufacturing — which was not the case before — it has come to account for a progressively higher share of GDP. The slowdown in productivity growth within these sectors has, therefore, been reinforced by the fact that a larger proportion of output has been produced in sectors where the growth of productivity is relatively low.

This leaves open the question of what caused the slowdown in productivity growth within these two sectors. Reductions in the average time worked per person employed might be a very small part of the answer, but for non-manufacturing rather than manufacturing and mainly it would seem for the most recent years (Graphs 64 and 65).

Other explanations might lie in measurement problems, in a systematic underestimation of constant price value-added in services, in particular. It is possible, for example, that improvements in the quality and range of service, associated partly with technological advance and computerisation, are not adequately captured in the constant price measure of value-added. It is also possible that constant price value-added has been depressed to some extent by the increasing proportion of women in employment, since their wages — the major element of value-added — tend to be considerably lower than those of men. The maximum plausible size of this effect, however, is considerably smaller than the reduction in productivity growth witnessed. Neither explanation, moreover, gives a plausible answer to the question of why there was a sudden slowdown in productivity growth in the mid-1970s.

A further factor underlying these developments is technology itself and, in particular, the information technological revolution which has broadly coincided with the slowing

down of productivity growth. While the coincidence of the two may appear paradoxical, in practice, it is arguable that, as well as the possible effect on the measurement of value-added, the new technology has been difficult to implement and exploit fully, precisely because of the far-reaching nature of its potential effect on the production process and the organisation of work. The potential large-scale gains in productivity have, on this argument, been slow to be realised but may materialise with a vengeance over the coming years as the learning process is completed, the structure of production changes and businesses adapt to take full advantage of the possibilities created.

Whatever the explanation, the evidence of developments in Japan, and also in the EFTA countries, indicates, however, that the Community has not been the only economy experiencing such a slowdown. In all the economies, the slowdown was arguably, in some sense, a result of the decline in GDP growth, which effectively meant that productivity growth had to fall if sufficient jobs were to be created for the increasing numbers of people wanting to work.

This is consistent with labour market forces operating to drive down productivity in response to the excess supply of labour in order that the excess should be absorbed. The absorption, however, seems to have occurred in Japan and the EFTA countries without a fall in wages to encourage employers to take on more labour and without a period of high unemployment. This suggests other mechanisms were at work, such as deliberate policy action or an autonomous change in behaviour on the part of employers.

In the Community, the same kind of mechanisms may have come into play but were less powerful, while in the US, market forces seem to have played a larger role in pushing down wages in the non-manufacturing sector and stimulating the creation of substantial numbers of additional jobs.

Output and employment in manufacturing in Member States

Changes in the relationship between output growth and employment in manufacturing in the Community as a whole disguise some differences between Member States. As at the Community level, the numbers employed have tended to vary in line with production in each of the largest four economies. However, whereas in Germany, France and Italy, there are signs of a progressive slowdown in underlying productivity growth since the 1960s, this does not seem to be the case in the UK. If anything, trend productivity growth seems to have been higher in the 1980s — at around 4% a year — than in the 1960s and higher still than in the second half of the 1970s, though during the earlier period, manufacturing output grew in only two years, and then by under 2%, which makes for difficulty in establishing any trend at all (Graph 74).

The figures for output per person, however, tend to exaggerate productivity growth in the UK in the 1980s, since at times of increasing production, in particular, average hours worked tended to increase. Underlying productivity growth, therefore, appears to have been closer to 3% a year than 4%.

Growth of manufacturing value-added and employment in Germany, France, Italy and UK, 1962 to 1993

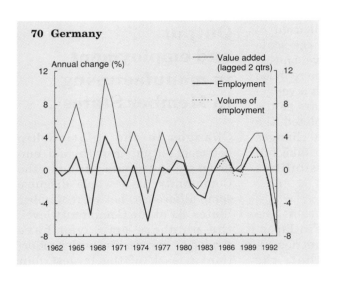

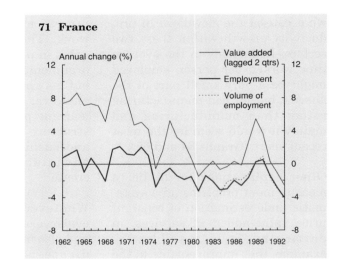

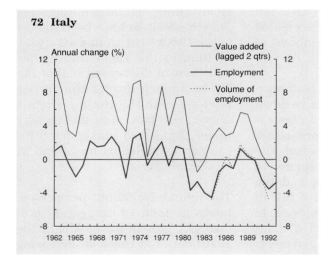

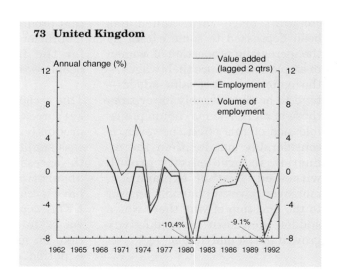

Growth of non-manufacturing value-added and employment in the Member States, 1962 to 1993

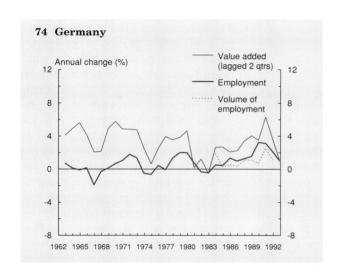

74 Germany

Annual change (%)

Value added (lagged 2 qtrs)
Employment
Volume of employment

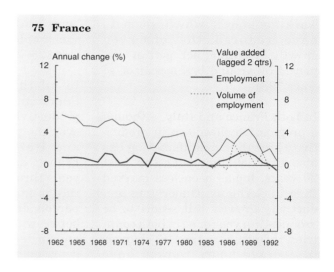

75 France

Annual change (%)

Value added (lagged 2 qtrs)
Employment
Volume of employment

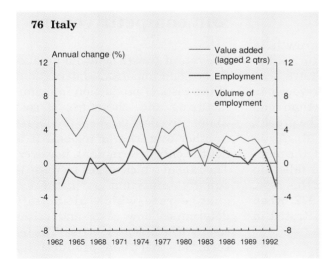

76 Italy

Annual change (%)

Value added (lagged 2 qtrs)
Employment
Volume of employment

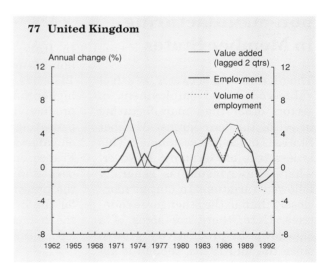

77 United Kingdom

Annual change (%)

Value added (lagged 2 qtrs)
Employment
Volume of employment

The progressive decline in productivity growth in manufacturing is most pronounced in Germany, where the underlying rate of increase seems to have fallen from around 5% a year in the 1960s to 4% a year in the 1970s and to only just over 2% a year in the 1980s. Part of this fall, however, can be explained in terms of reductions in working hours, which seem to have reduced the observed growth in output per person employed by around ¹/₂% a year or so since 1984.

In both France and Italy, although a progressive slowdown in productivity growth in manufacturing has also been evident over the past 20 years, it has been less marked than in Germany. Underlying productivity growth still seems to be around 4% a year or so in both countries, though, as in the UK, changes in average hours worked have tended to boost the observed growth in output per person employed.

Output and employment in non-manufacturing in Member States

The relationship between growth of value-added and employment in sectors other than manufacturing in all of the four largest Member States is much less systematic. This is less true of Germany, however, where employment has generally followed variations in output more closely than in the other three countries. Here, there are signs of a slowdown in productivity growth since the mid-1970s, though it appears to be less marked than for manufacturing (Graph 74).

This is particularly the case if employment is measured in terms of total hours worked rather than the number of people in work, since reductions in working time have been significant in the past few years. Adjusted for this, underlying productivity growth seems to have been running at around 3% a year since the mid-1980s — as much as in manufacturing. Nevertheless, because of reductions in average hours worked, value-added per person employed has risen by only some 2% a year or less.

In all three of the other large Community countries, apparent productivity growth has also fallen over the past 20 years, in France and Italy, particularly so. In France, having been around 4% a year throughout the 1960s, the rate of growth in value-added per person employed has fluctuated between 1% and 3% since 1975, and in terms of hours worked by even more (Graph 75). Overall, however, the rate of job creation in non-manufacturing sectors in this period has been greater than before, though during the present recession, the numbers employed have declined significantly for the first time.

In Italy, employment growth in non-manufacturing sectors since 1975 has also tended to have been higher than before, the slowdown in productivity growth more than compensating for the fall in the growth of value-added (Graph 76). As in France, on the other hand, the numbers employed have also fallen in the present recession, in this case, for the first time since 1972, when the reduction was concentrated in agriculture.

In the UK, the underlying rate of increase in value-added per person employed in non-manufacturing sectors, which was already much lower than elsewhere in the Community before 1973, appears to have fallen to under 2% a year since then (Graph 77). As a result, as in the other countries, employment growth has been higher on average over this period than before (though as compared with elsewhere, the growth in value-added has declined by less).

To sum up, in all four of the largest Member States, a slowdown in productivity growth in non-manufacturing sectors over the past 20 years has helped to meet the need for a higher rate of job creation, resulting partly from job losses in manufacturing and partly from the higher rate of growth in the labour force. Reductions in average hours worked have contributed to this in Germany in particular, and in all four countries during the present recession. However, neither factor has been sufficiently powerful, especially in France, Italy and the UK, to avoid high levels of unemployment.

Productivity growth in manufacturing and competitiveness

The rate of growth of labour productivity is an important determinant of the costs of production in manufacturing and, therefore, of cost competitiveness *vis à vis* producers in other countries or regions. It is not the only determinant, however. The rate at which wages increase is equally important as is the exchange rate which ultimately determines how costs and prices compare between countries. The interaction between productivity growth, wage rises and the exchange rate is critical to trade performance and inflation and, through these, to economic growth and employment.

If wage increases are to avoid pushing up prices, they need to be no higher than the rate of growth in labour productivity. If this is achieved, labour costs per unit of output will remain constant in nominal terms. In a world of inflation, however, things are not so simple. If prices generally are going up and wages in manufacturing only rose in nominal terms in line with productivity, there would almost certainly be a reduction in real wages (unless the growth of productivity in manufacturing was sufficiently higher than in the rest of the economy to compensate for inflation). In such a case, an increased share of value-added would go to profits. Clearly, the extent of the real reduction in pay would tend to be greater the higher the rate of inflation.

In an inflationary context, wage rises no higher than the growth of productivity plus the rate of increase in prices will not add to inflationary pressure — ie they will not cause higher inflation. Nor will they reduce the share of value-added going to profits.

It is important to recognise in this regard, however, that to maintain the share of profits in manufacturing, wages per unit of output (ie wages adjusted for productivity growth) need to increase in line with the price of manufactured goods rather than that of goods and services as a whole. Moreover, if non-wage labour costs were to increase in relation to value-added, the wage element of labour costs would need to adjust to prevent the share of profits falling.

It is also important to recognise, of course, that there may be circumstances when it is desirable for wages — ie average labour costs multiplied by the numbers employed — to fall as a share of value-added either because the share of profits is too low in relation to investment needs or because there is an increase in the capital-intensity of production (and a corresponding fall in labour-intensity).

Real wages and real product wages

In practice, over the past 20 years or so, nominal labour costs in manufacturing (ie wages plus employers' contributions and other non-wage labour costs) rose on average by around 11% a year in the Community as a whole — more in the 1970s, less in the 1980s and even less in the 1990s. (Average labour costs here, it should be noted, relate to men and women combined.) The rate of growth of labour productivity over this period averaged just under 4% a year. Prices of manufactured goods went up by an average of 7% a year (much the same as the excess of wage rises over productivity) so that the share of profits in value-added in manufacturing was broadly maintained. In other words, what is known as the real product wage (ie wages plus non-wage labour costs adjusted by the price of manufactured goods) rose in line with labour productivity (Graph 78).

There were, however, marked differences between what happened in the 1970s and what has happened in the period since. Between 1970 and 1980, real (product) wages in manufacturing in the Community rose at a higher rate than the growth in

productivity — by around 1% a year more. Although real wages (plus non-wage costs) measured in terms of consumer goods went up by less than this, there was a significant shift of value-added from profits to wages.

Since 1980, the real product wage has risen at a slower rate than productivity growth, so causing value-added to shift back towards profits. Thus, the real product wage rose by just over 2% a year while labour productivity went up by around 3%. In terms of consumer goods, real wages in manufacturing went up on average by under 2% a year. At the same time, inflation slowed appreciably from an average in the 1970s of over 10% a year in the Community as a whole to one of $6^{1}/_{2}$% in the 1980s and to 4–5% since. Wage moderation clearly contributed to this process as did the reduction in energy and primary product prices.

Although there are some differences in the pattern of change over time in individual Member States, over the period 1970 to 1991 as a whole, the real product wage rose broadly in line with productivity in the four largest countries (Graphs 79, 80, 81 and

78 Growth of productivity and real labour costs in manufacturing in EUR7, 1970-91

Index: 1970=100

— Productivity

···· Real labour costs (Manufacturing price deflator)

—·— Real labour costs (Consumer price deflator)

EUR7 = B, DK, D, F, I, NL, UK

Growth of productivity and real labour costs in manufacturing in Germany, France, Italy, UK, US and Japan 1970 to 1991

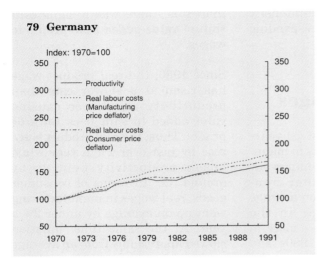

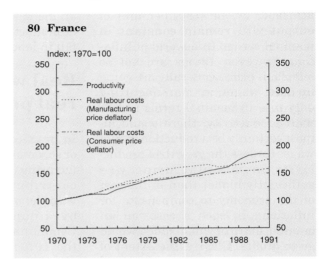

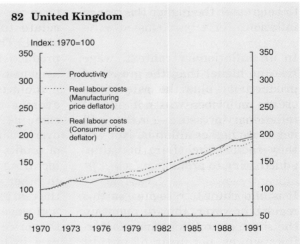

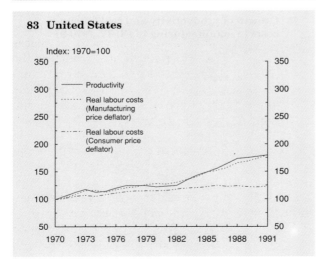

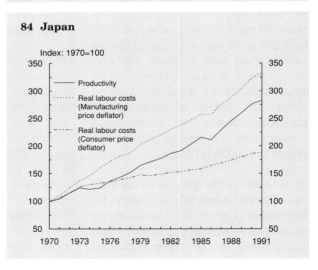

82). In each case, therefore, increases in labour productivity were passed fully into wages — or more accurately into labour costs — and the share of wages and profits in value-added remained much the same. Since 1980, however, in all countries, labour costs adjusted for inflation have risen by less than productivity and profits have taken a greater share of value-added, thereby recouping what they lost in the 1970s.

At the same time, in terms of the growth of real labour costs (ie measured in terms of consumers' expenditure), there were some differences between countries, with an average increase over the period as a whole of just over 2% a year in France and Germany, just over 2¹/₂% a year in Italy and just over 3% a year in the UK.

The differences have been more pronounced since 1980. Whereas in the 1970s, real labour costs increased on average by a similar rate in all four countries (by around 3% a year) between 1980 and 1991, the rate of growth of real labour costs was significantly lower in each case, apart from the UK. In this later period, real labour costs in France went up by only just over 1% a year, in Germany by just under 2% a year and in Italy by around 2% a year. Only in the UK did these increase by some 3% a year — much as in the previous decade.

These differences partly reflect differences in productivity growth over this period. But since this was higher in Italy than in the UK, they also reflect differences in the rate of increase in the price of manufactured goods relative to that of consumers' expenditure generally. In Italy, the price of manufactures rose at a much slower rate than general inflation, especially over

the 1980s, while in the UK the two rose more or less together. A given rise in the real product wage, therefore, was worth much less in terms of purchasing power in Italy than in the UK. As such, keeping the real product wage in manufacturing in line with productivity growth involved a significantly greater degree of wage moderation in the former than the latter.

The degree of wage moderation was also significant in France, where both the real product wage in manufacturing and real labour costs in terms of purchasing power went up by almost 2% a year less than the growth of productivity.

The relationship between productivity growth and real wages in manufacturing has been somewhat different in the US and Japan, though there are some similarities with the experience in Europe. In particular, the real product wage (the average wage deflated by manufacturing prices) in the US went up very much in line with productivity between 1970 and 1991, just as in Europe, with wages increasing slightly faster than productivity in the 1970s and slightly slower in the 1980s (Graph 83).

In Japan, on the other hand, the real product wage in manufacturing increased by around 1% a year more than productivity between 1970 and 1991 — 6% as opposed to 5% — implying a decline in the share of profits in value-added, though after 1980, the two rose at much the same rate (Graph 84). As in Italy, however, real labour costs (in purchasing power terms) increased by much less than the real product wage — by 3% a year instead of 6% — by only slightly more than the Community average and by less than in the UK.

This reflects, as in Italy, a much slower rise in the price of manufactured goods compared with consumers' expenditure as a whole. This was also the case in the US. There, real labour costs in manufacturing increased by an average of only 1% a year over the period 1970 to 1991 and by less than 1% a year after 1980. Indeed, between 1985 and 1991, there was no growth at all in average real labour costs in manufacturing, though the real product wage went up at the same rate as productivity. The degree of wage moderation seems, therefore, to have been substantial in both the US and Japan.

Unit labour costs in manufacturing

The above analysis suggests that the real product wage in manufacturing in the Community, as in the US and Japan, has risen broadly in line with productivity over the past 20 years and by slightly less since 1980. This implies that real labour costs per unit of output have remained unchanged over the period as a whole, though they have fallen a little over the past decade. It also implies that, in nominal terms, labour costs per unit of output have gone up at much the same rate as the price of manufactures and by a slightly lower rate since 1980. Since manufactured prices have risen at different rates in the different countries, however, nominal unit labour costs have also diverged when measured in national currencies.

In national currency terms, nominal unit labour costs in the Community increased on average by just under 7¹/₂% a year between 1970 and 1991, though by only around 3¹/₂% a year in the second half of the period as inflation fell

(Graph 85). By contrast, in the US, prices of manufactures rose by under 4% a year over the period as a whole and increased only marginally after 1982. The differential rate of increase between the Community and the US, therefore, narrowed only slightly in the 1980s as compared with the 1970s.

In Japan, nominal unit labour costs rose by an average of only 3% a year between 1970 and 1991, most of the increase being concentrated in the first five years of the period. After 1975, nominal unit labour costs went up only marginally and declined slightly in the 1980s. Between 1975 and 1991, there was a fairly consistent difference between the rate of increase in the Community and that in Japan of around 4% a year.

In themselves, these differences in inflation rates imply a steady deterioration in the cost competitiveness of Community manufacturers *vis à vis* their main competitors in the rest of the world. To a major extent, however, exchange rates have adjusted to compensate for the differences, especially so far as Japan is concerned.

When measured in terms of a common currency — in this case the ECU — therefore, unit labour costs in Japan went up in most years between 1970 and 1991 at a faster rate than in the Community (Graph 86). This was true over the period up to 1986, in particular, when the rise in unit labour costs in Japan averaged over 2% a year more than for the Community. From 1986 to 1991, however, unit labour costs in Japan declined in ECU terms, restoring much of the loss in cost competitiveness *vis à vis* the Community in the years before.

The fact that nominal unit labour costs in manufacturing in Japan have been consistently lower than in the Community has, therefore, been negated by exchange rate movements between the ECU and the Yen. It is these movements, rather than the rate of wage rises or productivity growth, which have primarily determined changes in the cost competitiveness of European manufacturers relative to their Japanese counterparts.

Moreover, exchange rate movements have been far from smooth. At various times over the past 20 years, they have caused the relative cost competitiveness of European and Japanese manufacturers to fluctuate wildly. Between 1978 and 1981, for example, manufacturing unit labour costs in ECU terms in Japan declined by over 30% relative to those in the Community, more than restoring the loss in cost competitiveness over the preceding 8 years. They then rose by almost 40% in relative terms between 1982 and 1986, before falling by 30% between 1986 and 1991. During this period, Japanese nominal unit labour costs in terms of Yen changed relatively little, while between 1982 and 1991, those in the Community rose steadily at around $3^{1}/_{2}$% a year.

The scale of fluctuations in US unit labour costs when measured in terms of ECUs has been similarly large and again is in marked contrast to the relative stability of the same costs in national currency terms. Having fallen significantly in the 1970s, unit labour costs in US manufacturing relative to those in the Community increased by over 50% between 1980 and 1985. They then fell by over 40% over the next three years.

These extreme fluctuations in cost competitiveness are due almost entirely to fluctuations in exchange rates, especially between the US Dollar and the Yen, and are very difficult to rationalise in economic terms. They would be even more difficult to offset by changes in the rate of growth of productivity or pay.

Over the long-term, however, there is a broad tendency for exchange rate movements to adjust for differential rates of inflation. At the same time, long-term exchange rate movements also tend to compensate for differences in underlying competitiveness and trade performance, which are not directly related to the unit costs of production. The long-term appreciation of the Yen against both the ECU and the Dollar, and the relative increase in unit labour costs which this has caused, is due in large measure to the comparative success of Japanese manufacturers in world export markets. Conversely, the long-term depreciation of the Dollar reflects the deterioration in the trade performance of US manufacturers relative to their European and Japanese rivals.

Unit labour costs in Member States

This marked difference in the behaviour of unit labour costs when measured in domestic currency or ECU terms is also a feature within the Community. Since 1970, there have been significant differences in rates of inflation between Member States which have shown up in equally large differences in the increase in unit labour costs, though since 1980, inflation has slowed down everywhere and differences have tended to narrow.

Nominal unit labour costs in national currency and ECU terms in the Community, US and Japan, 1970 to 1991

85 EUR7, US and Japan - national currency

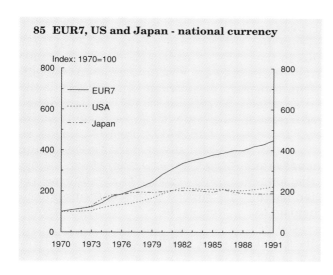

86 EUR7, US and Japan - ECU

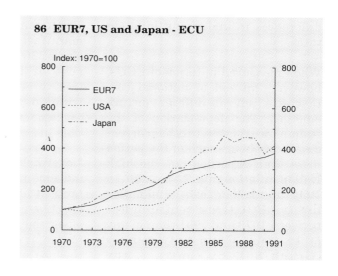

87 Member States - national currency

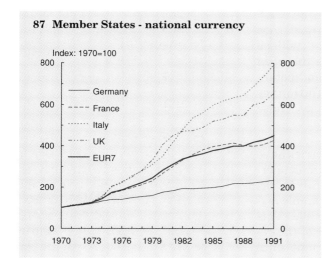

88 Member States - ECU

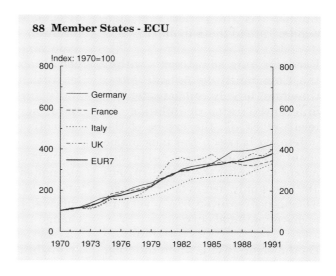

Between 1970 and 1991, nominal unit labour costs in manufacturing in Italy rose by an average of 10% a year and in the UK by over 9% a year, more than twice the increase in Germany of only 4% a year and significantly above the rise in France of 7% a year (Graph 87). In each case, as noted above, these differences largely reflect similar differences in underlying inflation rates.

When measured in terms of ECUs, however, instead of national currencies, a radically different picture emerges. The depreciation of the Italian Lire relative to other currencies throughout much of the period more than cancelled out the high Italian inflation rate. As a result, in Italy, unit labour costs in manufacturing in ECU terms went up by less between 1970 and 1991 than in any other major Community country (Graph 88). By contrast, the strength of the Deutschmark more than offset the low inflation rate in Germany causing unit labour costs of German manufacturers measured in ECUs to increase by more than those in other parts of Europe over the period, and at a similar rate to those in Japan.

Exchange rate adjustments within the Community as outside have, therefore, largely compensated for differential rates of inflation. In terms of ECUs, the extent of the difference between the four major countries in the average rise in unit labour costs over the period 1970 to 1991 was only just over 1% a year, as opposed to over 6% a year in terms of national currencies.

By the same token, when inflation rates differ significantly between countries, as they did throughout this period, the failure of the exchange rate to adjust can cause a rapid deterioration in cost competi-

tiveness. For example, between 1988 and 1991, the Italian Lire was maintained at a constant value against the ECU as part of EMS policy, at a time when Italian inflation exceeded that in most other Community countries and, more significantly, at a time when the real product wage in manufacturing in Italy increased markedly. As a consequence, unit labour costs in manufacturing in Italy rose by almost 20% relative to those in the rest of the Community over this three-year period. This contributed to the pressure on the exchange rate which proved irresistible in September 1992.

Nevertheless, though exchange rate movements seem, over the long-term at least, to have acted as an effective adjustment mechanism to offset the impact of differential inflation, it has to be recognised that the use of this mechanism is not necessarily costless. To the extent that exchange rate depreciation increases the price of imports in terms of national currency, it is liable to increase production costs and raise the general rate of inflation. Moreover, if wages rise in line with inflation and profit margins are maintained, this increase will be perpetuated, resulting in the need for further depreciation and potentially initiating an inflationary spiral as prices and wages chase each other upwards.

To avoid this danger, countries have attempted, through judicious operation of monetary and fiscal policies, to maintain a stable exchange rate if at all possible. This has served to throw most of the responsibility for adjustment onto wages and there has been a general tendency, as noted above, for real wage increases in manufacturing at least to moderate over the past 10 years. This approach has helped

to bring down inflation in the Community.

Part II **Follow-up to White Paper on growth, competitiveness, employment: background analysis of key areas for labour market action**

Part II Growth, competitiveness, employment: background analysis of key areas for labour market action

In response to the analysis contained in the Commission White Paper, *Growth, competitiveness, employment*, published towards the end of 1993 and the strategy outlined in the document, the European Council identified seven areas of action which Member States should address. The focus of this part of the report is on these areas.

The following chapters present background information and analysis on five of these areas for action, namely:

- labour market flexibility — in Chapter 4, which examines the sectoral mobility of labour;

- the reorganisation of working time within enterprises — in Chapter 5, which considers recent changes in working time;

- targeted reductions in indirect cost of labour — in Chapter 6, which analyses the importance of employers' social contributions and the gap between labour costs and the net earnings received by employees;

- better use of public funds set aside for combating unemployment — in Chapter 7, which examines the changing nature of the problem which labour market policies have to address and the scale and distribution of funding;

- developing employment in connection with new requirements — in Chapter 8, which examines new areas of job growth in the Community.

In addition, Chapter 7 considers in some detail the problem of youth unemployment which was a particular concern of the White Paper. Indeed, the European Council stressed the need to ensure that young people have access to adequate training to improve their chances of finding work as one of the main areas for action which Member States should address.

Wherever available, comparable Community-wide data and information is used in order to clarify issues and inform the debate. Such information, however, is far from comprehensive. Many issues, such as changes in internal work organisation in companies, are in any event not easily amenable to quantitative analysis. Moreover, for issues — such as the growth of new areas of employment — available data throw only a limited amount of light on key aspects. Nevertheless, as much use as possible has been made of the data which are available to try to provide an improved understanding of the issues involved and, thereby, to contribute to a more informed debate in which discussion is focused on matters where there are genuine and legitimate differences of opinion rather than on matters of fact.

Chapter 4 Mobility, labour turnover and labour market flexibility

Changes in employment conceal much larger flows of people moving into and out of work and between jobs. The scale of these movements varies with the rate of job creation, but it is consistently higher in some Member States than others and much higher for women than for men.

Introduction

European producers operate in increasingly competitive markets, many of which are now global in scale, where the ability to adapt to continuously changing market and technological pressures and to ensure that the products supplied appeal in terms of quality, design and after-sales service as well price is critical. Such an ability depends not only on the knowledge, judgement and organisational expertise of the decision-makers in an enterprise, but on the competence and adaptability of the existing workforce and on the possibilities of hiring new people with the requisite skills.

It is widely perceived that, in many parts of Europe, these conditions are not adequately met, that firms are slow to adapt to changing imperatives, that it is difficult to change methods of working and the jobs which people do, and that too often there is a lack of people with suitable skills to recruit. Blame is commonly levelled at the labour market, both internal and external, which is judged insufficiently flex-

ible to enable businesses to organise production and their workforce in the most cost effective way and to hire — and fire — employees when and where needed.

The evidence which exists on this, however, is largely anecdotal and, in practice, it is not easy to assess the extent to which an inflexible labour market in various parts of the Community is damaging the competitiveness of European producers, obstructing the shifts of manpower, and capital, between different areas of production to meet changing patterns of demand and global competition.

A major problem of evaluation is that the concept of labour market flexibility is not easy to define and, consequently, to measure. The only viable approach is to try to build up an understanding of the way the labour market in any part of the Community functions by examining individual features one by one and then putting the pieces together.

This analysis exploits the Community Labour Force Survey in order to contribute to this task. It should be stressed, however, that it

deals only with the external labour market and not the internal one within firms, which is equally as important, if even more difficult to assess in terms of flexibility. The chapter focuses on:

- the process of job creation and destruction;

- the flows into and out of employment;

- the extent of labour mobility between sectors of activity;

- the overall rate of labour turnover.

Flows into and out of employment

Figures for overall changes in employment from one year to the next conceal much larger movements of people into and out of work. The aim here is to examine the size of these flows and how they vary over time and between different parts of the Community. The evidence covers the period 1983 to 1992, which includes years of low employment growth at the

Data on sectoral mobility and job turnover

The data on which the analysis in this chapter is based come from the Community Labour Force Survey for successive years from 1983 to 1992. Essentially they relate to the replies given by respondents to questions about their employment status one year earlier — whether they were employed and, if so, in what NACE 1-digit sector they worked or whether they were unemployed or economically inactive.

The usual qualifications apply to this kind of data insofar as they are based on individual recollection of events one year before which might not always be accurate. Nevertheless, the figures derived seem to be reasonably consistent from year to year which provides some reassurance about their reliability.

The data used in the final section of the chapter on job turnover are based on replies to the question included for the first time in the 1992 LFS on how long respondents had been in their present employment. The analysis relates specifically to those who had been in their present employment for less than a year.

beginning, of declining employment at the end and years of substantial net job creation in the middle (see Box for an explanation of the data used).

For the countries taken together over the period 1983 to 1992 as a whole, an average of just over 7% of those in work at the time of the survey were either unemployed or inactive the year before, half of whom because they were still being educated or trained (Graph 89).

Although there is some tendency for the numbers of people finding work to be higher in years of high employment growth, the difference between years of recovery and years of recession is smaller than might be expected. The largest number of new entrants was recorded in 1989 when employment increased by 2%, and when 7.6% of those in work were unemployed or inactive the year before. This, however, is only 1 percentage point higher than in 1991, when employment declined slightly. Moreover, whereas the rate of new entry in the years of high growth from 1987 to 1990 — when employment rose by over 2% a year — averaged 7.4%, it still averaged 7.0% when employment rose by only $\frac{1}{2}$% a year.

The proportion finding work after being unemployed or inactive is not much lower in years of low net job creation than in years of high net job creation. However, although the difference in the rate of inflow into employment might be small, in terms of the number of people affected — ie the unemployed and inactive — it is significant. A difference of 1 percentage point in the rate of new entry translates into a difference of 10–15% in the numbers of unemployed.

89 Rates of entry into and exit from employment and employment growth in the Community (EUR8), 1984 to 1992

EUR8 = B, DK, D, GR, F, IRL, L, UK

At the same time, since the rate of new entry into employment varies comparatively little between years, it follows that the rate of exit varies more. Indeed the figures imply that, over the period examined, the proportion of people leaving employment to become unemployed or inactive varied by twice as much as the proportion entering employment. In the years of high net job creation, an average of 5.3% of people who had been in employment the year before were no longer in work at the time of the survey, the figure reaching a low 4.9% in 1990. This compares with an average of 6.7% in the other years and a high of 7.3% in 1992.

Typically, therefore, years of low net job creation are associated more with a high rate of job loss than a low rate of new recruitment, some two-thirds of the variation in employment change between years being attributable to the variation in the proportion of people leaving employment and only a third to the variation in the proportion entering.

These conclusions remain unaltered if the analysis is extended to Spain and Portugal, data for which are available only for the period from 1986. A consistently high rate of entry into employment in Spain over this period and a correspondingly high rate of job loss (as detailed below), however, pushes up the Community figures for movements of people into and out of work. For the 10 Community countries, excluding Italy and the Netherlands, the proportion in employment in any given year between 1986 and 1992 who had previously been unemployed or inactive averaged just over 8% — around one in 12 — with a similarly small variation as for the 8 countries.

Changes in male and female employment

Between 1984 and 1992, employment of women expanded by significantly more than that of men. Over the period as a whole, the numbers in employment increased by around 8% in the 8 Member States for which a complete set of data is available. Women accounted for some two-thirds of this increase. Moreover, the gap between the growth of female employment and that of men was particularly wide in the years of low net job creation at the beginning and end of the period — women accounting for 90% of the addition to the numbers in employment during these years — while in years of high net job creation there was relatively little difference between the two.

This pattern of experience is repeated in the figures for the gross movements into and out of employment. For the 8 Member States, the proportion of women moving from being unemployed or inactive into a job was consistently higher than the proportion of men, averaging over 9% a year of those in employment between 1984 and 1992, as compared with under 6% of men (Graph 90). At the same time, the proportion of women leaving employment in any year was also higher than that of men, especially during years of relatively high net job creation. High employment growth of men, therefore, tends to be associated with fewer numbers leaving jobs rather than with more entering work.

The more unstable nature of male employment is due to the fact that, in contrast to women, men are

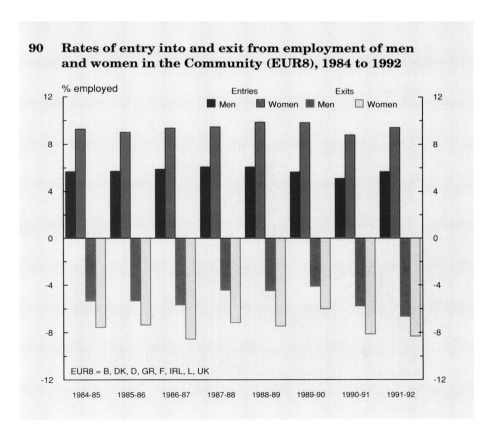

90   Rates of entry into and exit from employment of men and women in the Community (EUR8), 1984 to 1992

employed in much larger proportions in industry, where output is more sensitive to the rate of economic growth than is the case for services. Accordingly, job creation and job loss fluctuate more from year to year in industry than in services. Moreover, given the long-term decline in employment in industry, it is really only in years of relatively high growth that there is any net job creation at all in this sector.

The relationship to unemployment

The size of flows into and out of work are both influenced by the prevailing level of unemployment and have important implications for the problem of joblessness. Other things being equal, the higher the rate of unemployment, the greater the chances of someone

in work at the time of the survey having been unemployed the year before. In parts of the Community with high unemployment rates, therefore, flows into employment would also be expected to be high on this basis.

However, other things are not necessarily equal. In particular, the time it takes for someone unemployed to find a job, and, therefore, the probability of being recorded as out of work in two consecutive surveys, tend to vary across the Community. Equally, competition for jobs is not only confined to the unemployed but also extends to young people entering the labour market for the first time and those re-entering after a spell of inactivity — in a number of Member States, the UK and Germany, for example, women with family responsibilities, in particular.

Leaving aside variations in the importance of the latter, a comparison of the size of flows into employment with the rate of unemployment in the preceding year provides an indication of the ease with which someone without a job can find work and, conversely, of the scale of the potential problem of long-term unemployment. In other words, the larger the flows into employment relative to the rate of unemployment, the higher the turnover among the unemployed is likely to be and the shorter the spell they tend to spend out of work. Small flows in relation to unemployment, by contrast, imply that a high proportion of the unemployed fail to find a job within a year or, if they do, that they lose it before the year is out. Unemployment, in this case, therefore, as compared with the former, tends to affect only a relatively narrow group of people.

Employment changes across the Community

The pattern of flows into and out of employment that is evident at the Community level — ie the relative numbers entering work tend to increase when employment expands and to decline when it contracts — is also apparent in individual Member States. Nevertheless, the scale of the flows in both directions varies considerably and consistently between countries, bearing very little relationship to differences in the rate of employment growth. Though there is some relationship to differences in unemployment, it is by no means a uniform one.

Throughout the period 1984 to 1992, the size of flows was relatively large in the UK, France, Denmark, Ireland and, above all, in Spain (in

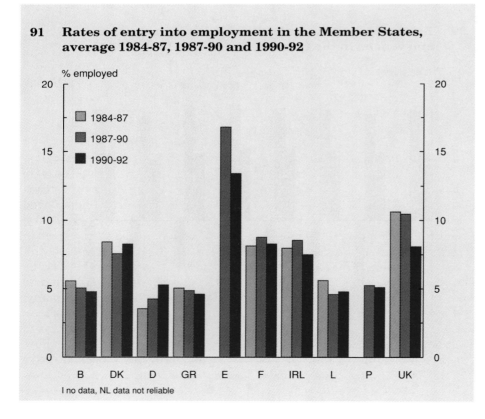

91   Rates of entry into employment in the Member States, average 1984-87, 1987-90 and 1990-92

% employed

Legend:
- 1984-87
- 1987-90
- 1990-92

I no data, NL data not reliable

this case from 1986) and relatively small in Belgium, Greece, Portugal (also from 1986), Luxembourg and most especially in Germany (Graph 91). (Although the Netherlands also shows substantial movements into and out of work, the figures seem implausibly high for women, almost one in three of those in employment in each year between 1987 and 1992 seeming to have been unemployed or inactive the year before. This contrasts with a figure of 9–10% in 1983 and 1985, which could reflect a tendency after 1987 for the LFS to record more short-time casual work than before.)

The former group includes the two countries — Spain and Ireland — where unemployment was much higher than the Community average throughout the period. But it also includes two countries — France and the UK — where unemployment was below average for half the time and one country — Denmark — where, except for 1991 and 1992, it was consistently below the average, in most years significantly so. The latter group, where flows into and out of work were low, includes the countries with the lowest rates of unemployment in most years — Luxembourg, Germany and Portugal — and Greece where the rate was also below the Community average, but it also includes Belgium, where for 5 of the 8 years, unemployment was above the average. Moreover in a number of cases, the difference in the size of flows into and out of work between countries in the two groups is much larger than the difference in unemployment rates.

The difference between the countries with the largest flows in the former group and those with the smallest flows in the latter was

around 2 to 3 times. In Spain, an average of almost 17% of those in employment in the years of high net job creation between 1987 and 1990 had been unemployed or inactive the year before — only slightly below the average rate of unemployment. In contrast, the figure was only around 5% or less in each of the countries in the group with a low rate of entry into employment. This includes Greece and Belgium, where 5% is significantly below the prevailing level of unemployment over this period.

In the latter two countries, therefore, it appears to have been considerably more difficult for those out of work to find a job than in Spain. This is reflected in the high level of long-term unemployment in Belgium, where an average of almost 65% of the unemployed over the period had been out of work for a year or more, as against a figure of just over 50% in Spain. It is also reflected in the much larger increase in activity rates over the period in Spain as compared with either Belgium or Greece, where the entry, or re-entry, of women into the labour market was significantly less than in other Southern Member States.

Large differences in the rate of entry into employment are mirrored by equally large differences in the rate of exit. In Belgium and Greece, as well as in Germany and Portugal, an average of only around 3–4% of people left work each year to become unemployed or inactive between 1987 and 1990 — not much more than the natural rate of retirement. In Spain, in comparison, the figure was 13%.

The contrast is equally marked between Spain and Ireland. In the latter, where unemployment was only slightly lower than in Spain,

the rate of entry into employment was only some 8½% between 1986 and 1990, only around half the Spanish rate. This is reflected, as in Belgium, in a high rate of long-term unemployment, an average of 60% of the unemployed being out of work for a year or more over this period.

Similarly, although the UK had a higher rate of unemployment than Germany throughout the period 1984 to 1992, the chances of someone without work finding a job in the UK — whether unemployed or inactive — seem to have been greater than in Germany. In the UK, the rate of entry into employment was around 10–11% in each year between 1984 and 1989, 2–3 times higher than in Germany, where the rate in most years was only 3–4%. Even in 1991 and 1992, when employment fell by over 2% in the UK, there was still an average of around 8% of those in work who had moved into a job after being unemployed or inactive the year before. Moreover, even in years of high net job creation, the rate of people leaving employment remained relatively high at over 7% — substantially above the rate of 2–3% in Germany.

Again, this difference is mirrored in rates of long-term unemployment. Despite the comparatively low level of unemployment in Germany, over 45% of the unemployed had been out of work for at least a year throughout the period, even in 1991 after 7 years of net job creation. By contrast, in the UK, by 1991, this figure had declined to under 30%. Moreover in Germany, to a greater extent than elsewhere, the unemployed not only faced competition for jobs from those who had previously been inactive or in education but also from new immigrants from the East.

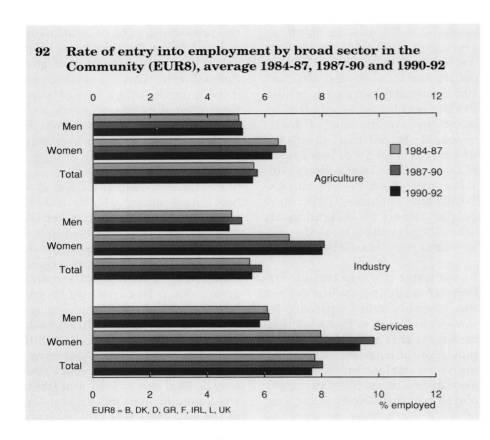

92   Rate of entry into employment by broad sector in the Community (EUR8), average 1984-87, 1987-90 and 1990-92

1984-87
1987-90
1990-92

Agriculture

Industry

Services

EUR8 = B, DK, D, GR, F, IRL, L, UK

% employed

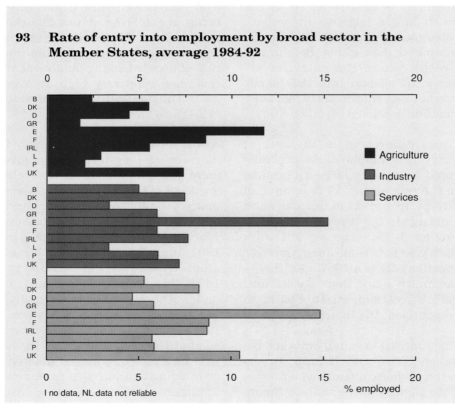

93   Rate of entry into employment by broad sector in the Member States, average 1984-92

Agriculture
Industry
Services

I no data, NL data not reliable

% employed

In France, the rate of entry into employment was only slightly less than in the UK, at 8–9% of those in work, though the net increase in the numbers employed was much lower in most years (never being much above 1% as against $3^1/_2$% in 1988 and 1989 in the UK). The proportion of those leaving employment annually was, therefore, much the same as in the UK. Just as in the UK as well, this relatively high rate of movement into and out of work was reflected in a comparatively low level of long-term unemployment, which in spite of the low rate of net job creation had fallen to under 40% of the total number of jobless in 1991, less than in Germany.

Flows into employment by sector

The inflow of people into employment in services from being unemployed or inactive was consistently higher than into other sectors throughout the period 1984 to 1992, reflecting relative rates of net job creation. For the 8 Community countries for which a complete set of data is available, an average of just under 8% of those employed in services in any given year had been unemployed or inactive a year earlier (Graph 92). The variation between years was small (at only around half a percentage point between years when employment increased by $2^1/_2$% or more and years when it went up by 1% or less). For the 8 countries plus Spain and Portugal, the average rate of entry into services between 1986 and 1992 was just over $8^1/_2$% of those employed, with a similarly small difference between high and low growth years.

Entry into industry was over 2 percentage points lower than into services for the 8 Community countries, at around 5½% of those in employment, reflecting the lower rate of net job creation, but only around 1½ percentage points lower, at 6½–7% if Spain and Portugal are included. Indeed in Spain, the rate of entry of the unemployed and inactive into jobs in industry over the period was more than for services (Graph 93). This was also the case in most years in Greece and Portugal, which like Spain have so far experienced less of a shift in employment from industry to services than other Community countries.

For these three countries, moreover, the rate of entry into industry of women as well as men was higher than for services, a phenomenon which in a number of years was also evident in Denmark and Belgium.

Perhaps unexpectedly, the rate of entry into agriculture of those without jobs was much the same over the Community as a whole as into industry. This contrasts with the frequent portrayal of agriculture as a sector where there are few new entrants and the only real mobility takes the form of people leaving, either because they are made redundant or because they reach retirement age. For the 8 Community countries, in every year between 1984 and 1992, between 5½ and 6% of those in employment in agriculture had been unemployed or inactive one year earlier, and between 6 and 7% for these countries plus Spain and Portugal. In a number of countries in the North of the Community, moreover, the rate of entry of people out of work into jobs in agriculture over this period was higher than for industry. This was the case in France, where an average of 8½% of those working in

agriculture during these years had been unemployed or inactive the year before — some 1½ percentage points higher than the figure for industry — and in Germany, where the average proportion was 4½% as opposed to just over 3% in the case of industry.

In these two countries, therefore, given the net job losses in the sector, the rate of exit from agriculture was substantially greater than from other sectors of activity.

Similarly in the UK, in around half the years over the period, the rate of entry of those out of work into jobs in agriculture exceeded that for industry, though here unlike in the other two countries, the numbers employed in agriculture declined by less than those employed in industry between 1984 and 1991. Moreover whereas in

France and Germany, a higher rate of entry into agriculture than industry applied to both men and women, in the UK, it was only true of men. Indeed in every year over the period, except for 1985, but especially in years of low growth or decline in employment, a higher proportion of men working in agriculture had been out of work one year earlier than was the case for industry.

In the Southern Member States, where agriculture is a much more important provider of jobs, though a rapidly diminishing one, the rate of entry into the sector was significantly less than that into industry over this period. This was especially the case in Greece and Portugal where only around 2% or less of those employed in agriculture in any year were not in work the year before. It was also true of Spain and Ireland. In the former,

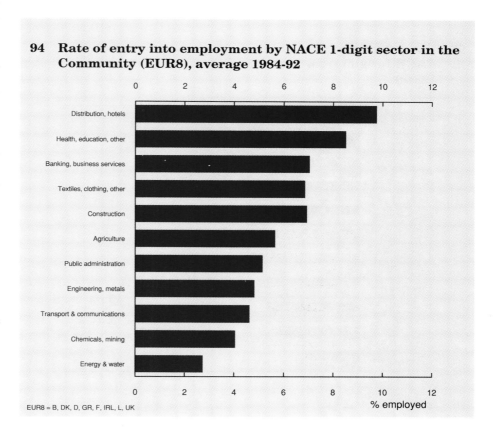

94   Rate of entry into employment by NACE 1-digit sector in the Community (EUR8), average 1984-92

EUR8 = B, DK, D, GR, F, IRL, L, UK

% employed

however, the proportion was well over 10% in every year, indicating a rapid rate of job turnover in the sector, and in the latter, it was around 5–6%, though this was wholly due to an extremely high rate of entry of women.

Indeed in Ireland, in most years over the period, more than one in every four women employed in agriculture — in some years more than one in three — was unemployed or inactive one year earlier, as compared with only around 3% of men, and substantially higher than the same figures for industry and services. (A similar pattern is evident for the Netherlands, where similarly high figures also apply to other sectors and where there are doubts about the reliability of the data.) The rate of entry into agriculture is, therefore, extremely high for women which, given the high rate of exit, also means that the rate of

turnover among women is equally high.

Within the service sector, distribution and catering stands out as having a high rate of new entrants from among the unemployed and inactive. On average for the 8 Community countries examined here, in the years between 1984 and 1992, just under 10% of those employed in distribution and catering were unemployed or inactivity the year before, and around 11% if Spain and Portugal are added (Graph 94). This applies fairly generally in all Member States, with the proportion reaching 17–18% in Spain and 14–15% in the UK. It also applies to women in particular, for whom the average proportion of new entrants was around 12% for the 8 Community countries (13% with Spain and Portugal included), though the figure for men was also higher than

other sectors, averaging 8–9% (Graph 95).

The other services category, which includes education and health as well as a range of personal services, is only slightly less important as a point of entry into employment, though unlike distribution and catering, the numbers employed rose significantly between 1984 and 1992. Over the period as a whole, 8–9% of those working in this sector in the 8 Community countries were unemployed or inactive one year earlier (9–10% with Spain and Portugal).

Within industry, the other manufacturing sector, which predominantly includes basic products such as food and drink, textiles and clothing and footwear, and construction consistently had a proportionately higher rate of new entry than other areas over the period, though again these were not sectors of correspondingly high rates of employment growth. In these two sectors, an average of 6–7% of those in work in each year between 1984 and 1992 had been unemployed or inactive the year before in the 8 Community countries (8–9% with Spain and Portugal).

Moreover in both cases, as for all other sectors, the figures for women were higher than those for men, an average of 9–10% of women employed in these two sectors having been out of work one year earlier in the 8 Community countries over this period (10–11% with Spain and Portugal), much the same proportion as in services — though in the case of construction this translates into comparatively few jobs (only around 800 thousand women worked in this sector in the Community as a whole in 1992).

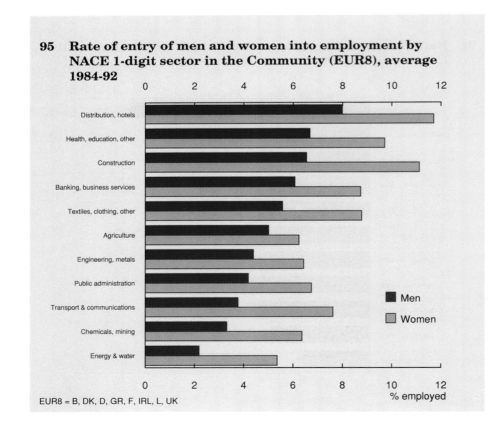

95   Rate of entry of men and women into employment by NACE 1-digit sector in the Community (EUR8), average 1984-92

EUR8 = B, DK, D, GR, F, IRL, L, UK

% employed

Movements between sectors

As has been increasingly argued in recent years, a major implication of the accelerating pace of technological advance in processes of production and continuous changes in the structure of economic activity is that people can no longer count on being employed in one job throughout their working lives. Indeed, many may be obliged to change what they do, and acquire new skills accordingly, several times during their working lives. Both the willingness and ability of the workforce to adapt in this way are likely to be important determinants of economic competitiveness.

Direct evidence on the prevailing extent of job mobility is difficult to obtain. Data on occupations (as pointed out in Chapter 8) are among the least comparable labour market indicators as between countries. Moreover, there is a lack of cohort-type information which might enable the movements of individuals to be tracked and analysed.

The analysis here is based on movements of workers between sectors of activity from one Labour Force Survey to the next, sectors being defined at the NACE 1-digit level which essentially means dividing the economy into 11 broad industry or service groups (listed in Graph 95). This is not an entirely satisfactory basis of analysis since a number of the groups contain very different activities — health and education are included with personal services, such as hairdressing, for example, retailing with hotels and mining with chemicals, and shifts between these will not be registered. Moreover, while

shifts between similar jobs in different groups will be registered — though the broad nature of the groups defined here reduces the likelihood of the jobs being the same — shifts between different jobs in the same sector will not be.

Nevertheless, the figures provide some indication of the scale of job mobility and the way in which this varies across the Community, as well as over time. Indeed the fact that groups are widely defined should imply that the figures understate actual mobility and, even more, the rate of job turnover (some evidence on job turnover for 1992 is presented below).

For the 8 Community countries for which data are available throughout the period, an average of around 4% — one in 25 — moved from one sector of activity to another each year between 1983 and

1992 (Graph 96). This figure, however, varied from under 4% in the early, low growth, years of the period (as well as in 1992) to over 5% — one in 20 — in 1990 after a period of high employment expansion, which suggests that a high rate of job creation encourages sectoral mobility.

Adding Spain and Portugal in this case tends to reduce the figures marginally, since in both countries sectoral mobility is below the Community average, at just over 3% in most years in both cases, despite their relatively high rates of employment growth. Greece and Ireland also registered low rates of movement, in the former an average of only around 2% a year of those in employment changing the sector in which they worked over the period, while in Ireland the average was under $1\frac{1}{2}$% a year, the lowest in the Community (Graph 97).

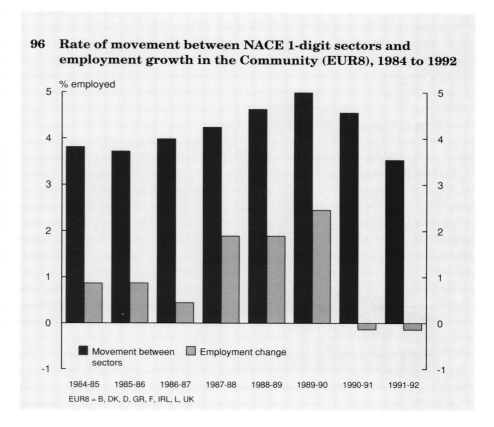

96   Rate of movement between NACE 1-digit sectors and employment growth in the Community (EUR8), 1984 to 1992

EUR8 = B, DK, D, GR, F, IRL, L, UK

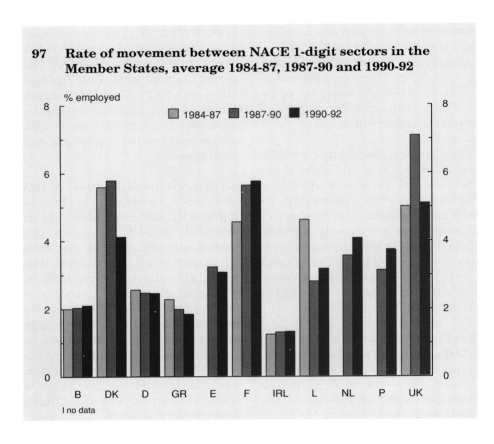

97   Rate of movement between NACE 1-digit sectors in the Member States, average 1984-87, 1987-90 and 1990-92

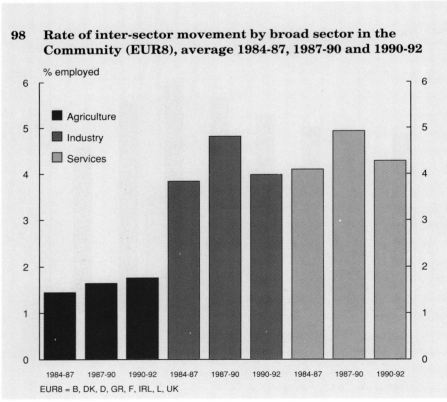

98   Rate of inter-sector movement by broad sector in the Community (EUR8), average 1984-87, 1987-90 and 1990-92

In the more developed Member States, the rate of mobility tends to be higher, the main exception being Belgium where the proportion moving between sectors over the period was much the same as in Greece (just over 2% a year). In Germany also, however, the average figure was only around $2^1/_2$%, well below the Community average. By contrast, in the UK, France and Denmark, the figure averaged over 5%, and indeed almost 6% in the UK, where the movement of workers between sectors was in most years the highest in the Community. (In the Netherlands, where there is less doubt about these figures than about those for new entrants, the average proportion moving between sectors was just under 4% between 1987 and 1992.)

In most of the countries, as at the Community level, some tendency is evident for the rate of sectoral mobility to increase with the rate of employment growth, though it is not particularly pronounced in all cases. In the UK, for example, an average of 5% of those employed moved from one sector to another in 1991 and 1992, years when employment declined by over 2%, as compared with an average of 7% in the years between 1987 and 1990 when employment rose considerably. On the other hand, in Germany, the average rate of mobility during the high growth years between 1987 and 1990 was much the same as over the preceding three years or the subsequent two years, when employment growth was much less.

Mobility by sector

As would be expected, considerably fewer people moved into agriculture than into other sectors. In the

Community as a whole (for the 10 countries as well as the 8), an average of only around $1\frac{1}{2}$% a year of those working in agriculture moved into the sector from another job between 1984 and 1992 (Graph 98). For Ireland and Greece, the proportion was under 1% and in Belgium only marginally higher (Graph 99). In the UK, on the other hand, the figure rose to 4% at the beginning of the 1990s (from around $2\frac{1}{2}$% in the mid-1980s), while in Denmark, it averaged $2\frac{1}{2}$% over the period as a whole.

The high figure for the UK may reflect the fact that, almost alone in the Community, it experienced some growth in agricultural employment over this period, though it may also reflect the fact that very few people were employed — only around 2% of the workforce. Nevertheless, in the Netherlands, where employment in agriculture also increased and where the proportion employed in the sector was not much higher than in the UK, the average movement into the sector was around the Community average.

Despite the very different rates of employment growth, the rates of inter-sectoral mobility in industry and services were very similar between 1983 and 1992. For the 8 Community countries over this period, an average of just over 4% of those employed in the five industrial sectors moved into one of these sectors each year. (This includes those moving from one industrial sector to another as well as those moving from services or agriculture.) For the five service sectors, the average was $4\frac{1}{2}$%.

For industry, there was some tendency for the proportion moving between sectors to be higher in years of high employment growth — between 1987 and 1990, the

average was almost 5%, between 1983 and 1987, it was under 4%. In services, the difference was less marked, though still evident. In both sectors, the rate of mobility seems to have increased over time, though not by much.

For both sectors also, the variation in the scale of movement between Member States evident at the aggregate level and for agriculture is apparent for both industry and services. Indeed there is a high degree of uniformity between sectors in the relative rates of mobility shown by different countries.

In the UK, Denmark and France, the rate of inter-sectoral movement was higher than elsewhere in the Community in both industry and services, the proportion moving averaging 6–7% a year between 1986 and 1992 in each case in the former two countries and $5\frac{1}{2}$% a year in

France. Similarly, Ireland, Greece, Belgium and Germany had much lower than average rates of mobility in both sectors over the period, in each case the figure being around $2\frac{1}{2}$% a year or less and only around $1\frac{1}{2}$% a year in Ireland, though the rate for services in Belgium was not much higher.

Within industry and services, the rate of entry into individual sectors by those who were employed elsewhere shows a significantly different pattern than entry by those who had previously been unemployed or inactive. For the latter, the main flows were into basic industries and services, like textiles and retailing. For those who already have a job, the highest rate of entry occurred in finance and business services, where the proportion in employment who had been working in another sector a year before averaged over 6% a year

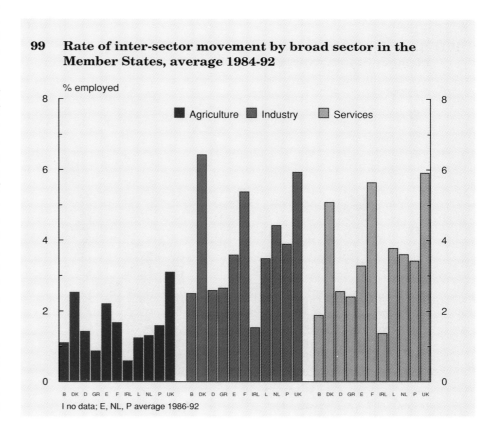

99   Rate of inter-sector movement by broad sector in the Member States, average 1984-92

% employed

Legend: ■ Agriculture ■ Industry ■ Services

I no data; E, NL, P average 1986-92

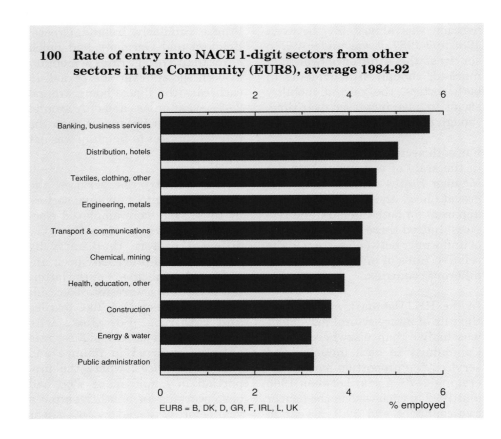

100   Rate of entry into NACE 1-digit sectors from other sectors in the Community (EUR8), average 1984-92

EUR8 = B, DK, D, GR, F, IRL, L, UK

% employed

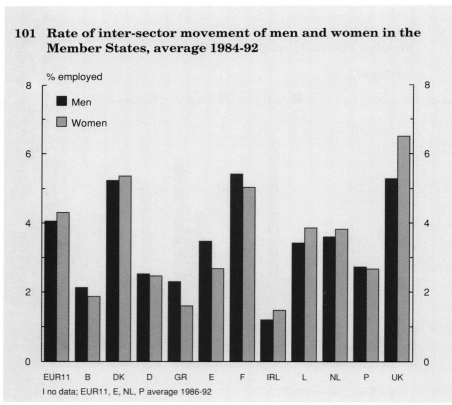

101   Rate of inter-sector movement of men and women in the Member States, average 1984-92

I no data; EUR11, E, NL, P average 1986-92

in the Community between 1986 and 1992 — in the UK, the average was over 9%, in Germany under 3% (Graph 100). Moreover in industry, the rate of entry was much the same in engineering, as in the other manufacturing group, with an average of around 5% a year over the period (in Denmark and the UK, 7–8%, in Germany, under 3%).

At the other extreme, public administration showed the smallest inflow into employment from another sector, the rate averaging only around 3% a year in the Community as a whole between 1986 and 1992 — though the figure was over 4% a year in the UK and under 1% a year in Ireland.

Mobility of men and women

Over the Community as a whole, there was a greater tendency for women to move between sectors than men over the period 1984 to 1992. The difference, however, was very small — the average proportion for women being just over 4%, for men 4% (Graph 101). Moreover, the difference was predominantly accounted for by one country — the UK — where inter-sectoral mobility among women was on average almost $1\frac{1}{2}$ percentage points higher than for men over the period ($6\frac{1}{2}$% of women in employment moved between sectors each year, just over 5% of men). For all other countries, either there was little difference in rates of mobility between men and women or mobility among men was consistently higher.

At the sectoral level, an interesting and somewhat unexpected pattern emerges. In agriculture, mobility is higher among men than women in all countries except the UK

— where the rate of entry of women from other sectors averaged over 4% — and, in the later years of the period, Denmark and Ireland. In industry, however, mobility was significantly higher among women than among men — almost 1½ percentage points higher on average over the period for the 8 Community countries (slightly less for the 10). This, moreover, was true in all countries in most years, except Greece, Portugal and Spain — in the latter case only for half the years (Graph 102).

In services, on the other hand, the reverse is the case. Though the differences are not so marked as for industry, in most countries the mobility of men was consistently higher than that of women over the period 1984 to 1992 (Graph 103). Almost the only exception is the UK where proportionately more women than men already in employment moved into one of the service sectors over the period, though again the difference was much smaller than in the case of industry.

Mobility by age

The chances of someone moving from one sector to another decline with age. For young people under 25, an average of just over 7% of those in employment in the Community changed the sector in which they worked in every year between 1984 and 1992, the figure rising to almost 9% in 1989 and 1990 at the end of the period of high job creation (Graph 104). In Denmark, the proportion was over 10% and in the UK and France not much lower, while in contrast it was only just over 2% in Ireland, not much above 3% in Greece and under 4% in Germany.

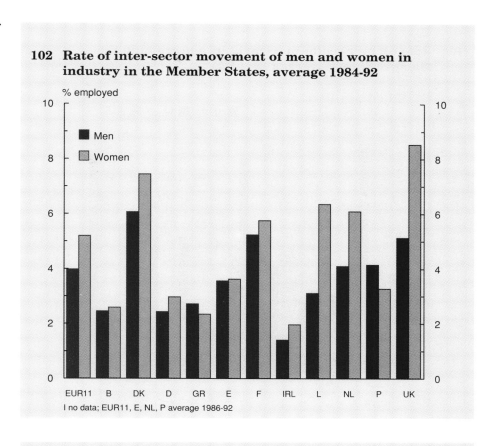

102   Rate of inter-sector movement of men and women in industry in the Member States, average 1984-92

% employed

I no data; EUR11, E, NL, P average 1986-92

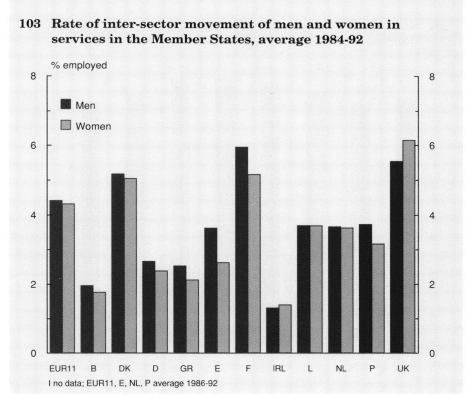

103   Rate of inter-sector movement of men and women in services in the Member States, average 1984-92

% employed

I no data; EUR11, E, NL, P average 1986-92

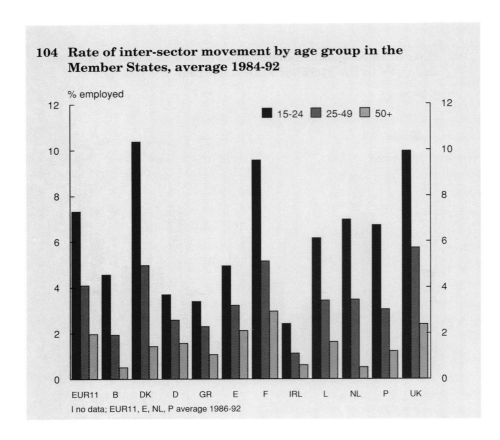

104   Rate of inter-sector movement by age group in the Member States, average 1984-92

% employed

15-24   25-49   50+

EUR11   B   DK   D   GR   E   F   IRL   L   NL   P   UK

I no data; EUR11, E, NL, P average 1986-92

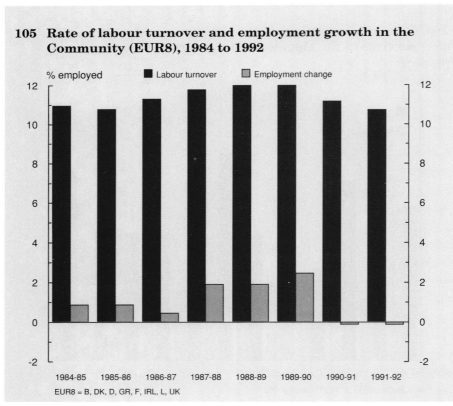

105   Rate of labour turnover and employment growth in the Community (EUR8), 1984 to 1992

% employed   ■ Labour turnover   ■ Employment change

1984-85   1985-86   1986-87   1987-88   1988-89   1989-90   1990-91   1991-92

EUR8 = B, DK, D, GR, F, IRL, L, UK

For those aged between 25 and 49, the average proportion moving between sectors was 4% over this period in the Community, rising to 5% in 1990, but falling back to under 4% in 1992. A similar variation emerges between Member States, with the UK, France and Denmark having the highest rate of movement — with 5% or more of people a year changing sectors — and Ireland the lowest at barely over 1% a year, though this time joined by Belgium as well as Greece.

For those aged 50 or over, the average proportion of those in employment moving was only around 2% a year in the Community, with figures of just over $\frac{1}{2}$% a year in Belgium and Ireland as well as in the Netherlands. In France, however, the average was almost 3% a year and in the UK and Spain not far below.

Much the same pattern of variation is in this case true for both men and women.

The probability of someone moving from employment in one sector to a job in another, therefore, declines by around 50% as the person passes from the 15–24 age group to the 25–49 age group and falls by another 50% or so as they pass into the over 49 age group.

Labour turnover

The figures examined above on flows into employment from unemployment and inactivity and on movements between sectors provide, in combination, an indication of the overall extent of labour turnover in the Community. Specifically, they show the number of people employed in a particular sector at a given time who were not working there one year earlier.

Between 1984 and 1992, an average of $11\frac{1}{2}\%$ of those in employment — more than one person in 9 — had entered a new job during the preceding year in the 8 Community countries for which complete data are available. For the 10 Community countries, including Spain and Portugal, the average for the period 1986 to 1992 rises to $12\frac{1}{2}\%$ or one in 8 (Graph 105).

The proportion also rises in the high growth years between 1987 and 1990 — to 13% for the 10 Community countries and to almost $12\frac{1}{2}\%$ for the 8, compared with an average of under 11% in the other years. On average, around 60% of those entering a new job were previously unemployed or inactive, 40% were employed in another sector.

Given that the data on inter-sectoral movements encompass only those moving between broad sectors of activity, these figures clearly understate the actual proportion of people entering a new job each year and the extent of job turnover. They suggest, however, a significant degree of fluidity in the Community labour market taken as a whole.

Nevertheless, the extent of labour turnover varies markedly between Member States. Spain has the highest rate with an average of over 18% a year — almost one in 5 — of those working in a particular sector over the period 1986 to 1992 not having been employed in that sector one year earlier (Graph 106). The UK has the second highest rate with an average figure of almost 16% — one in 6 — for the same period, while France and Denmark, the only other two countries with rates above the Community average, come some way behind with averages of 13%.

Although Spain and the UK have similarly high rates of labour turnover, the proximate reasons for this are significantly different as noted above. Whereas in Spain, the high rate is due almost entirely to a much larger than average flow of people from unemployment and inactivity into work, the rate of inter-sectoral movement being less than the Community average, the UK has relatively high figures for both new entrants into work and those moving between sectors. France and Denmark are similar in this respect.

At the other extreme, in Germany and Greece, the countries with the lowest rates of labour turnover, over the same period an average of under 7% of those in employment — one in 15 — were not employed in the same sector one year earlier, while in Belgium, the average was only slightly higher at 7%. (In Germany,

it should be noted, a higher proportion of jobs than elsewhere are likely to have been filled by immigrants over this period — people who one year earlier had not been living in the country at all and who, therefore, are left out of account here. However, including immigrants would add an average of less than $\frac{1}{2}\%$ to the proportion of those entering employment in any year — not enough to make a significant difference to the comparisons.)

Labour turnover by sector

At the sectoral level, the rate of labour turnover is lowest in agriculture, as would be expected in view of the large and continuous reduction in employment which has been experienced. Even in this sector, however, new entrants are far from rare. For the 8 Community

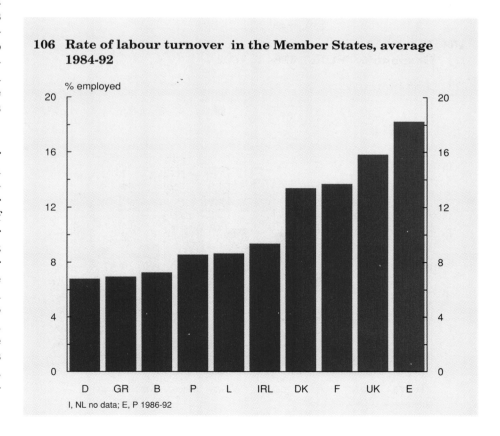

106   Rate of labour turnover in the Member States, average 1984-92

% employed

I, NL no data; E, P 1986-92

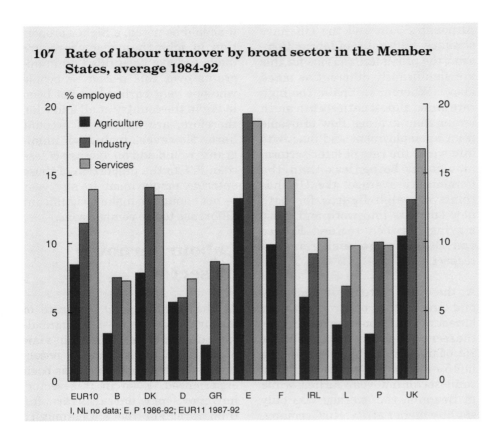

107   Rate of labour turnover by broad sector in the Member States, average 1984-92

% employed

Agriculture
Industry
Services

EUR10   B   DK   D   GR   E   F   IRL   L   P   UK

I, NL no data; E, P 1986-92; EUR11 1987-92

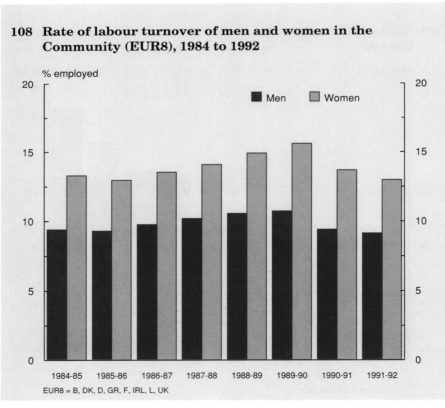

108   Rate of labour turnover of men and women in the Community (EUR8), 1984 to 1992

% employed

Men   Women

1984-85   1985-86   1986-87   1987-88   1988-89   1989-90   1990-91   1991-92

EUR8 = B, DK, D, GR, F, IRL, L, UK

countries, between 1984 and 1992, an average of 7% of those employed in the sector in any year were not working in agriculture a year earlier, most of them (80%) having been unemployed or inactive. At the same time, over 10% of workers left the sector each year (Graph 107).

The variation between countries, however, is considerable. In Spain, the rate of entry into agriculture averaged over 13% a year between 1986 and 1992, while in the UK over the same period it was over 11% a year. In contrast, the average figure for Greece was only $2\frac{1}{2}$% and for Portugal and Belgium, $3\frac{1}{2}$%.

For the industrial sectors, the rate of entry averaged 10% in the 8 Community countries between 1984 and 1992 — and over 11% if Spain and Portugal are added — with an average rate of exit only slightly lower than this. Spain again had the highest rate, with an average of over 19% of people entering industry each year between 1986 and 1992. The UK, France and Denmark were the only other countries with rates consistently above the Community average (at $12\frac{1}{2}$–14%), though this was also true of Portugal in a number of years, while Ireland was not far below the average.

At the other end of the scale, Germany had by some way the lowest rate of entry into industry, with an average of less than 6% a year of those employed in an industrial sector between 1984 and 1992 not having worked there a year before.

Services, not unexpectedly, had the highest rate of entry, with an average of $11\frac{1}{2}$% a year starting to work in a service sector in the 8 Community countries between 1984 and 1992 (14% if Spain and Portugal are added). It also, however, had a higher rate of exit than in industry and one which was similar to that in agriculture — ie the chances of someone in a service sector leaving their job in any year were much the same as someone in agriculture.

The same general variation in rates of labour turnover between Member States applies as for industry. Spain had the highest rate of entry into a service sector, with an average of around 19% moving into a service job each year between 1986 and 1992, the UK the second highest rate, with an average of almost 17% in the same period, in this case, significantly higher than in France (15%) or Denmark (14%). Germany, with Belgium, had the lowest rates, with an average figure of only around 7%.

Labour turnover of men and women

On average, over the Community as a whole, men accounted for a higher proportion of the people moving into new jobs over the period 1984 to 1992 than women. The difference, however, was very small, men accounting for 51% of labour turnover, women for 49%. Given the relative numbers of men and women in the workforce, however — over 60% men, under 40% women — women were on average 50% more likely to be involved in moves, whether entering or re-entering employment or moving from one sector to another, than men (Graph 108). Moreover, partly reflecting the growing participation of women in the labour force, the proportion of moves involving women increased significantly over the period. Indeed between 1989 and 1992, women accounted for a higher proportion of labour turnover than men.

Labour turnover of women, therefore, exceeded 15% in the high growth year of 1990 and averaged only just under 15% between 1987 and 1990, when there was significant net job creation. Even in years of recession, such as 1991 and 1992, labour turnover was still around 13%. In contrast, labour turnover among men exceeded 10% only in years of high employment growth and fell to under 9% in 1992.

The marked difference between rates of labour turnover for men and women is true of all Member States. This is particularly the case for Ireland, where the average turnover of women each year between 1984 and 1992 was around 14% of those in employment, double the rate for men (Graph 109). In the UK and Luxembourg, the annual turnover of women was around 50% higher than for men, while only in Portugal and Greece was the

difference between the two rates less than 20%.

The implications for flexibility

Conclusions about overall labour market flexibility can be drawn from the above evidence only with a great deal of caution.

Although the inflow of people into employment from the ranks of the unemployed or inactive is much higher in some countries — Spain, the UK, France and Denmark, in particular — than others — Germany, Belgium, Greece and Portugal — part of the difference can be attributed to differing levels of unemployment. This is clearly the case in respect of Spain *vis à vis* Portugal or Germany. However, it is less true of Spain *vis à vis* Ireland or Belgium or of the UK, France or

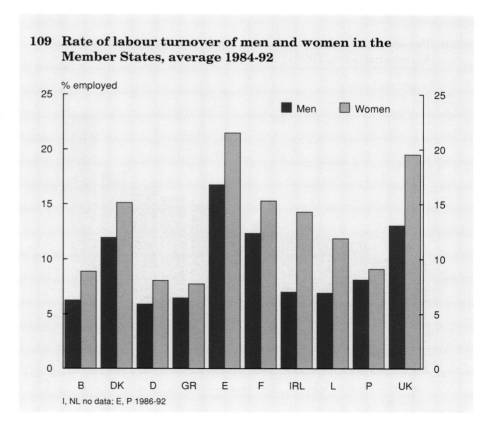

109 Rate of labour turnover of men and women in the Member States, average 1984-92

I, NL no data; E, P 1986-92

Denmark relative to most other countries. Here, the turnover among the unemployed seems to have been higher than elsewhere and the chances of someone unemployed finding work correspondingly greater.

The implications of the similarly large variation in movements between sectors seem less unequivocal. The scale of labour mobility, in a sectoral rather than a spatial sense, is significantly greater in the UK, France and Denmark than in other parts of the Community and significantly lower in Germany, Belgium and Greece. In Greece, this is due in large measure to the size of the agricultural sector which has a very low rate of entry. In Germany, the low rate of sectoral mobility may reflect in part the influence of the vocational training system and the requirement that people need to have gone through the training system before working in a particular sector. Whatever the underlying reason, in terms of sectoral mobility, the external labour market can be said to be much more flexible in the former three countries than in the latter three.

On the other hand, flexibility in this sense does not necessarily imply greater efficiency. In all three of the former countries, as well as in Spain, a high proportion of those working in a particular sector of activity were not working in that sector, or not working at all, the previous year. A high proportion, therefore, are comparative newcomers, whose productivity could well be lower than more experienced workers.

Moreover, there is some evidence that investment in training tends to be discouraged if labour turnover is high, since firms financing the investment are less sure of recouping the benefits. More fundamentally, labour market flexibility in its broadest and most meaningful sense, can only be fully assessed by considering the internal as well as the the external market, which essentially means examining at the same time the adaptability of labour organisation within firms. In a number of the Member States with low sectoral mobility, Germany and Belgium, in particular, the internal labour market structure seems to be well developed, with investment in training a key element.

Job turnover within sectors

The above analysis, based as it is on movements between sectors, leaves out of account job changes in the same sector. The 1992 Labour Force Survey, for the first time, provides some evidence on this since it included a question on how long the respondent had been in their present employment. Collating the replies from all those who had been in their present employment for less than a year gives an indication of the number of people who had either changed jobs during this time, or had began working after being unemployed or inactive — though this still leaves out of account people changing their jobs within the same enterprise.

The results broadly confirm the above findings, in the sense that those countries which had high rates of labour turnover between sectors also have high rates of job turnover within sectors, and vice versa for countries with low rates of turnover. For the Community as a whole, some 17% of those in work — around one in six — had not been in their present job one year earlier

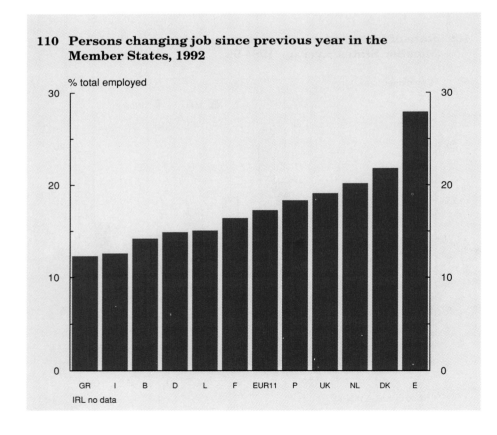

110 Persons changing job since previous year in the Member States, 1992

% total employed

GR   I   B   D   L   F   EUR11   P   UK   NL   DK   E

IRL no data

(Graph 110). This compares with the above figure of just under 11% in the same year if those moving within sectors are excluded, which implies that the latter — those moving to another job in the same sector — amounted to around 6% of the total numbers in employment in 1992.

As in the above analysis, Spain, Denmark and the UK — as well as the Netherlands — had the highest proportions of people in work who had not been in the same employment one year before — in Spain, the figure being as high as 28%, implying that over one in four people in work either entered employment or changed their place of work over the preceding year, while in Denmark, it was over one in five.

At the other end of the scale, the rate of turnover was under 13% in Greece as well as in Italy (for which there were no data for the foregoing analysis) and only around 15% in Belgium, Germany and Luxembourg — countries which also had a low rate of turnover if intra-sector movements are left out of account.

Overall, there seems to be some tendency for the scale of movement within sectors to be relatively high in countries with low rates of movement between sectors. Greece, Belgium and Germany, all with low rates of inter-sector mobility, had a slightly higher than average proportion of workers moving from one job to another within the same sector, while for both France and the UK the reverse was the case.

Countries with low mobility between sectors seem, therefore, to compensate to some extent through higher mobility within sectors, though this does not necessarily signify the same kind of structural change as the former. Moreover, even after taking account of intra-sector employment changes, the differences in overall rates of job turnover between Member States remain significant.

As noted above, countries with apparently low rates of labour mobility, may well compensate through higher rates of job turnover within companies — a flexible internal labour market substituting for a less flexible external one.

Relying on intra-firm mobility to achieve structural change might, however, be seen as a higher risk strategy than pursuing this through increased external labour market flexibility. On the other hand, the greater stability inherent in relying more on the internal labour market may be associated with higher potential productivity if it is managed correctly.

Chapter 5   Changes in working time

The normal working week in the Community has shortened over the past decade, but by much more in some countries than others. A reduction in full-term working hours has been widespread, but significant numbers still work long hours. While part-time jobs have increased, these do not always involve shorter working hours.

Introduction

Over many years, there has been a general tendency throughout the Community for the average time worked by those in employment to decline, so contributing to the growth in the number of people in work. However, the extent of the reduction has varied considerably between Member States as have the factors underlying the decline.

This chapter examines, in the first part, the changes in the average hours usually worked per week over the past decade. Specifically, the main focus is twofold: first, upon the changes which have occurred in what constitutes full-time weekly hours across the Community between 1983 and 1992 and, secondly, upon the growth of part-time working over this period.

It should be recognised that this leaves out of account any changes which have occurred in the number of weeks worked per year, the general trend towards increased numbers of holidays also being a factor reducing working time. Complete, up-to-date and comparable data on hours worked per year, however, are not yet available for the Community as a whole.

It should also be recognised that the chapter does not address the equally important issue of changes in working patterns over an employee's lifetime, in the form, for example, of time off for study, the pursuit of other interests or to take care of a family.

The second part of the chapter examines the importance of

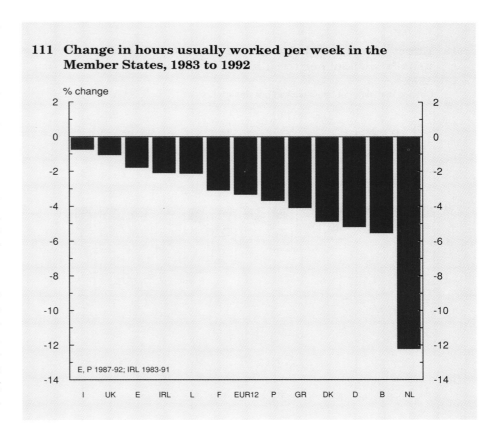

111   Change in hours usually worked per week in the Member States, 1983 to 1992

% change

E, P 1987-92; IRL 1983-91

I   UK   E   IRL   L   F   EUR12   P   GR   DK   D   B   NL

weekend and night working and the way that this varies across the Community.

Changes in average weekly hours, 1983 to 1992

Between 1983 and 1992, average hours usually worked per week in the Community declined by just under 4% — or by around an hour and half (Graph 111 — see Box for a description of the data on hours worked). By far the largest reduction occurred in the Netherlands, where average hours fell by 13% — by 4 hours a week (though a significant part of this is due to the change in the method of measuring employment in 1987 which led to a large rise in jobs with short hours). By contrast, in Italy and the UK, the

fall was only 1% or less — under half an hour a week — while in Spain, Ireland and Luxembourg, the reduction was around 2%. In the remaining countries, the decline in hours ranged from 5% or more in Denmark and Germany to 3% in France.

Overall, it is difficult to discern a consistent pattern in the relative rates of decline over this period. While the fall was relatively large in the Netherlands and Denmark, where the average working week was comparatively short, the fall was also above average in Greece and Portugal, where the average working week was relatively long and below average in Spain and Ireland, where it was also long. No trend towards convergence in the average hours worked per week was, therefore, evident over this period.

The reductions which occurred were the result of a combination of factors in each country. In the first place, most Member States have experienced a shift in employment from agriculture and industry to services. Since average hours worked tend to be less in services than in the other two sectors, especially in agriculture, this in itself tends to reduce average working time.

Secondly, over the past decade, all Member States have experienced a relative increase in the employment of women who tend to work fewer hours than men in individual countries (though women in some countries work longer hours than men in others). This trend is, therefore, also likely to have been accompanied by some overall reduction in average hours worked, though whether this is due to the employment of women *per se* or to the nature of the jobs which have been created — ie jobs involving shorter than average hours which have just happened to have gone to women — is a moot point. Both the relative growth of female employment and the expansion of services has gone along with a rise in part-time working.

These two developments tend to obscure the reduction in working time which has occurred within sectors of activity, as a result, on the one hand, of more part-time rather than full-time jobs being created and, on the other, of a reduction in full-time working hours.

Estimates of the effect of the two developments show that, on average, some 30% of the decline in hours worked in the Community as a whole between 1983 and 1992 was the direct result of structural changes in the economy — in other words, of a decline in agriculture

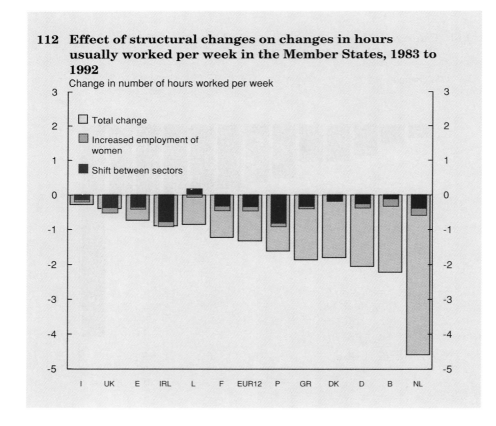

112 Effect of structural changes on changes in hours usually worked per week in the Member States, 1983 to 1992

Change in number of hours worked per week

Legend:
- Total change
- Increased employment of women
- Shift between sectors

Countries (x-axis): I, UK, E, IRL, L, F, EUR12, P, GR, DK, D, B, NL coupled with a growth of services (Graph 112). In Italy, the UK and Ireland, all, or almost all, of the reduction in average hours worked over this period can be attributed to such changes, while in Spain and Portugal over half of the reduction was due to sectoral shifts of this kind. In the four countries experiencing the largest falls, however — the Netherlands, Belgium, Germany and Denmark — very little of the decline was the result of sectoral shifts.

Although the increased employment of women was a less important factor, it can, nevertheless, explain 10% of the overall reduction in average weekly hours over this period. In absolute terms, the relative growth of female employment had the largest effect in reducing the average working week in Belgium and the Netherlands, though in both cases, the decline due to this factor was only 12 minutes over the 9-year period. In relative terms, however, it was most significant in the UK, where it amounted to 40% of the overall, very small, reduction in working time which occurred (signifying that if allowance is made for this factor and the shift between sectors average hours usually worked increased in the UK over this period). In contrast, in Denmark, Greece and Italy, because of the similar average number of hours worked per week by men and women, the effect was negligible.

Once allowance is made for the shift in employment between sectors and the relative growth in employment of women, only 5 of the 12 Member States showed a fall in average working time of more than one hour a week between 1983 and 1992 and only the Netherlands a fall of more than

two hours. In the UK and Ireland, there was a small increase in the average hours worked per week after allowing for these two factors.

The distribution of working time of employees

The figures for average working time discussed above say nothing about how this average is distributed across the workforce, about how many people normally work longer hours than the average and how many shorter hours. Nor do they reveal how the distribution of hours worked is tending to change over time.

In practice, the detailed figures on working time collected as part of the Labour Force Survey indicate that a large proportion of employees tend to work very similar hours and that in most parts of the Community a standard working week of a given number of hours is clearly discernible (though in a few Member States, the UK, in particular, this is far from the case).

In 1992, 58% of male employees in industry and services in the Community usually worked between 38 and 40 hours a week, while a further 13% worked between 35 and 37 hours (Graph 113). (The analysis here is confined to industry and services because of the difficulty of measuring normal working time in agriculture.) Only 6% of men had a normal working week which was less than 35 hours, which means that 23% of men employed in these two sectors worked more than 40 hours a week.

For a significant proportion of these, the normal working week

Data on hours worked

The data used in this chapter come from the Community Labour Force Survey and relate to the number of hours people responding normally worked each week, including any overtime or extra hours, whether paid or unpaid, if these were usual, as well as any work done at home. In cases where respondents are unable to give a figure for usual hours, the average of the hours actually worked over the preceding four week is used.

Because of the difficulty of measuring hours of work in agriculture (there is, for example, significant differences between the LFS figures on this and the Community farm survey), and because agriculture differs markedly in importance between Member States, the analysis is largely confined to industry and services. In addition, employees are distinguished from the self-employed since the issues are somewhat different in the two cases.

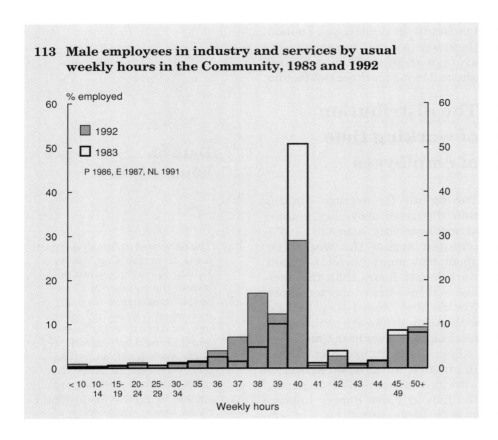

113   Male employees in industry and services by usual weekly hours in the Community, 1983 and 1992

% employed

■ 1992
□ 1983

P 1986, E 1987, NL 1991

Weekly hours: < 10 10-14 15-19 20-24 25-29 30-34 35 36 37 38 39 40 41 42 43 44 45-49 50+

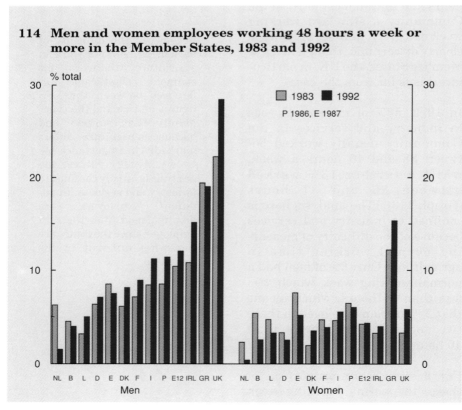

114   Men and women employees working 48 hours a week or more in the Member States, 1983 and 1992

% total

■ 1983   ■ 1992

P 1986, E 1987

Men: NL B L D E DK F I P E12 IRL GR UK
Women: NL B L D E DK F I P E12 IRL GR UK

was 48 hours or more. Indeed 12% of all men employed in industry and services in the Community in 1992, almost 7 million in total, usually worked at least 48 hours a week — in other words, in excess of the maximum number of hours which will be allowed, on average, under the Working Time Directive (Graph 114). At the same time, another 550 thousand men employed in agriculture had a normal working week of at least 48 hours.

Although women in most parts of the Community tend to work fewer hours than men, 41% of female employees in industry and services normally worked between 38 and 40 hours a week in 1992 (Graph 115). Only 10%, however, worked longer hours than this and only 4% 48 hours a week or more. Nevertheless, this amounts to some 2 million women in total, while another 500 thousand women worked these hours in agriculture. Just under 11 million employees in total in the Community in 1992, therefore, had a normal working week which exceeded the maximum allowed under the Working Time Directive.

Almost half of women in the Community in 1992, 49%, usually worked less than 38 hours a week and almost 30% normally worked under 30 hours. A significant proportion, over 4% — over 2 million — moreover, had a normal working week which was less than 10 hours. Over half of these — over 2% of all women employees in industry and services in the Community — usually worked 6 hours a week or less — that is, for less than one full day a week.

Such women are clearly in a different kind of employment than those who work longer hours, even though by working for at least one hour a week they conform to the international standard (ILO) definition of what constitutes someone being in employment. While it is important to have this information, when analysing the figures for employment some allowance needs to be made for those working short hours, perhaps by according the jobs concerned a lower weight than others. This is potentially important when making comparisons between countries, as noted below, or when assessing the rate of job creation.

More detailed comparisons of working time indicate that there is very little difference for men in the distribution of working time as between industry and services, while for women, a significantly higher proportion work less than 35 hours a week in services than industry, reflecting the more flexible working arrangements.

Variations in working time across the Community

While there are marked differences in the distribution of working time between Member States, there are also a number of common features. In particular, men tend to work longer hours than women in all countries, with very few working less than full-time and a significant proportion in a number of Member States working long hours. In addition, in all Member States, more women work part-time in services than in industry. Moreover, for most countries, for men much more than women, there is a narrow band of working hours which constitutes the normal full-time working week which covers the large majority of employees.

Male employees

For five countries in the Community — three of the Southern Member States Greece, Spain and Italy plus Ireland and Luxembourg — the normal working week for men in 1992 was 40 hours. In four of these countries, more than half of all male employees usually worked these hours — 75% in the case of Spain, 88% in the case of Luxembourg — while in Ireland over 40% did so (Graphs 119, 120, 123, 122 and 124).

In France the normal week was 39 hours — 54% working these hours (Graphs 121).

For three Member States — Belgium, Germany and Denmark — the normal working week in 1992 was between 37 and 38 hours — closer to 38 in the former two, 37 in Denmark (Graphs 116, 117 and 118).

In one Member State, the Netherlands, men seem to have been employed either to work 40 hours a week (32% of the total) or 38 hours a week (38%) (Graph 125 — where the data are for 1991 because of problems with the 1992 data).

In the other two Member States — Portugal and the UK — a less clearcut pattern is discernible. In both cases, particularly the UK, for a high proportion of men the normal working week was significantly longer than elsewhere in the Community. In Portugal, 27% of male employees usually worked 40 hours a week in 1992, while 21% worked a 44-hour week and 26% a 45-hour week or more, of whom 8% normally worked at least 50 hours a week (Graph 126).

The UK, however, stands out as having by far the longest working hours for male employees in industry and services in the Community.

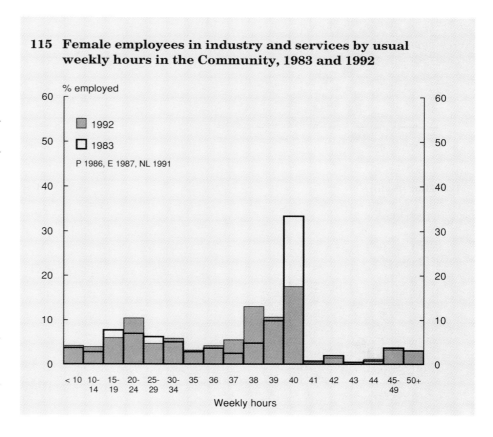

115   Female employees in industry and services by usual weekly hours in the Community, 1983 and 1992

Distribution of male employees in industry and services
by hours usually worked in the Member states, 1983 and 1992

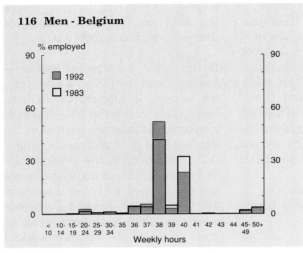

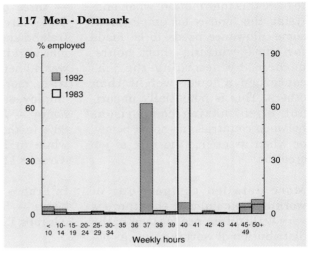

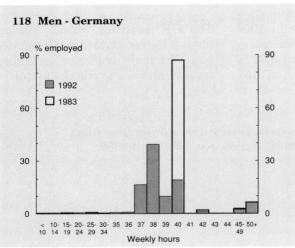

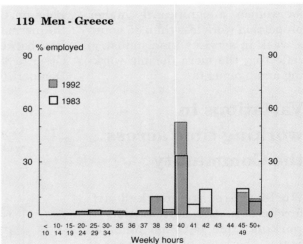

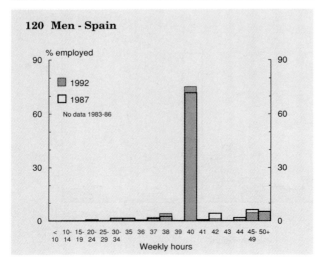

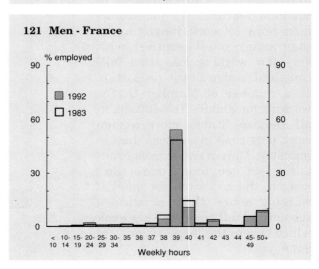

Distribution of male employees in industry and services
by hours usually worked in the Member states, 1983 and 1992

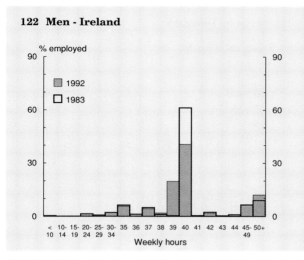

122 Men - Ireland

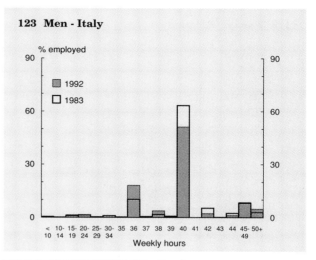

123 Men - Italy

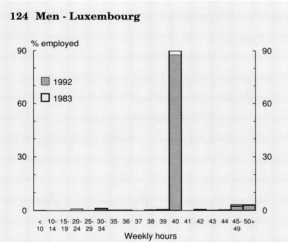

124 Men - Luxembourg

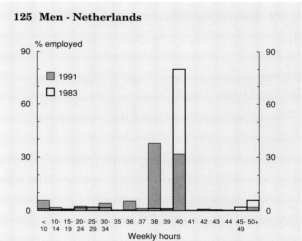

125 Men - Netherlands

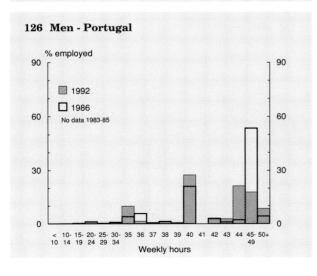

126 Men - Portugal

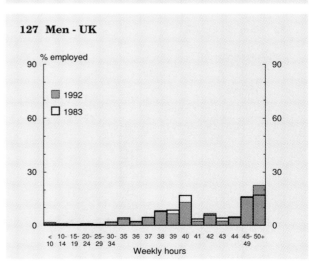

127 Men - UK

Distribution of female employees in industry and services by hours usually worked in the Member states, 1983 and 1992

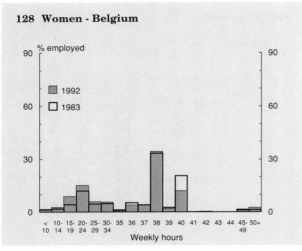

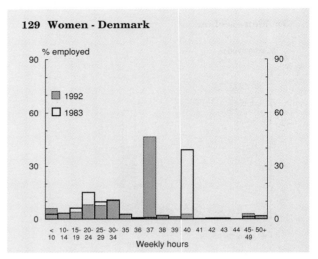

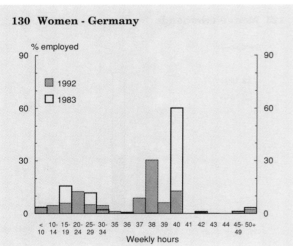

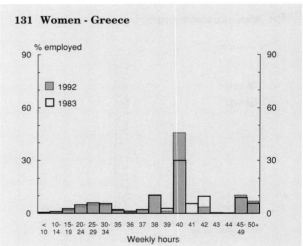

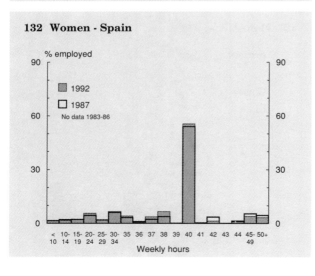

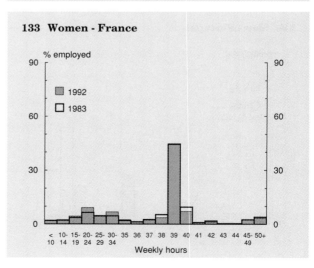

Distribution of female employees in industry and services
by hours usually worked in the Member states, 1983 and 1992

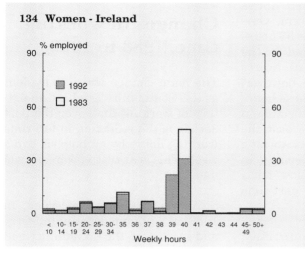

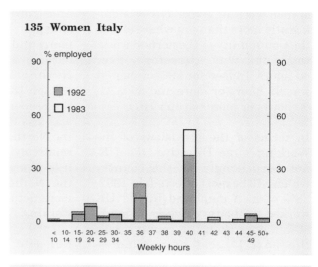

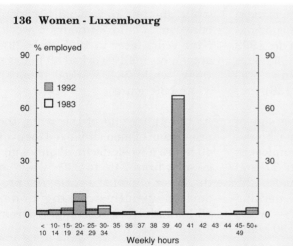

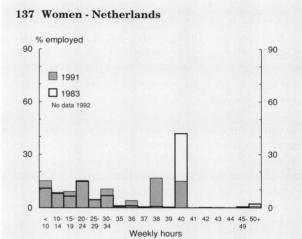

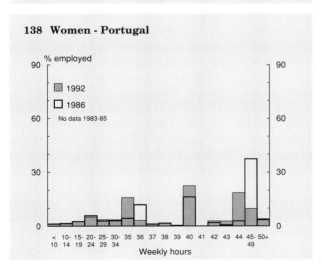

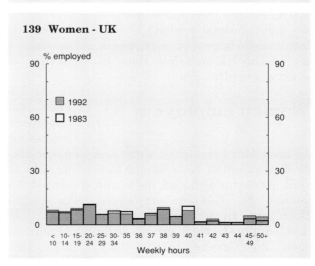

Only 32% of male employees in the UK had a normal working week of less than 40 hours in 1992 and another 13% one of 40 hours. For 55% of men working in the UK — significantly more than anywhere else in the Community — the normal working week was, therefore, over 40 hours. Indeed for 39% of men, it was 45 hours or more and for 22%, 50 hours or more (Graph 127).

In terms of the provisions of the Working Time Directive, the UK, not surprisingly, is the country which will be most affected. In 1992, 28% of men employed in the UK worked 48 hours a week or more, 50% higher than the country with the next largest proportion — Greece — and over three times higher than all but four Member States (Ireland, Portugal and Italy in addition to Greece). Indeed, as much as 44% of all male employees in industry and services usually working a 48-hour week or more were employed in the UK.

At the other end of the scale, a very small proportion of men in most Member States normally worked for less than 35 hours a week. Only in Denmark and the Netherlands was the proportion over 10% in 1992, and then only slightly so in the former. In the Netherlands, however, the figure was 18%, and as many as 6% had a normal working week of less than 10 hours (4% in Denmark, 2% in the UK and less than 1% everywhere else).

Women employees

In most Member States, there is a close association between the normal working time of men and women. For full-time employees, therefore, the countries can be divided into the same groups as for men. For Greece, Spain, Italy,

Ireland and Luxembourg, consequently, the normal working week for women employees was 40 hours in 1992 (Graphs 131, 132, 135, 134 and 136), for France 39 hours (Graphs 133), for Belgium, Germany and Denmark, 37 or 38 hours (Graphs 128, 130, 129) and for the Netherlands, 38 or 40 hours (Graph 137). In each case, however, the proportion working these hours was less than for men, reflecting in the Northern countries, at least, the relatively high proportions working less than full-time, especially in the Netherlands (see below for a more detailed analysis of part-time working).

For the other two countries, Portugal and the UK, as with men, the pattern of working time is more varied. In Portugal, the normal working week for women in 1992 seems to have been either 35 hours (16% of the total) or 40 hours (22%) or 44 hours (18%) (Graph 138).

In the UK, there is even less sign of any conformity in full-time hours. Here only 31% of women employees normally worked between 37 and 42 hours a week, while almost 12% worked longer hours — 9% working 45 hours a week or more — while 41% usually worked under 30 hours a week (Graph 139).Of these, one in five, or 8% of all women employees worked less than 10 hours a week in 1992, more than half of these having jobs of 6 hours a week or less.

In the UK, therefore, some allowance needs to be made for the importance of jobs with very short hours when assessing its rate of employment. This applies even more forcibly to the Netherlands, where almost 15% of women employees normally worked under 10 hours a week, just under half of these for 6 hours a week or less. In Denmark, also, the proportion of women

employed for under 10 hours a week was significant, at 6%, while for the other countries, only in Germany was it more than 3%.

Changes in working time, 1983 to 1992

The main change which is evident at the Community level in the pattern of working time over the past decade is the reduction in full-time working hours by an hour or two a week. This is as true of women as of men.

So far as men are concerned, in 1983, 51% of employees in industry and services in the Community had a normal working week of 40 hours, while another 16% usually worked between 37 and 39 hours a week. Nine years later in 1992, only 29% of men normally worked 40 hours a week, while 36% worked between 37 and 39 hours.

At the upper end of the scale, the proportion of men employed for over 40 hours a week declined only marginally, from 24% to 23%, while at the lower end of the scale, the proportion usually working under 35 hours a week rose slightly from 4% to almost 6%.

Nevertheless despite the small fall in those working over 40 hours a week, the proportion of men employed in jobs of 48 hours a week or more in industry and services increased between 1983 and 1992, from 10 to 12%. There was also a marginal increase in this proportion for women, so that if anything the trend in respect to working long hours is upwards rather than downwards.

For women, however, as for men, the most marked tendency over this period was for a small fall in normal full-time working hours. In 1983,

33% of women employees in the Community had a usual working week of 40 hours and 17% one of between 37 and 39 hours. In 1992, only 17% of women normally worked 40 hours a week, while 29% worked between 37 and 39 hours. Much the same proportions in the two years worked more than 40 hours a week (10%), while there was a small rise in those working under 30 hours (27% to 29%) — and an equally small rise in those working less than 10 hours a week.

Changes in working-time in Member States, 1983 to 1992

The reduction in full-time hours of work in the nine years to 1992 is most apparent in Germany, Denmark and the Netherlands. In these three countries, for women as well as men, normal weekly hours were reduced over this period from 40 to 38 or less. In Germany, for example, 87% of all male employees in 1983 worked a normal week of 40 hours; in 1992, only 19% did so, while 56% worked for 37 or 38 hours. In Denmark, 75% of men were employed for 40 hours a week in 1983, in 1992 only 6% and 62% worked a 37-hour week. In the Netherlands, 80% of men usually worked 40 hours a week in 1983, in 1991, 32%.

In Belgium, Italy and Luxembourg, a similar tendency is apparent, though less marked, while in France, the main change seems to have been a small reduction in the proportion of men working a 40-hour week (15% to 11%) and a small rise in those working a 39-hour week (49% to 54%).

In Spain, very little change is apparent (though in this case, the figures cover only the period 1987 to 1992), while in both Greece and Portugal, there was a significant reduction in the relative number of men usually working over 40 hours a week. This was most pronounced in the latter, where the proportion of men employed for 45 hours a week or more declined from 58% in 1986 to only 26% six years later.

Finally for men in the UK, in sharp contrast to all the other Member States, the prevalence of long hours of work increased between 1983 and 1992. In the former year, 51% of men normally worked over 40 hours a week, by 1992, this had risen to 55%. Moreover, the proportion of male employees working a 45-hour week or more, went up from 33% to 39%. A similar rise is evident over this period in the relative number of men normally employed for 48 hours a week or more — from 22% to 28%. The UK, however, is by no means alone in this respect, 7 other Member States showing an increase in the proportion of such jobs, with significant rises — around 3 percentage points or more — in Ireland, Italy and Portugal, and a rise of 2 percentage points in Denmark and France. Indeed only the Netherlands showed a significant fall — more than 1 percentage point — in the proportion of jobs of 48 hours a week or more between 1983 and 1992.

For women, much the same pattern of change — or lack of change — in the individual countries is evident as for men. In Germany, 60% of women employees usually worked a 40-hour week in 1983, only 13% in 1992. In Denmark and the Netherlands, around 40% did so in the earlier year, only 3% in the former and under 15% in the latter in the later year. There was much the same kind of reduction in Belgium, Ireland and Italy, though on a smaller scale, in Italy a decline in the proportion of women employed for 40 hours a week being matched by an increase in those employed for 36 hours a week.

In France, Spain and Luxembourg, normal hours for full-time women employees changed very little, while in Greece, there was a significant shift to women working 40 hours a week from them working longer hours (46% of women employees had a normal working week of 40 hours in 1992 as against 30% in 1983). Similarly in Portugal, there was a reduction in the proportion of women employed in jobs of 45 hours a week or more and a rise in those working between 40 and 44 hours a week (41% of women employees normally worked 45 hours a week or more in 1983, only 14% in 1992, while those working between 40 and 44 hours went up from 22% to 47%).

In the UK, again in contrast to other Member States, there are signs of an increase in the proportion of women employed in jobs involving long hours. In 1992, 9% of female employees in the UK were employed in jobs of over 45 hours a week as against 6% nine years earlier, while the proportion of women working under 35 hours a week remained virtually unchanged.

As for men, there was a rise in the UK in the relative number of women employees working 48 hours a week or more between 1983 and 1992 (from 3% to 6%). In this case, however, only four other Member States — Denmark, Greece, Ireland and Italy — showed an increase in the proportion of women working these long hours and only one, Greece, a rise comparable to that in the UK.

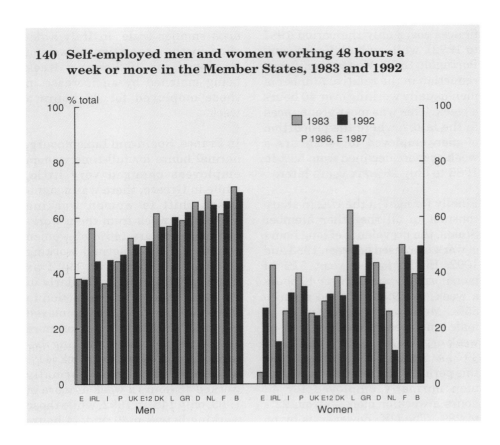

140   Self-employed men and women working 48 hours a week or more in the Member States, 1983 and 1992

% total

1983   1992

P 1986, E 1987

E IRL I   P UK E12 DK L GR D NL F   B   E IRL I   P UK E12 DK L GR D NL F   B
                Men   Women

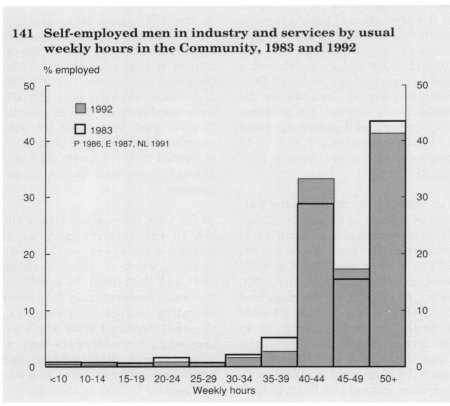

141   Self-employed men in industry and services by usual weekly hours in the Community, 1983 and 1992

% employed

1992

1983

P 1986, E 1987, NL 1991

<10 10-14 15-19 20-24 25-29 30-34 35-39 40-44 45-49 50+
Weekly hours

The self-employed

The major difference in working time is not between sectors — agriculture apart — or between men and women but between the self-employed and employees. A large proportion of the relatively high numbers of people working long hours are self-employed. Indeed over the Community as a whole, 51% of self-employed men in industry and services and 32% of self-employed women usually worked 48 hours week or more in 1992 (Graph 140). The self-employed, therefore, accounted for almost half of all those working very long hours in the Community.

The implication of these figures seems to be that self-employment in large numbers of cases necessitates long hours of work in order to ensure business success or even perhaps a decent level of income (see Chapter 7 which indicates that the self-employed are more likely to fall below the poverty line than wage-earners). Alternatively, the self-employed may derive more job satisfaction from what they do than employees and are therefore willing to work more. Whatever the reason, only 12% of self-employed men in the Community in 1992 worked less than 40 hours a week in 1992 (Graph 141), while under 35% of women did so (Graph 142).

At the same time, however, 5% of self-employed women in industry and services usually worked less than 10 hours a week in 1992, slightly higher than the figure for employees.

A high proportion of the self-employed work very long hours in all Member States. In only one country — Spain — did less than

40% of self-employed men in industry and services work for 48 hours a week or more in 1992, and in only three other countries — Ireland, Italy and Portugal — was the proportion less than 30%. In the Netherlands, Germany, Luxembourg and Belgium, the figure was over 60% — indeed in Belgium, almost 70%.

The figures for self-employed women are also high for most countries. In Belgium and Luxembourg, the proportion was over 50% in 1992, while in Greece, France and Portugal, it was 40% or more. Only in the Netherlands and Ireland was the proportion under 20%.

Changes in working-time of self-employed, 1983 to 1992

For both men and women self-employed, the changes in the pattern of working time were less marked than for employees. For men, there was a small reduction in the proportions working 50 hours a week or more and between 35 and 39 hours accompanied by an increase in those working between 40 and 49 hours a week. For women, the change was more pronounced, with proportionately more normally working 40 hours a week or more and less working under 40 hours.

At the Member State level, the pattern of change over the period was mixed, with half the countries showing a decline in the proportion of self-employed men working very long hours and 8 countries showing a decline in the proportion of women working these hours — the fall for both men and women being particularly pronounced in Ireland.

Part-time working and hours worked

There is a general perception that part-time working has increased in importance in the Community and, moreover, that there is scope for expansion as a means of increasing the numbers employed in many Member States where at present it seems to be underdeveloped. However, much of the policy debate on part-time working often takes place without a clear definition of what is meant by the term.

In the simplest sense, part-time employment means working less than full-time hours. Since, however, the latter can vary significantly both between countries, according to the prevailing conventions and working practices, and between occupations, it is compatible with a wide variation in actual hours worked. In some cases where a normal full-time job involves long hours, working part-time may mean working similar hours to a full-time employee in another occupation or country.

The term part-time may also be used, not so much to denote the actual hours normally worked, but to differentiate the person concerned from someone working full-time, in the sense that they are subject to different — often less favourable — terms and conditions of employment. A part-time worker in this sense may again, in practice, work hours which are not so different from a full-time worker.

These differences in conventions and practices make it difficult to compare the importance of part-time employment between countries, as well as to interpret changes over time. The data on

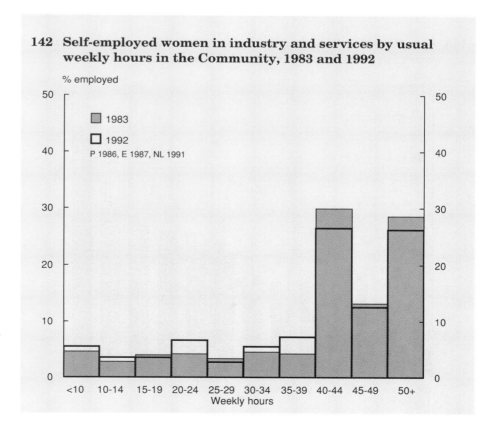

142   Self-employed women in industry and services by usual weekly hours in the Community, 1983 and 1992

% employed

1983
1992
P 1986, E 1987, NL 1991

Weekly hours

hours worked presented above, however, enable a clearer picture to be gained of those working fewer hours a week than the norm in different Member States and how the numbers have changed over the past decade. In addition, comparisons of the hours worked figures with the data on part-time working obtained from labour force or business surveys — the usual sources — gives an indication of how many hours a week are seen as constituting part-time employment in different parts of the Community.

Part-time employment of women

Although many men work part-time hours, it is women who make up the vast majority (85%) of part-time workers in the Community. In 1992, according to the Labour Force Survey, 31% of women employees in industry and services in the Community were employed on a part-time basis (ie they interpreted their job as being part-time when asked). In the same survey, 29% of women were recorded as normally working less than 30 hours a week and another 6% as working between 30 and 34 hours a week. The implication is that just over two-third of women in the Community with jobs of 30 to 34 hours a week regarded themselves as in full-time rather than part-time employment (Graph 143).

In addition, just over 4% of all women employed in industry and services, as noted above, normally worked under 10 hours a week, more than half of these 6 hours or less. If these are excluded from the figures as being in a somewhat different category of employment to other workers, just over 25% of women worked what can be termed part-time hours (10 to 29 hours a week) in 1992.

The number of women classified as being in part-time jobs varies enormously across the Community, from 59% in the Netherlands (see Box p. 117) and 44% in the UK to only around 8% in Italy and Portugal and 6% in Greece. The extent of variation in those working between 10 and 29 hours a week, however, though still wide, is much less. This is because of the different conventions which prevail in the Member States as to the interpretation of part-time working.

Thus in Ireland and Spain, all women normally working under 30 hours a week seem to have been classified as part-time employees in 1992 (the proportion in such jobs being the same as the proportion of part-timers). In France and the UK, all such jobs were similarly classified plus almost half of the jobs involving hours of work of between 30 and 34 hours a week. In Denmark, Germany and the Netherlands, most of the women working 30 to 34 hours a week seem to be classified as part-time together with those working under 30 hours.

In these seven countries, therefore, the two sets of figures give similar results. In the Netherlands, the UK and Denmark, however, as noted above, significant numbers of women classified as part-time worked under 10 hours a week. Excluding these and those normally working 30 hours a week or more — as being in more or less full-time employment — gives much lower figures for those working part-time hours than for part-timers as usually measured.

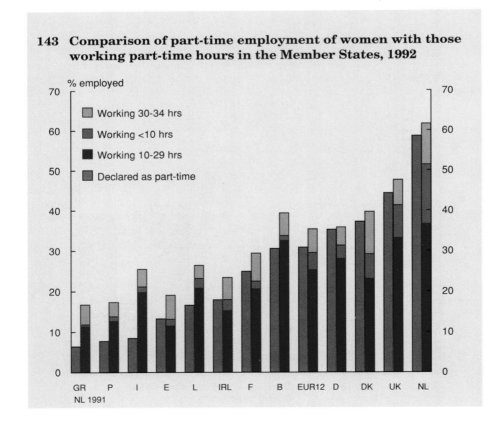

143 Comparison of part-time employment of women with those working part-time hours in the Member States, 1992

% employed

Legend:
- Working 30-34 hrs
- Working <10 hrs
- Working 10-29 hrs
- Declared as part-time

GR P I E L IRL F B EUR12 D DK UK NL
NL 1991

Part-time working in the Netherlands

Part-time working is much more common in the Netherlands than in other European countries. On average, about 5 workers do the equivalent of what would be 4 full-time jobs in most other Member States. Around one-third of all employees work part-time, most of them women, in services especially, in less skilled positions. The growth of part-time work, however, is above average for men in industry and in high skilled jobs.

The variety of working time arrangements which exists reflects the absence of government regulations. In general, while there are no legal or financial incentives to stimulate the growth of part-time working, there are also no major constraints on the creation of part-time jobs as compared with full-time ones.

For an employer, there are essentially three considerations when deciding whether a job should be full-time or part-time:

- the variability of work over the week — ie the extent of any peak in demand;

- the potentially higher productivity of employees who work the weekly hours of their choice, who therefore may be more motivated;

- the potentially higher overhead costs of part-time labour (in terms of office, management and training).

For an employee, the motivation for working part-time is to have more time for other obligations (like family responsabilities) and for leisure activities. Indeed, many people would like to vary the number of weekly hours worked at different stages of their life.

Part-time work has greatly expanded the number of people in employment. The Dutch central Planning Bureau has calculated that the growth of part-time work increased the numbers employed by 300 thousand between 1979 and 1990. Although the recent recession has led to a decline in full-time equivalent employment, the number of people in work has not fallen because of the continued growth of part-time working.

The historical explanation for the growth of part-time working lies in the response to the situation in the 1960s when there was an excess demand for labour. Up to then in the Netherlands participation of women was very low compared to other countries, and employers were forced to offer jobs to women which were tailor-made for them (given family responsibilities and the limited availability of childcare facilities) which in practice meant part-time jobs. From then on, part-time work became an accepted feature of the labour market and developed from providing second-class jobs for married women to fully acceptable jobs for all women and increasing numbers of men. Increasingly employers now use part-time employment as the best solution to meet particular labour needs instead of as a second-best option as in the 1960s.

Since 1980 or so, the Government has supported the use of part-time employment by research, information, dialogue with the social partners and legislation aimed at removing differences between part-time and full-time contracts. Part-time contracts in many areas now have the same legal status and conditions (job protection, social security, pensions and so on) as full-time ones. There have never been any financial incentives (or disincentives) in respect of part-time work, on the ground that these would distort employer and employee choice and so be liable to reduce economic efficiency. The introduction of a legal right of workers to part-time employment was rejected by the Parliament in 1993 mainly for these reasons.

There is an increasing consensus between the social partners on the value of part-time work and they have agreed to promote this as well as the quality and quantity of jobs.

The already high proportion of jobs which are part-time in the Netherlands is still growing relatively rapidly, stimulated in part by a lessening of prejudice against such jobs and the disappearance of cultural barriers to part-time work.

Recent research indicates that 21% of men and 23% of women would prefer to work fewer hours than at present for the same hourly rate of pay, while 14% of employees would like to work more hours. The implication is that 110 thousand additional 32-hour jobs could be created if all employees were able to work the hours they wished.

In the Netherlands, 36% of women employees worked 10 to 29 hours in 1992 as opposed to the 59% classified as in part-time employment, in the UK, 33% as opposed to 44% and, in Denmark, 23% as against 37%. In the other four of these 7 countries, the differences are less marked but in each case the proportion of women working 10 to 29 hours a week was significantly less than those classified as part-timers.

In the remaining five Member States — the Southern countries, excluding Spain, plus Belgium and Luxembourg — the position is very different, in that a significant number of those working under 30 hours a week in 1992 were classified as full-time rather than part-time employees. This was particularly the case in Italy, Greece and Portugal where the proportion

of women classified as part-timers amounted to half or less of those working between 10 and 29 hours.

In terms of usual hours worked, therefore, there is much less difference in the working patterns of women in these countries as compared with the rest of the Community than the figures for part-time employment seem to imply. In particular, the proportion of women working under 34 hours a week in Belgium was much the same as in the UK in 1992, except that there were very much fewer working under 10 hours a week (33% of women worked between 10 and 29 hours a week in the UK, 32% in Belgium, while 6% in both countries worked between 30 and 34 hours). Yet in Belgium, only 30% of women were classified as working part-time as against 44% in the UK.

Indeed, a much higher proportion of women worked between 10 and 29 hours a week in Belgium than in Denmark, where a significantly larger proportion of women are classified as part-time employees.

Similarly, the proportion of women employed in jobs with part-time hours was hardly any different in Italy than in France — 20% in both countries normally worked between 10 and 29 hours — yet almost three times as many women were classified as part-time employees in France as in Italy. Moreover, the proportions working 10 to 29 hours a week were very similar in Portugal and Greece as in Spain, even though only half the proportion of women were classified as part-time employees.

In the Southern countries, in particular, therefore — as also in Belgium and Luxembourg — the main difference with the rest of the Community in this regard is not so much the relative numbers of women working part-time hours but the way such women are classified. In other words, significant numbers are classified as full-time employees who in other countries would be classified as part-time.

Part-time employment of men

Only 4% of men employed in industry and services in the Community were classified as working part-time in 1992, as compared with 4% normally working under 30 hours a week and 1% working under 10 hours a week.

The same variation in practices regarding part-time employment also apply to men, and the Member States can be divided into the same

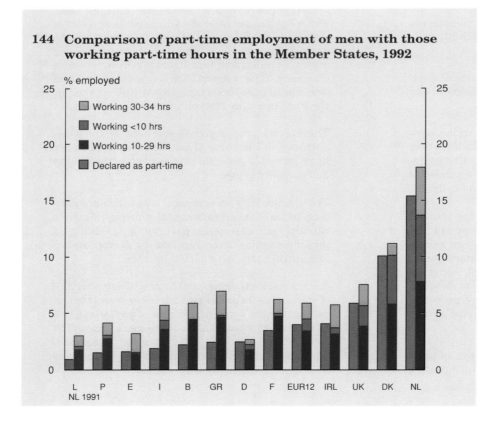

144   Comparison of part-time employment of men with those working part-time hours in the Member States, 1992

% employed

Working 30-34 hrs
Working <10 hrs
Working 10-29 hrs
Declared as part-time

L   P   E   I   B   GR   D   F   EUR12   IRL   UK   DK   NL
NL 1991

groups as for women, with the sole exception of France. Thus in the North of the Community, apart from in Belgium, Luxembourg and France, but together with Spain, a part-time job is broadly equivalent to one of under 30 hours a week, though in a few countries, the Netherlands, in particular, some of those working 30 hours a week or more are classified as in part-time employment (Graph 144).

In the Southern Member States except Spain but together with Belgium, France and Luxembourg, a significant proportion of men working under 30 hours in industry and services are classified as in full-time work. In terms of hours worked, therefore, as in the case of women, there is much less difference in the proportion of part-time employees between these countries and the rest of the Community than the usual figures suggest.

Indeed, though Greece and Belgium had under 2% of male employees classified as part-time in 1992 as opposed to 6% in the UK, a higher proportion worked between 10 and 29 hours a week (5%) in the former two countries than the latter (4%). Similarly, Italy had almost the same proportion of men working these hours as the UK, but under a third of the proportion of men classified as part-time.

Moreover, in the Netherlands and Denmark, where part-time working as usually measured is much more important than elsewhere (accounting for over 15% and 10% of male employees in industry and services, respectively), only around half of these were actually in jobs with part-time hours, a significant proportion (6% and 4%) being in jobs of under 10 hours a week.

Changes in part-time working, 1983 to 1992

The proportion of people normally working 10 to 29 hours a week in industry and services increased by much less in the Community between 1983 and 1992 than the proportion classified as in part-time employment. In other words, a significant part of the apparent growth in part-time working seems to have been due to more jobs being interpreted as part-time rather than full time rather than to an increase in the relative numbers of people in jobs with part-time hours.

In the nine years to 1992, the number of women employees in industry and services in the Community classified as working part-time increased from 26% of the total to

31%. Over the same period, the proportion of women working part-time hours in these two sectors only went up from 23% to 25% (Graph 145). At the same time, the proportion of women in jobs of under 10 hours and in those of between 30 and 34 hours increased slightly (by under 1 percentage point in each case)

Whereas in all Member States, apart from Denmark and Greece, the number of women employees classified as part-time increased between 1983 and 1992 as a share of the total, in most cases significantly, in only five countries was the rise in the share of those working 10 to 29 hours a week more than 2 percentage points. The largest increase was in Belgium, where the proportion of women working 10 to 29 hours a week went up from 23% to 32%, while in the Netherlands, which registered a substantial rise

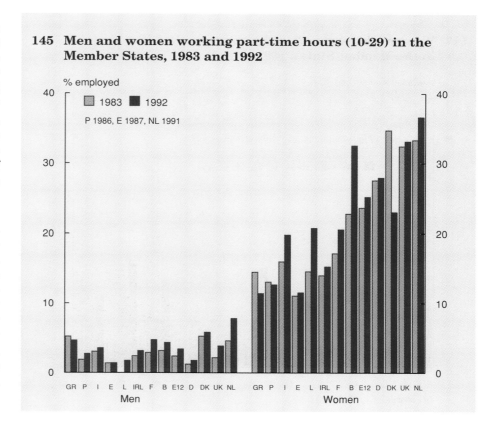

145   Men and women working part-time hours (10-29) in the Member States, 1983 and 1992

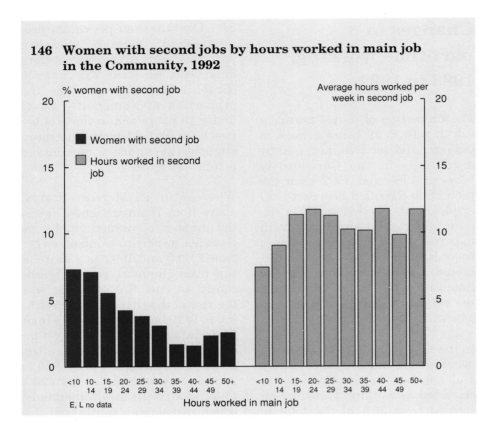

146   Women with second jobs by hours worked in main job in the Community, 1992

% women with second job

Average hours worked per week in second job

- Women with second job
- Hours worked in second job

Hours worked in main job

<10 10-14 15-19 20-24 25-29 30-34 35-39 40-44 45-49 50+

E, L no data

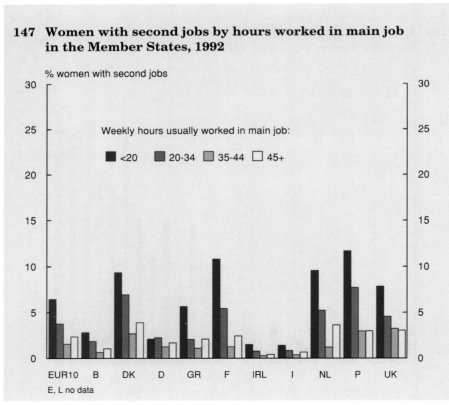

147   Women with second jobs by hours worked in main job in the Member States, 1992

% women with second jobs

Weekly hours usually worked in main job:

- <20
- 20-34
- 35-44
- 45+

EUR10   B   DK   D   GR   F   IRL   I   NL   P   UK

E, L no data

on the usual measure, the increase was considerably less, from 33% to 36%.

In Germany, Spain, Ireland, Portugal and the UK, there was either a very small increase in the proportion working 10 to 29 hours a week or a small fall, while in Denmark and Greece, the reduction was significant (almost 12 percentage points in Denmark).

For men, on the other hand, there was an increase in the proportion of employees working 10 to 29 hours a week between 1983 and 1992 in all Member States apart from Greece — by over 1 percentage point in Belgium, France, the Netherlands and the UK.

The above analysis strongly suggests that figures for part-time employment need to be treated with a good deal of caution, especially when comparisons between Member States are made or when policy conclusions are drawn.

Second jobs

The interpretation of the above analysis is potentially affected by the fact that the figures on hours worked relate only to main jobs. It is possible that a number of those working relatively few hours a week also have second — or even third — jobs. In practice, however, only a very small proportion of men and women employed in the Community reported that they had more than one job (about 3% in 1992 in each case) — at least according to the Labour Force Survey. Second jobs are, therefore, not nearly important enough to affect the conclusions.

Nevertheless, for women at least, there is some tendency for the proportion of those in employment with second jobs to be higher the fewer the number of hours worked in the main job. Some 7% of women working under 10 hours a week in their main job in 1992 had a second job — which on average involved them working an additional 8 hours — as compared with under 4% of those working over 20 hours and under 2% of those with full-time jobs (Graph 146). At the same time, there is also some tendency for the few people with second jobs to work longer in these if they work more than very few hours in their first job.

The tendency for the proportion of women with second jobs to be higher if they work short hours in the first job is general throughout the Community. It is especially pronounced in France, the Netherlands and Portugal, in each of which women employed for under 20 hours a week in their main job were four times as likely to have another job as women working full-time (Graph 147). In only France and Portugal, however, did more than 10% of women working under 20 hours in 1992 have a second job.

For men, on the other hand, the proportion of employees with second jobs tends to be highest for those working "normal" part-time hours — between 15 and 29 hours a week (Graph 148). Around 10% of these had second jobs in the Community in 1992, in which they worked an average of around 16 hours a week. For these men, therefore, the two jobs effectively involved them working full-time hours in total.

This pattern, however, is less typical across the Community than that for women. While it is true of five Member States — Denmark, Germany, Greece, Italy and the

148 Men with second jobs by hours worked in main job in the Community, 1992

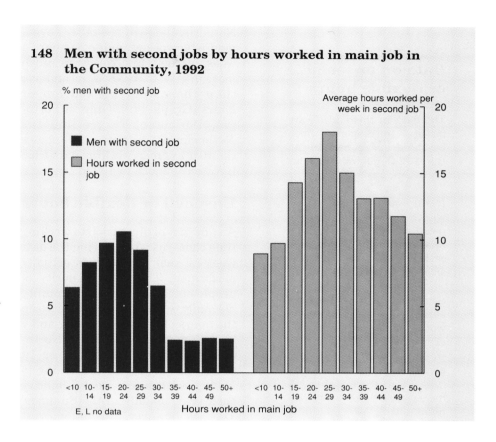

149 Men with second jobs by hours worked in main job in the Member States, 1992

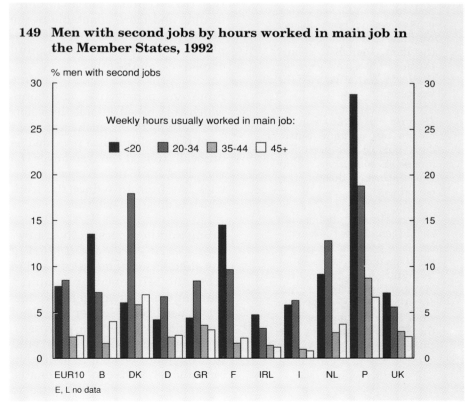

Data on unsocial or flexible hours

The data in this section are based on the responses given by those questioned during the 1992 Community Labour Force Survey.

Night work is defined as work carried out during usual sleeping hours, which implies that the person concerned has an abnormal sleeping pattern.

Someone who *usually* works at night means someone who worked nights on at least half of the days during the four week preceding the reference period; someone who *sometimes* works at night will have worked at least one night during the preceding four weeks.

Saturday and *Sunday* work is intended to relate to formal working arrangements and the data, therefore, should exclude those who work on their own initiative over the weekend.

Usually in this context means two or more Saturdays during the preceding four week, *sometimes* means one Saturday during this period.

Nevertheless, while the data should conform to these criteria, it is possible that there were some differences in interpretation between the Member States in carrying out the survey, especially since this was the first year these questions were included.

Netherlands — in the other seven, men who worked under 20 hours a week in their first job were much more likely to have a second job than those who worked longer hours (Graph 149). Only in Portugal, Denmark, France and the Netherlands, however, did more than 10% of men working part-time have second jobs in 1992.

Unsocial or flexible hours

An additional dimension to working time concerns when during the day, week or year the work is actually performed. The great majority of people employed in the Community normally work sometime between the hours of 8 in the morning and 7 in the evening — earlier in Northern Member States, later in Southern ones — from Monday to Friday, with a few weeks' holiday each year, usually in the Summer. There is, however, growing interest in a number of countries over making this typical pattern more flexible and more adaptable to the individual circumstances of employers, on the one hand, and employees, on the other.

From one perspective, any hours which are worked outside these normal working times, such as at night or at the weekend, are regarded as unsocial. Indeed the trend over the very long-term in advanced countries has been to reduce the work which is done at such times.

From another perspective, however, work carried out during so-called unsocial hours can add to economic efficiency by enabling plant and machinery to be productively used for a longer length of time (indeed in certain processes, such as steel-making, it is vital that the plant be kept in operation continuously). It can also enable consumer demands for service to

be met at any time of the day, week or year. Moreover, it also gives individuals more choice over the hours and days they work so that they can better organise their leisure time.

From the latter perspective, therefore, a larger amount of work performed during unsocial hours can be seen as a sign of the greater flexibility of the productive system and one which is not necessarily to the detriment of workers — provided, of course, that workers are willing participants in the working-time arrangements.

Up to now it has been difficult to obtain information on the numbers of people working non-standard hours across the Community. The Labour Force Survey for 1992, however, included for the first time questions on night and weekend working which provides a partial insight into the scale of the phenomenon, how it varies between Member States and the sectors of activity in which it is most prevalent (see Box for data details).

Night working

In 1992, some 7% of men employed in the Community — around 5 million — usually worked at nights, while 3% of women — just under 2 million — did likewise (Graph 150). In addition, a further 11% of men and 5% of women sometimes worked at night, making a total of over 16 million employees working at night at least occasionally.

Night working is most prevalent in transport and communications, where around 14% of men in 1992 usually worked nights and another 20% sometimes did, in the energy and water industry and in mining and chemicals (these days mainly chemicals), in both of which 12% of men usually worked nights. When occasional night working is also taken into account, night working is also important in public administration (almost 30% of men at least worked sometimes at night), which includes policing. Apart from construction, where there are obvious constraints on working nights, night working is least prevalent in financial and business services, but even here some 3% of men in 1992 usually worked at nights.

For women, only in transport and communications and other services — which includes healthcare — did more than 10% either usually or sometimes work at night.

The prevalence of night working varies a good deal between Member States, both in total and in individual sectors, bearing no clear relationship to the level of economic development or prosperity. Indeed, if anything, there is some tendency for the relative numbers usually working at night to be higher in the more developed than the less developed countries, though it is by no means systematic. Moreover, the countries with relatively high proportions of men working nights also tended to have relatively high proportions of women doing likewise.

The proportion of wage-earners who usually worked nights in 1992 was higher for men in Germany than anywhere else in the Community, at 11% (this figure includes those working in the New Länder), while for women, Germany (with a figure of 5%) was second only to Denmark (6%), which, in turn, had the second highest proportion of men working nights (Graph 151). By contrast, only 2% of men usually worked nights in the Netherlands and only around 1% of women, while in Portugal, the figure for men was

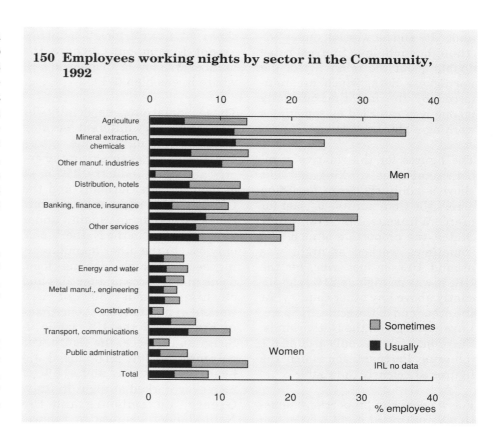

150 Employees working nights by sector in the Community, 1992

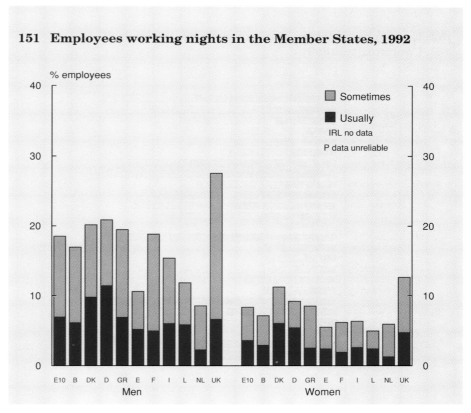

151 Employees working nights in the Member States, 1992

under 1% and for women, under $\frac{1}{2}$% (though such low figures raise doubts about the reliability of the Portuguese data, which are reinforced by the fact that virtually no-one was recorded as sometimes working nights).

The figures for the relative numbers sometimes working at night show a similarly large variation across the Community, at least for men. Whereas for 6 Member States, the proportion of men who sometimes worked at night was around 10% or just over, for the UK, it was as high as 21%, significantly above any other country. At the other end of the scale, in Spain, Luxembourg and the Netherlands, the proportion was only around 6% (ignoring Portugal, for which the figures are clearly unreliable).

For women, the proportions sometimes working at night were much

closer, at 4 to 6% for all countries except Luxembourg, where the number was low (2%) and the UK, where it was high (8%).

These variations, especially for men, imply very different working arrangements in the same sectors of activity. For example, in the energy and water industry, 45% or so of men in both Germany and the UK, worked at night at least sometimes, whereas in Spain, under 20% did so and in the Netherlands, only 5%. In the other manufacturing sector (which includes food, drink and tobacco and textiles and clothing), almost 30% of men worked at night at least sometimes in France and the UK, while in Spain and Greece, the figure was only just over 10%. In financial and business services, under 5% of men ever worked at night in Italy, Greece, Luxembourg and the Netherlands, whereas in France,

Germany and Denmark, over 10% did, and in the UK, over 20%.

Saturday working

Almost half the men employed in the Community in 1992 had jobs which involved them working Saturdays at least some of the time, while over 20% of men usually worked Saturdays (Graph 152). The proportion of women usually working Saturdays was even higher at 25%, while another 17% sometimes did.

For both men and women, Saturday working, as might be expected, was most prevalent in agriculture and distribution and catering (which includes hotels). In the latter, almost half of women employed in 1992 usually worked Saturdays and another 20% sometimes did. As also might be expected, the proportion of employees working Saturdays tended to be higher in service activities than in industry, though financial and business services, where only around 30% of wage-earners ever worked on Saturday (40% of men, 20% of women — similar to the figure for manufacturing sectors), is a partial exception.

The greater importance of Saturday working in services than in industry is the reason why the overall proportion of women usually working Saturdays is higher than for men, despite the fact that in every sector apart from distribution and catering, proportionately more men than women work Saturdays. Since women tend to work predominantly in services, there is more chance of them working on Saturdays than there is for men who work a much greater extent in industry.

In the case of men, there is some tendency for the proportion

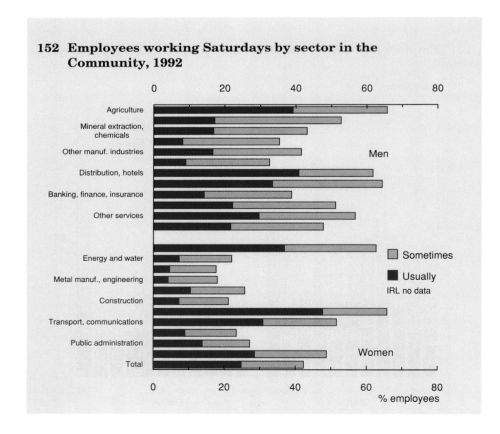

152 Employees working Saturdays by sector in the Community, 1992

usually working on Saturday to be higher in the Southern Member States than in the North, something which seems to be true in most sectors of activity — ie it is not a reflection of a difference in the structure of employment. In both Italy and Spain, around 30% of men usually worked Saturdays and in Greece, just under 25%, while in most Northern countries, the figure was under 20% — in Belgium under 10% — the UK being the main exception with a figure of 23% (Graph 153).

In the UK, moreover, a significantly higher proportion of men than elsewhere in the Community sometimes worked on Saturdays — some 40% overall — which apart from agriculture holds for all sectors of activity. Indeed in virtually every sector, around 60% or more of men either usually or sometimes worked Saturdays in 1992, even in metal manufacturing and engineering and construction, where the average figure for the Community was 35% or less. Except for Italy, where the average proportion was 55%, in all other Member States, under 50% of men ever worked on Saturdays and in three countries, Belgium, Luxembourg and Portugal, under 30% did so.

This marked difference implies significant variations in working arrangements across the Community, even in areas of activity, such as distribution and catering, where there is a widespread need for services to be provided on Saturdays (in the latter three countries, for example, only some 40% or less of men in this sector had jobs which involved working on Saturdays as opposed to 60% or more in most other countries). The differences in the proportions sometimes working Saturdays also implies large variations in the

degree of flexibility of these arrangements, with Spain and Portugal, in particular, where the proportion was under 10%, seeming to have relatively inflexible arrangements, especially compared to the UK, France and Denmark, where it was 30% or more.

The variations between Member States in the prevalence of Saturday working are much the same for women as for men. Both Italy and Spain had the highest proportion of women usually working on Saturday in 1992, at over 30%, though in contrast to the position for men, the figure for Greece was among the lowest in the Community. Indeed, apart from Portugal and the UK, Greece was the only Member State where the proportion of women usually working Saturdays was lower than for men.

On the other hand, in all Member States without exception, proportionately fewer women than men sometimes worked on Saturday, which seems to imply that working arrangements for women are less flexible than for men. This is particularly so for the UK and France, where there was a difference of 12–15 percentage points in 1992 in the two proportions, though where, nevertheless, significantly more women employees sometimes worked Saturdays than anywhere else in the Community.

As for men, the differences in the importance of Saturday working between Member States is fairly uniform across sectors of activity, though in all countries apart from Luxembourg, the proportion of women employed in distribution and catering was generally high throughout the Community — around 60% or more.

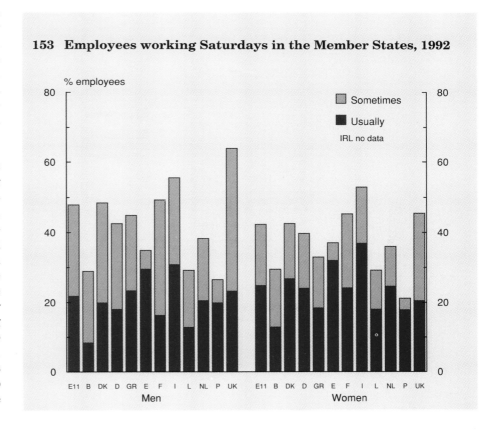

153   Employees working Saturdays in the Member States, 1992

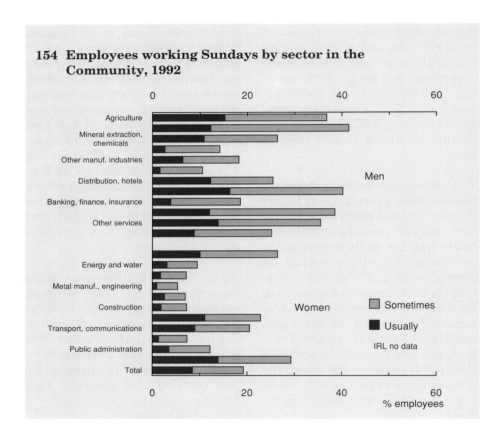

154 **Employees working Sundays by sector in the Community, 1992**

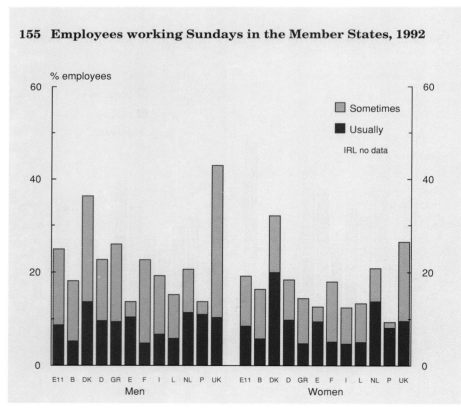

155 **Employees working Sundays in the Member States, 1992**

Sunday working

Under half as many employees usually work Sundays in the Community than work Saturdays. In 1992, around 8% of both men and women had jobs which involved regular Sunday working — giving a total number of some 9 million. Another 15% or so — 18 million — occasionally worked on Sunday (Graph 154).

Sunday working varies less between sectors than Saturday working. In the case of men, the proportion usually working Sundays in 1992 was over 10% in 7 of the 11 sectors of activity and only in metal manufacturing and engineering, construction and financial and business services was it less than 5%. For women, the proportion usually working Sundays was less than for men in all sectors and was over 10% in only three — agriculture, distribution and catering and other services — and in 7 other sectors it was less than 5%. Again, however, the concentration of women in service activities — and in distribution and catering and other services, in particular — meant that the overall proportion of women working Sundays was much the same as for men.

The pattern of Sunday working across the Community is somewhat different than for Saturday working. In particular, there is little sign of any tendency for Sunday working to be more — or less — important in the South than in the North. Italy, where Saturday working is most prevalent, had among the lowest proportions of both men and women regularly working on Sundays in 1992, whereas the Netherlands, which is below the Community average for Saturday working, has among the highest proportions of men and women usually working on Sundays.

In the case of both men and women, the proportion of employees *usually* working Sundays was highest in Denmark in 1992, at around 15% for men and 20% for women, the latter figure in particular being substantially more than in any other country (Graph 155). At the other end of the scale, in Belgium, France, Italy and Luxembourg, the proportion for both sexes was only around 5–6%.

As for Saturday working, the proportion of employees *sometimes* working Sundays is considerably higher in the UK than elsewhere. In 1992, over 30% of men and 17% of women occasionally worked on Sunday, with remarkably little variation between sectors of activity, the proportion being as high for men in engineering — 35% — as in transport and communications or other services, and not much lower for women in financial and business services than in distribution and catering.

As many as 43% of men in the UK, therefore, had jobs which involved at least some Sunday working, whereas apart from in Denmark, where the figure was 37%, and Greece, where it was 27%, in all countries, the proportion was only around half or less of this. For women, the UK, Denmark and the Netherlands were the only countries where the proportion ever working on Sundays was more than 20%.

Again as in the case of Saturday working, in all Member States proportionately fewer women *sometimes* worked on Sundays than men, so confirming the impression that they tend to have more regular working patterns. Moreover, unlike

in the case of men, there is some tendency for the proportion of women who ever work Sundays to be lower in the Southern Member States than in the North of the Community.

The pattern of variation in the importance of Sunday working between sectors is similar across countries — in all Member States, the proportion of employees at least occasionally working Sundays was relatively low in engineering and construction and, in most, it was relatively high in transport and communications, distribution and catering and other services. The difference in the absolute values of these proportions, however, in a number of cases is extreme, implying that there are marked differences in working arrangements between countries.

For example, in the Benelux countries, distribution and catering services operate with under 20% of those employed ever working on Sunday, whereas in Denmark and Greece, over 50% of men and over 25% of women sometimes work Sundays. This clearly may reflect differences in institutional and social conventions which affect the pattern of consumer demand — such as the demand for Sunday shopping, for example — and is not necessarily a sign of less flexible working. On the other hand, there are instances of equally wide differences in respect of other service sectors as well as manufacturing where variations in consumer preferences between countries ought to have relatively little effect.

In engineering, for example, under 10% of men ever work on Sundays in most Member States, in some cases, such as Spain and Portugal, under 5%, but in Denmark, the figure is 25% and in the UK, 40%.

Similarly, in other services — which includes healthcare as well as various personal and recreational services — over 35% of women sometimes work on Sunday in the latter two countries as well as in Germany, whereas in Spain, Portugal and Italy, the figure is under 20%.

Chapter 6   Labour costs, social contributions and taxes

The cost of labour to businesses is substantially greater than the take-home pay of employees in many Member States, even at low pay levels, with possible adverse effects on the employment of the less skilled. The challenge is to encourage more job creation for these without adding to the working poor.

Introduction

A distinguishing feature of most Community economies is the high level of social protection provided by the State. This is associated, moreover, with charges on business made by government to fund systems of social protection — specifically, social security contributions paid by employers — being higher than in other developed countries. As international competition has become more intense, there has been concern that the effects on labour costs are such as to put European companies at a competitive disadvantage relative to those located in other countries, and to discourage them from employing people.

There is also a concern about competition between producers located in different European countries because of the large variations in the scale of charges which exist. Countries where employers are required to pay substantial amounts to finance social welfare benefits, it has been argued, are likely increasingly to lose business and employment to those where this requirement is lower.

The effects of the costs imposed by systems of social protection on European producers raise at least three kinds of question :

- first, how far social contributions paid by European employers add to labour costs and thereby discourage firms from taking on more workers;

- secondly, whether a different method of financing social expenditure would have less of an effect on labour and production costs and thereby provide an inducement to increase employment;

- thirdly, whether a less extensive, less generous and, therefore, less costly system of social protection would reduce labour costs;

- fourthly, whether a shift in the structure of the charges to relieve the burden on lower paid employees would increase the numbers in work.

In response to these questions, the Commission has suggested a reduction in social contributions and taxes on employment, especially on the employment of less skilled workers, of 1–2% of GDP, though the exact figure would depend on the fiscal situation in individual Member States.

The impact of employment taxes

The extent to which charges on employers increase the costs of employment and production cannot be judged simply on the basis of their initial impact. Charges on business may be borne by the business itself (reducing profits and the incentive to employ people) may be passed on to customers (raising prices) or may be passed back to employees (reducing wages). Which of these outcomes predominates, and all three will generally occur to some extent, depends on the balance of economic forces in the product and labour markets concerned.

In none of the cases – leaving aside possible disincentive effects – need there be any depressing effect on aggregate demand and output in the economy, so long as the revenue raised from charges is matched by equivalent government expenditure, and so long as exchange rates adjust appropriately to keep price and cost levels in line between countries.

The composition of demand and output would, however, stand to change since the effective cost imposed on businesses will vary according to the characteristics of the market in which they operate and the labour intensity of the production process. Similarly, the increased cost of employing labour provides some incentive to choose less labour-intensive methods of production, insofar as the techniques of production allow such a choice to be made.

To a major extent, the social contributions paid by employers appear to be passed back to employees and, therefore, to lead to wages being lower than they otherwise would have been. Thus, countries with similar levels of productivity (ie with similar levels of value-added per person employed) tend to have similar levels of labour costs, irrespective of the rate of social contribution imposed on employers, but often very different levels of gross earnings. The respective shares of labour costs and profits in value-added, therefore, are also similar and appear not to be affected to any great extent by the relative importance of employers' contributions in total labour costs.

To the extent that this is the case, it is employees as a group who provide much of the finance for the systems of social protection designed to support them when they are unable to do so because of sickness, invalidity, old-age or unemployment. As such, their position may not be so different from workers in other developed countries with less developed public

systems who rely on private schemes to provide protection.

Alternatively, or additionally, companies, especially large enterprises, may provide employee protection on a voluntary rather than statutory basis. Outside the Community, this is most notably the case in Japan, where the largest companies provide a level of social protection to their workers which is on a par with that provided by the State in the most advanced European countries. However, such expenses do not always show up in the data on non-wage labour costs. Though only a minority of workers in Japan are employed by such companies, these are, nevertheless, the ones most actively engaged in international trade where cost competitiveness is a major consideration. On the other hand, large Japanese companies also tend to rely on smaller companies acting as sub-contractors to undertake a significant part of the production process, and workers in these firms are very much less well protected in this respect.

At the same time, there are also a number of European countries in which marital status or family circumstances are reflected in gross wages. Equally, though the effects on labour costs of statutory or voluntary contributions may be similar, their social effects are likely to be very different, since less skilled workers and part-time employees, who are predominantly women, tend to benefit less from voluntary schemes.

Nevertheless, the evidence would seem to imply that reducing their contribution to the cost of social protection in Europe would not necessarily benefit European producers as much as it might seem in relation to their counterparts in other countries, where State

systems are less extensive, but where private or company schemes are more developed. Much depends on how the reduction is financed and, in particular, whether it is accompanied by an equivalent reduction in the level of social protection provided to workers or whether other taxes are raised to compensate for the loss in revenue. To the extent that workers are worse off, either because the real value of social protection declines or because they pay more in tax, then over the long-term, there is likely to be pressure for wages to adjust to compensate for this loss of real income combined with a tendency for companies to increase the voluntary element in benefit provision. At the end of the day, when economic forces have fully worked themselves out, the difference in overall labour costs between Europe and elsewhere may be little altered.

However, though this may be true over the long-term, reductions in employers' contributions could serve to reduce the cost of labour and provide an incentive to increase employment over the period when this adjustment is taking place, which might well be a great many years.

The effect on labour costs of such a reduction is likely to be strengthened by the fact that businesses in most parts of Europe perceive employers' contributions as an important addition to their labour costs. Moreover, the contributions paid by employers and employees together, when combined with taxes levied on wages, represent a sizable 'wedge' between what employers pay to hire labour and what workers receive in the form of take-home pay. As such, they represent a major incentive for both employers and employees to avoid these payments by seeking other arrangements outside the formal economy. Any narrowing of the difference between labour costs and take-home pay will reduce the incentive to avoid or evade the payment of state levies and may, therefore, lead to a reduction in the size of the informal, or grey, economy and to an increase in GDP and employment as officially recorded.

Furthermore, contributions and taxes are not necessarily neutral as regards the incentive to employ people at different wage levels — and, therefore, at different skill levels — nor, as noted above, as between different kinds of goods and service produced. Any change in the rate of contribution is likely, as a result, to affect the composition of demand and output and, if it is not proportional to earnings, the employment of people at different wage levels.

In this regard, employers' contributions cannot be passed back to workers without limit. At the bottom end of the pay scale, earnings cannot in most cases be reduced below a certain point without running foul of minimum wage legislation or of conventional standards as to what constitutes a living wage or, if these are not effective, below the level of social benefits available to someone out of work.

Equally, if contributions are passed on in higher prices or borne by the company, the costs of production might be such as to affect the willingness of consumers to pay or the company's willingness to employ people who contribute only marginally to production. Reductions in employers' contributions, in other words, can lead to marginal production becoming profitable and the employment of workers with low productivity becoming viable.

The concern here is not to undertake a detailed investigation of the links between social contributions and employment. Instead it is to examine the levels of contributions and taxes levied on wages in different parts of the Community and their proximate effect on comparative labour costs and net earnings and to relate these to levels in other countries. The concern is also to indicate the size of the wedge between labour costs and take-home pay and the way that it varies with wages.

Tax and contribution rates

The rate of social contribution paid by employers — including both statutory and voluntary amounts — varies considerably across the Community. In 1991, for an employee receiving the average wage

paid to male workers in manufacturing, it ranged from close to 30% of labour costs in France, Italy and Belgium to under 20% in Ireland and Luxembourg, under 15% in the UK and under 5% in Denmark, giving an average rate for the Community of around 22% (Graph 156 — see Box for a description of the data used).

This is not so different from the rate in the US for the same kind of employee — 21% — though above the 15% rate in Japan. In Japan, in particular, however, part of what in Europe are social welfare benefits funded through employers' contributions — such as family allowances — tend to be consolidated into the wage. The recorded rate of employers' contributions in Japan is likely to understate the social element in the wage and to distort the comparison with Europe.

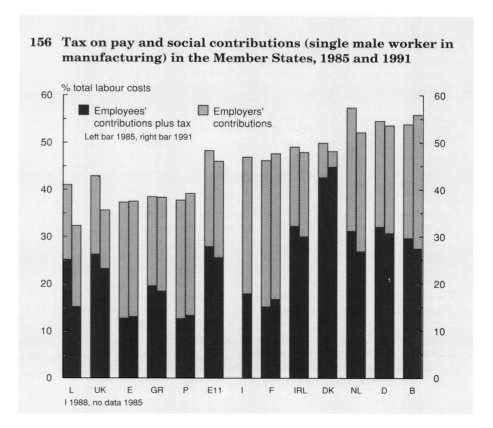

156   Tax on pay and social contributions (single male worker in manufacturing) in the Member States, 1985 and 1991

Data on earnings, social contributions and taxes

The data which form the basis of the analysis in this chapter have been compiled mainly by Eurostat supplemented by information on social contribution regulations published in MISSOC. They relate, first, to the taxes and social contributions which would be paid in each of the countries, on the basis of the tax and contribution schedules in operation, by each of six categories of employee, defined in terms of marital status, dependents and level of earnings in relation to the average wage of a manual worker in manufacturing industry (taken from Eurostat, *Net earnings of manual workers in manufacturing industry in the Community*). As such, they are theoretical rather than actual amounts. They, therefore, do not allow for individual circumstances beyond these basic characteristics and may accordingly differ from the actual amounts someone might pay in practice. No data are available on this aspect for Italy, which means that it is excluded from the analysis.

Secondly, these data have been combined with figures on employers' social contributions from the survey of labour costs published by Eurostat (updated to 1991 — Eurostat, *Labour costs: updating 1989–1991*), which give for each Member State the average contributions paid by employers in manufacturing. Information published in MISSOC on the rates of employers' contribution payable at various levels of earnings have been used to estimate contributions at other than average earnings in those countries where the rate is not proportional over the range of earnings considered (ie Denmark, the Netherlands and the UK). Since this only covers statutory contributions, it has been assumed for all countries that voluntary contributions vary in proportion to earnings, which may not, of course, be the case in practice. Comments in the text on the variation in social contributions with earnings, it should be emphasised, are based on national regulations relating to contributions.

The analysis leaves out of account taxes on expenditure which are more difficult to incorporate both in practice and in principle since, as they manifest themselves in higher prices, along with a range of other factors — including perhaps employers' contributions in part — they tend not to be perceived in the same way as deductions from gross wages. Their incidence also depends on the spending pattern of the individual concerned.

The analysis also largely leaves out of account the benefits and services received which are financed by the taxes and social contributions paid and which can be considered as part of net earnings in a broad sense.

In the main, variations in employers' contributions in the Community reflect differences in the statutory levies imposed on businesses when taking on labour, though they may also be due to non-statutory contributions paid by employers to employee pension funds, health insurance schemes and the like. Such contributions, while often voluntary, are not wholly so in a number of countries, in that they are often the result of collective agreements between employer and employee representatives. The importance of this element varies from around 40% of the total contribution paid in the UK and Ireland (where it is voluntary for the most part), 30% in France and the Netherlands (where it is mainly the result of collective agreements), to under 5% in Belgium, Italy and Luxembourg.

In the US, the non-statutory element is more important than in Europe, accounting for about a third of the 21% of labour costs represented by the non-wage element (around 7% of labour costs).

In most Member States, rates of employers' contribution have not changed much over many years. In only three countries — Belgium, Denmark and the UK — did the effective rate change by more than 1% of labour costs between 1985 and 1991. In Belgium — the only country where there was a significant increase — the rate for someone on average earnings in manufacturing went up from just over 24% to over 28% of labour costs, while in Germany, Ireland, Greece and Luxembourg, there was also an increase, but much smaller. By contrast in Denmark, the rate fell from 7% to 3% and in the UK, from almost 17% to 12%. The result, for the Community as a whole, was that the average rate in

1991 was virtually the same as six years earlier.

This stability has changed somewhat recently. In the second half of 1993 and the first half of 1994, changes have taken place in a number of Member States, mostly designed to reduce employers' charges for unskilled workers or young workers.

In Japan, social contributions appear to have increased between 1985 and 1991, but only by around 1% of labour costs.

Differences between the Community, on the one hand, and the US and Japan, on the other, seem more pronounced in respect of employees' contributions and taxes on wages (though because the latter are affected to a considerable extent by individual circumstances, it is more difficult to identify effective rates and compare these between countries). In the US and Japan these in combination amounted to only around 10–15% of labour costs in 1991, whereas in the Community, they averaged over 20%. Together with employers' contributions, therefore, they represent a significant wedge between the cost of employing labour to companies and the net earnings which workers receive.

On average, the total social contributions and income tax paid in the Community by a single person on the average wage of a male worker in manufacturing was some 45% of labour costs in 1991 — ie such a person received less than 55% of what it cost the company to employ them.

The size of the wedge, however, varies considerably across the Community — broadly, but not entirely, in line with the level of prosperity,

as measured by GDP per head. For a single person, as defined above, the overall rate of tax plus contribution was under 35% in Spain, Portugal and Greece in 1991, but over 50% in Belgium, Germany and the Netherlands, and not far below this in Denmark and France. On the other hand, the overall rate was lowest, at just over 30% in Luxembourg, while in the UK, it was 35%.

In most Member States, the taxes and social contributions paid by wage earners either declined or remained broadly unchanged between 1985 and 1991 in relation to pay. The only two countries where there was much of an increase were France and Denmark. (In the latter, this was partly a reflection of a shift in the tax burden from employers to employees, though overall the wedge between labour costs and net earnings was

reduced slightly.) In Luxembourg, the UK and the Netherlands, there were significant reductions in taxes on employees which were coupled with a substantial narrowing of the difference between labour costs and net earnings. In Belgium, on the other hand, a reduction in taxes on employees was combined with a widening of the difference because of the increase in employers' contributions. However, this was only one of three countries — the others being Portugal and France — where the tax wedge increased over this period.

Focusing on a single person on average earnings gives only a partial indication of the scale and variation of effective rates across the Community. Though social contributions tend to be related solely to gross earnings, taxes on wages vary in most cases with individual circumstances — notably the

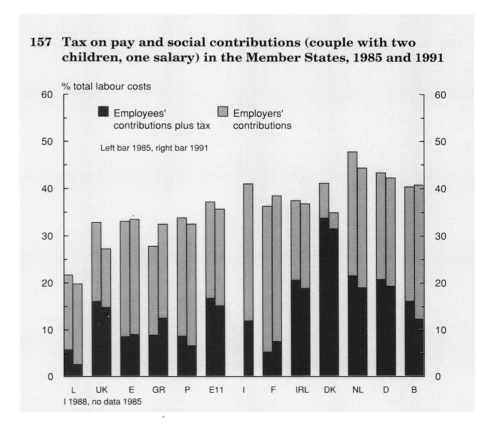

157   Tax on pay and social contributions (couple with two children, one salary) in the Member States, 1985 and 1991

number of dependents. Thus, in all countries, apart from Greece, taxes on wages are lower if the person concerned has a dependent wife or husband than if they are single. Moreover, allowances are payable to families with children in all countries, though at significantly differing rates.

For a married person with two children earning the average wage of a male worker in manufacturing, for example, the average taxes and contributions paid in the Community as a whole in 1991 were 5% of labour costs less than for a single person, and around 10% less if family allowances are treated as an offset to tax (Graph 157). In Belgium (partly because of the high level of family benefits) the overall tax rate was over 15% less and in Luxembourg and Denmark, some 13% less. On the other hand, in the poorer countries in the South of the Community, the difference was very much smaller — 4% less in Spain and Greece, 6% less in Portugal.

The effective tax wedge, therefore, is smaller for workers with dependents, net earnings for most Member States averaging around 65% or more of labour costs in 1991. As for a single person, the wedge was reduced between 1985 and 1991, though the reduction in most cases was less — the main exceptions being Denmark and Portugal — while only Greece showed a significant increase in the size of the wedge.

Labour costs and earnings

The average monthly cost of employing a male manual worker in manufacturing in the Community varied from around 2,750 ECUs in Germany and just over 2,500 ECUs in Belgium to just under a 1,000 ECUs in Greece and under 600 ECUs in Portugal — a difference at the two extremes of over 4 to 1 (Graph 158). This is broadly in line with the difference in value-added per person employed.

In terms of net earnings, the difference is narrower, measured in ECUs, since the rate of tax and social contributions tends to be less in the poorer, lower productivity economies. However, this understates differences in living standards since in the latter, workers have less generous welfare benefits and less well developed health services.

On the other hand, ECU figures overstate differences because they fail to take account of variations in price levels which are not reflected in the exchange rate. In terms of purchasing power standards (PPS), differences in net earnings between Member States are greatly reduced — monthly take-home pay in Luxembourg being on average less than three times greater than in Portugal in 1991. In these terms, a single male worker in manufacturing in Spain on the average wage has a higher level of take-home pay than a comparable worker in Denmark, though their standards of living are not necessarily equivalent.

The variation of effective tax rates with earnings

In most Community countries, social contributions are regressive — in the sense that their effective rate declines as earnings increase. This is true of both employers' and employees' contributions. This

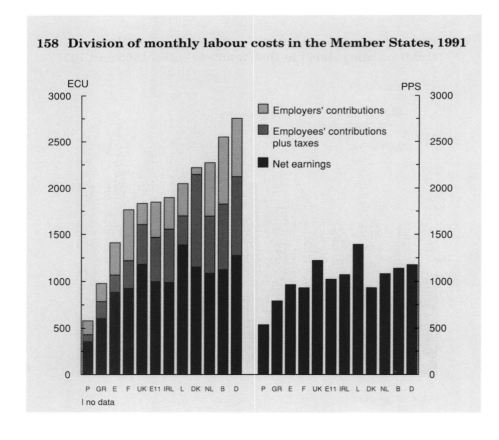

158 Division of monthly labour costs in the Member States, 1991

ECU

Employers' contributions

Employees' contributions plus taxes

Net earnings

PPS

P GR E F UK E11 IRL L DK NL B D

I no data

contrasts with the fact that in all countries, taxes on wages are progressive, in that they rise more than in proportion to earnings.

The extent to which either is the case, however, differs significantly between Member States. Unfortunately, the data available enable only a partial Community-wide analysis to be made of the degree to which contributions and taxes vary with wage levels, since they cover only a relatively narrow range of earnings, from 80% of the average wage of men working in manufacturing to 125%. This leaves out of account less skilled workers near the bottom end of the pay scale who represent a major proportion of the unemployed and who represent the main focus of concern as regards job creation. It also leaves out of account a large proportion of women whose average wage in manufacturing in many countries is below 80% of the male average and is even lower in many service activities in which women predominantly work.

Within this relatively narrow range of wage variations, the social contributions levied by the state on employers in most Member States — 8 of the 12 — are proportional to earnings (Graph 159). In three countries, Denmark, the Netherlands and Italy contributions are slightly regressive (though in the latter, they only become so on earnings above the average), bearing more on low paid workers than higher paid ones. This is especially the case in Denmark where contributions are fixed in nominal terms and where they therefore decline markedly in relation to wage levels, although, since they are so small, the effect is marginal. The UK is the only country in the Community where contribution rates are progressive within this or any

earnings range and where for those on very low wages — and/or those working relatively few hours a week — nothing at all is payable.

Above 125% of the average wage, however, rates in most Member States become regressive at some level of earnings. In Germany, Greece and Ireland, this happens at between average earnings and twice average earnings, with rates declining continuously as wages increase — at 4 times average earnings, the rate in each case becoming only around half that on wages below the average. In France as well as Italy, the same is true, though the decline in relation to earnings is considerably less. In Spain and Luxembourg, contribution rates become regressive only at above twice average earnings, though the decline is as steep as in the former three countries. Only in Belgium and Portugal is the rate

proportional at all levels of income and only in the UK, is the rate progressive, but then only marginally so (at above 1½ times average earnings, the marginal rate of employers' contribution remains constant).

In 9 of the 12 countries in the Community, therefore, the non-wage labour costs imposed by government bear proportionately more on workers at the lower end of the earnings scale than on those at the higher end. In two of the other three, the addition to costs is the same in percentage terms, in both cases the rate being higher than the Community average. The only country where differential contributions provide any incentive for employers to take on lower paid workers is the UK.

In practice, it appears, the schedule of contribution rates in most

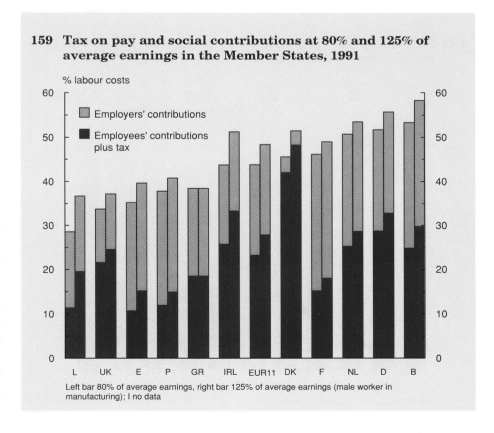

159 Tax on pay and social contributions at 80% and 125% of average earnings in the Member States, 1991

Left bar 80% of average earnings, right bar 125% of average earnings (male worker in manufacturing); I no data

countries has been determined without much regard to the potential effects on employment. The apparent reason why rates are regressive is that the social benefits to which the payment of contributions gives entitlement are also effectively regressive relative to earnings, in that there are limits on the amount payable to recipients. Since benefits decline in relation to earnings as salaries increase, it was considered appropriate that contributions should do likewise. However, as statutory benefits these days seldom reflect the actual contributions which individuals have paid, or have had paid on their behalf, the logic of this state of affairs is now questionable. It is even more questionable in the light of the high level of unemployment in most of the countries concerned.

Employees' contributions have much the same characteristics as those imposed on employers, in that they are either proportional to earnings or, especially towards the upper end of the earnings scale, regressive. This is also true of the UK in this case, where the rate of contribution declines continuously as pay increases above $1\frac{1}{2}$ times the average wage.

On the other hand, taxes on wages are progressive in all Member States, though the extent to which this is so is much less marked within the range of earnings for which comparable data exist than at higher wage levels.

Only in Greece, was the same rate of tax levied on earnings at 125% of the average as on those at 80% (Graph 159). In all other Member States, the effective tax rate increases as wages go up within this range, with the result that overall the rate of tax plus contributions is progressive. The extent of this, however, varies significantly across the Community, being most pronounced in 1991 in Luxembourg, Ireland and Denmark (in the latter, the progressive nature of the tax system much more than offsetting the regressive nature of social contributions) and least so in the UK, Portugal, France and the Netherlands.

At 80% of average earnings, taxes and contributions in combination still amounted, on average, to close to 45% of labour costs in the Community as a whole in 1991 for a single person, not much below the rate at average earnings. In the Netherlands, Germany and Belgium, they amounted to over 50%. At 125% of average earnings, the combined rate averaged just under 50% of labour costs in the Community and was over 55% in Germany and Belgium.

Tax and contribution rates for men and women

For tax and contribution purposes, single women are treated in the same way as single men in all Member States. Since, in all countries, women tend on average to earn less than men — over the Community as a whole, around 28% less for manual workers in manufacturing in 1991 (though it should be stressed that this is a difference between two averages and does not relate to a man and woman in the same job) — tax rates for a woman on average earnings are generally below those of a man on average earnings, reflecting the progressive nature of the tax schedule.

The rates of contribution are the same, apart from in Denmark and

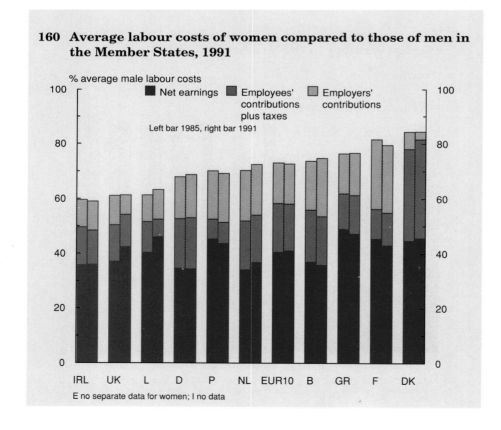

160   Average labour costs of women compared to those of men in the Member States, 1991

% average male labour costs

Net earnings   Employees' contributions plus taxes   Employers' contributions

Left bar 1985, right bar 1991

IRL   UK   L   D   P   NL   EUR10   B   GR   F   DK

E no separate data for women; I no data

the Netherlands, where they are marginally higher and in the UK, where they are slightly lower, reflecting the variation of rates with income in these countries. On average, therefore, the wedge between labour costs and net earnings is similar to, though slightly less than, that for a male worker on 80% of average earnings discussed above.

The relative level of labour costs for women employees compared with men, however, varies a good deal across the Community. In the case of manual workers in manufacturing, the average labour costs for women in 1991 ranged from 85% of those of men in Denmark and just under 80% in France to only 61% in the UK and 59% in Ireland (Graph 160). A similar range of differences exists for other workers in other sectors · of activity.

The net earnings received by a woman on the average wage, on the other hand, shows a somewhat different pattern of variation, being highest relative to male earnings in Greece and Luxembourg, where the combined tax and contribution rate is relatively low and lowest in Germany and Belgium, where it is relatively high.

Between 1985 and 1991, the average level of labour costs for women relative to men remained virtually unchanged over the Community as a whole, increasing slightly in Germany and the Benelux countries and declining in France but hardly changing at all in the other Member States. Net earnings relative to labour costs, however, rose marginally over this period in Denmark, the Netherlands and Ireland and more significantly in the UK and Luxembourg, but declined in all the other Member States.

Overall, therefore, the relative labour costs for men and women seem to have changed very little between 1985 and 1991, as does the relative tax wedge. Since the data available, however, is restricted to women on the average earnings of female manual workers in manufacturing, this conclusion needs to be treated with a great deal of caution. Most women are employed in services and most earn less than the average in manufacturing. Most women in employment, moreover, are married rather than single and for these a somewhat different tax regime applies in a number of the Member States.

While in the Community overall, a man and woman on average earnings, treated as a couple for tax purposes, pay much the same tax and contributions as if they were treated singly, in six of the

10 Member States for which comparative data are available, the amount they paid was different in 1991 (Graph 161). In Greece and the UK, a couple on average earnings (ie receiving the average wage of a male manual worker in manufacturing plus the average of a female) paid less in tax and contributions than a man and woman treated singly. In Belgium and France, however, they paid marginally more and in Ireland and Portugal, significantly more, reflecting the combining of their incomes for tax purposes and the higher rate of tax charged accordingly.

In the latter four countries, therefore, and in Ireland and Portugal, in particular, the tax system seems to discriminate against married women who work and, accordingly, is liable to have a deterrent effect on them seeking employment

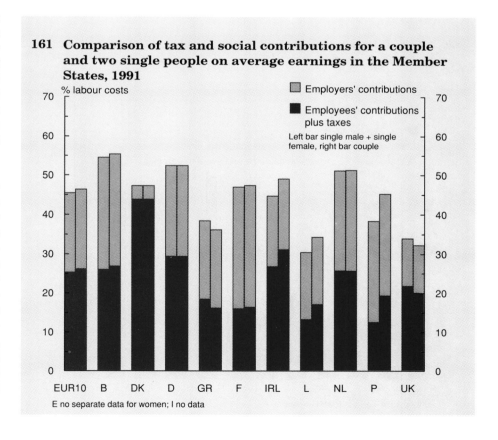

161 Comparison of tax and social contributions for a couple and two single people on average earnings in the Member States, 1991

% labour costs

Employers' contributions

Employees' contributions plus taxes

Left bar single male + single female, right bar couple

EUR10   B   DK   D   GR   F   IRL   L   NL   P   UK

E no separate data for women; I no data

(or perhaps on them seeking marriage).

Marginal rates of tax

Progression in the combined tax and contribution rate means, of course, that marginal rates are above average rates in most countries. One consequence is that, as employers increase the wages paid to their workers, progressively less of the increase goes to the employee and progressively more to the State, so potentially affecting both the incentive to work and the inducement to reward higher levels of productivity. Insofar as this is the case, it gives rise to a potential conflict between considerations of economic efficiency and equity.

In 1991 the combined marginal rate was highest in Belgium — the country with the highest average

rate — with 63% of any increase in labour costs above 80% of the average going to the State (Graph 162). This means, in more comprehensible terms, that if an employer wishes to increase an employee's take-home pay, he or she must be prepared to pay almost twice as much as the employee receives to the State. In other words, the total cost of raising an employee's pay is nearly three times the addition to their net wage.

This, moreover, is the position towards the lower end of the wage scale. As wages increase above average earnings, then the marginal income tax rate also goes up, reflecting the progressive nature of the tax, so that the overall marginal tax plus contribution rate can rise to well above 63%.

The marginal rate was only just below the Belgian level in Ireland,

even though the average rate was significantly lower than in Belgium, and was also above 60% in Germany. Moreover, Luxembourg which had the lowest average combined rate had a marginal rate above that in Spain, Portugal and Greece as well as that in the UK, these five countries being the only ones in the Community with a marginal rate below 50%.

With the exception of Belgium, where it rose slightly, and France, where it remained unchanged, the combined marginal rate was reduced in all Member States between 1985 and 1991, though in Portugal, Spain and Ireland, the reduction was very small. The largest reductions, of 5 percentage points and more, occurred in the Netherlands and Greece, predominantly because of a smoothing of the tax schedule, while reductions of around 3 percentage points occurred in Luxembourg and the UK, in the latter largely due to lower employers' contributions.

These marginal tax plus contribution rates are higher in the Community than in either the US or Japan. In the US, the combined marginal rate in 1991 was around 40% at the average wage of a production worker (according to OECD estimates), a little lower than in the UK, which had the lowest rate of all Community countries, while in Japan, it was only around 30%.

In the US, in particular, the marginal rate for many workers was significantly lower at lower wage levels. This is not only because the rate of income tax at low wages is low, but more importantly because of the relatively small size of statutory social contributions imposed on employers and the correspondingly greater discretion which employers have over the level of

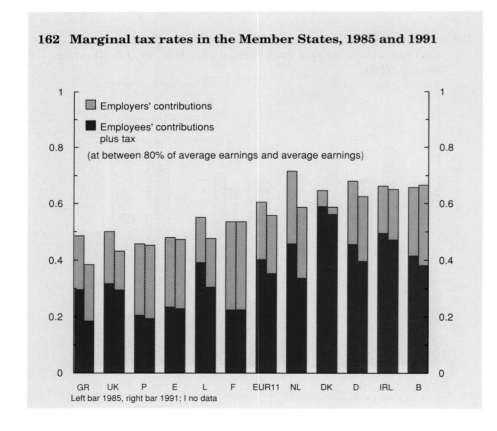

162 Marginal tax rates in the Member States, 1985 and 1991

Employers' contributions

Employees' contributions plus tax

(at between 80% of average earnings and average earnings)

GR   UK   P   E   L   F   EUR11   NL   DK   D   IRL   B

Left bar 1985, right bar 1991; I no data

non-wage labour costs. Employers in the US, therefore, have the option of taking on workers at costs which are not far above the take-home pay which they receive, since they can — and often do — reduce the voluntary element in social contributions to a minimum, especially in sectors where trade union representation is relatively low or non-existent.

This, in practice, applies particularly to women who in many cases are employed on a part-time basis and are not covered by health insurance.

In most European countries, this option is not available — or at least was not until very recently. Since, irrespective of the level of wages, both employers and employees are required to pay statutory social contributions at the same — or in some cases a higher — rate as on the average wage, this imposes a limit on the extent to which the non-wage element in labour costs can be reduced.

In a number of European countries — Belgium, Germany, France, Italy and the Netherlands, in particular — the tax wedge as defined here still amounted to 35% of labour costs or more even in respect of workers on wages too low to attract income tax. In the UK, on the other hand, the low rates of statutory contribution levied on those at the bottom end of the earnings scale mean that the non-wage element in labour costs — and, therefore, the tax wedge — can be reduced to a very small amount. As a consequence, the overall costs of employing people at the lower end of the scale are much less in the UK than in most other parts of the Community, even leaving aside the absence of minimum wage legislation which itself imposes a lower

limit on the costs of employment in other countries.

Very recently, however, measures have been introduced in a number of other countries to reduce the level of contributions on less skilled workers and on young people. Given that a high proportion of the unemployed are unskilled, with few qualifications and a low level of education, the costs of employment at the lower end of the earnings scale are particularly relevant for any policy aimed at bringing down unemployment. This was specifically recognised in the Commission White Paper on *Growth, competitiveness, employment*.

It was also recognised, however, that there is a need to prevent any measures taken from worsening the income prospects among those already in the weakest position in

the labour market. The challenge for policy is to bring about a reduction in the costs of employing low skilled workers so as to encourage employers to take on such people, while at the same time avoiding any significant reduction in their income and any increase in the working poor.

This latter objective is important, especially in view of the many people in the Community who already fall below the poverty line despite being in employment and earning a wage — a combination of circumstances which social protection systems in most Member States fail to address.

Many of these people are women, who still in a number of Member States earn significantly less than their male counterparts and who make up the bulk of low-paid workers. The challenge for policy,

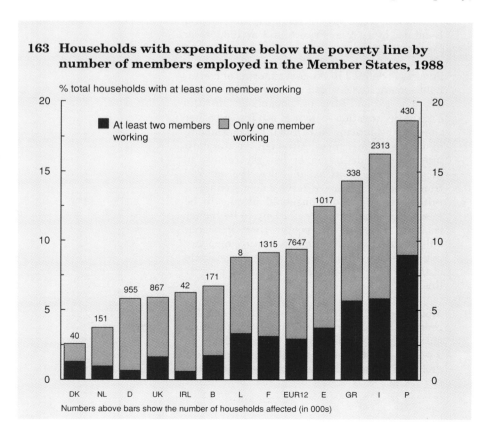

163   Households with expenditure below the poverty line by number of members employed in the Member States, 1988

% total households with at least one member working

■ At least two members working   ▨ Only one member working

Numbers above bars show the number of households affected (in 000s)

Data on poverty

The data on which the analysis of low pay and poverty is based are derived from national surveys of family budgets, or household expenditure, in the Member States. More specifically, they are taken from "Poverty statistics in the late 80s: research based on micro-data" a study carried out for Eurostat by Aldi J.M. Hagenaars, Klaas de Vos and M. Asghar Zaidi of the Department of Economic Sociology and Psychology, Erasmus University, Rotterdam (to be published towards the end of 1994).

Although the data have been harmonised in some degree, significant differences exist between the national surveys in the way the survey was conducted, in the sample size and in the definitions and concepts used. These mean that the results should be regarded as very much approximate and preliminary only and as broadly indicative of the numbers of households with expenditure below 50% of the average expenditure in the different Member States.

The national surveys were carried out in 1988 in six of the Member States, in 1986/87 in Luxembourg, in 1987 in Denmark, Ireland and Belgium, in 1989 in France and in 1989/90 in Portugal.

Poverty is defined in the text in terms of household expenditure which is below 50% of the average expenditure of households in the country in question — ie it is a *relative* rather than an absolute measure and is just one among many of such measures. Although the standard international definition of poverty relates to income rather than expenditure, the surveys from which the data are derived do not enable a reliable estimate of household income to be made. Since expenditure is likely to be higher relative to income in poorer than in richer households, the use of an expenditure measure is likely, if anything, to give an underestimate of the number of households below the poverty line.

Members of households are weighted to enable comparisons to be made of households of different size, with the head of the household having a weight of 1, the second member a weight of 0.5 and each subsequent member a weight of 0.3.

therefore, is not only to provide incentives for creating jobs, but also to protect women's earnings.

Low pay and poverty

While there is some difficulty from the data available to estimate the number of people in employment in the Community with low earnings, evidence from household and family budget surveys suggests that low pay is associated with poverty in many Member States. (The preliminary nature of this evidence, however, should be emphasised since the data on which it is based are not fully harmonised between Member States and, moreover, relate to expenditure rather than income — see Box for details.)

Towards the end of the 1980s, almost 10% of households in the Community with at least one member working had a level of expenditure below 50% of the average for households in the country concerned, which can be taken as an indicator of poverty in a relative sense. This represents a total of around $7^{1}/_{2}$ million households or an estimated 19 million people (Graph 163). Moreover, around 30% of these households had at least two members in work and yet wages from employment were still not sufficient to bring their expenditure above the poverty line. (Although the analysis here is in terms of households, which is the usual unit for measuring the incidence of poverty, this should not be taken to mean that the income, or wages, of individuals *per se* is not also of relevance, especially since low pay may make the individual concerned reliant on the income of the rest of the household and, therefore, less independent.)

As might be expected, the working poor are particularly numerous in the less developed Southern Member States. In 1988, 19% of Portuguese households where at least one person was in employment had a level of expenditure below the poverty line (almost half of these having at least two members in work), while in Italy, the figure was 16%, in Greece, 14% and in Spain, over 12%. At the same time, in France, which has one of the highest levels of income per head in the Community, 9% of households with someone working had a level of expenditure below 50% of the average.

On the other hand, in the Netherlands, under 4% of households with at least one person in employment had expenditure below this level and in Denmark, under 3%.

Low pay is not the primary source of poverty in any Member State. In most countries, old-age and consequent retirement from paid activity is a much more important reason for poverty levels of expenditure. However, in a real sense, this partly reflects wages being too low to produce an adequate retirement pension when the person concerned was in work. It also partly reflects the large number of women who are left alone in old age with insufficient pension entitlement to bring them above the poverty line.

Nevertheless, in one third of the households with expenditure below the poverty line in the Community in 1988, the head of the household was in employment. This represents 5% of total households in the Community (Graph 164). Of these, 30% on average were households where the head was self-employed rather than a wage-earner. This is significantly higher than the proportion of self-employed households in the total (21%), which implies that there is a much greater chance of someone who is self-employed having income

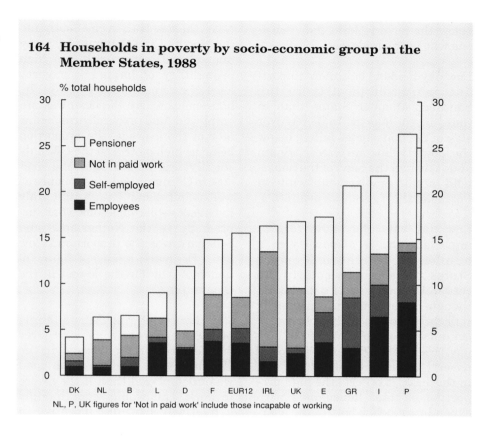

164   Households in poverty by socio-economic group in the Member States, 1988

% total households

Legend:
- Pensioner
- Not in paid work
- Self-employed
- Employees

NL, P, UK figures for 'Not in paid work' include those incapable of working

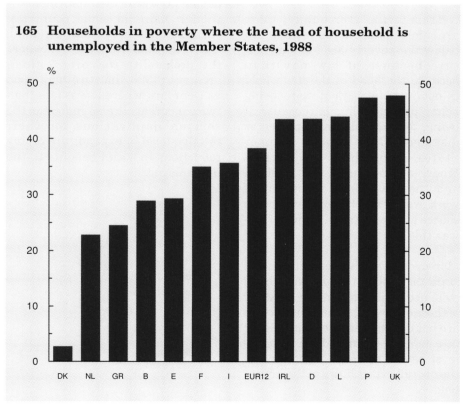

165   Households in poverty where the head of household is unemployed in the Member States, 1988

%

below the poverty level than someone who is an employee.

Low pay tends to be a more important source of poverty in the Southern Member States than in those in the North. In 1988, over 40% of the households falling below the poverty line in Greece, Spain and Italy had the head of the household in paid employment, while in Portugal, the figure was over 50%.

Low pay was also, however, an important source of poverty in a number of Northern Member States. This is particularly the case in Denmark and Luxembourg, though, in the former this primarily reflects the low incidence of poverty overall. By contrast, in the UK, low pay is a relatively minor source of poverty levels of expenditure, but, in this case, it reflects the high proportion of total households with expenditure below 50% of the average (17% in 1988).

Overall in the Community, there are more households which fall below the poverty level of expenditure because of low pay than because the head of the household is not in paid work despite being below pensionable age (because of being, for example, unemployed or disabled). Only in four Member States — Belgium, the Netherlands, and most especially, Ireland and the UK, where being out of work was a much more important source of poverty than elsewhere — was this not the case.

Moreover, even this tends to understate the problem of low pay. Other evidence indicates that the majority of those on low wages are women who are not usually the sole wage-earner in a household and whose poverty-level pay is, therefore, concealed in the overall expenditure of the household.

Nevertheless, both in the South and the North of the Community, being unemployed brings with it a high probability of having a poverty level of income. In 1988, 38% of the households where the head was unemployed had expenditure below 50% of the average, the proportion being as high as 48% in the UK, only slightly less in Portugal and over 40% in Germany and Luxembourg as well as in Ireland (Graph 165). Only in Greece — perhaps somewhat surprisingly — the Netherlands and Denmark was the proportion below 25%, Denmark having a figure of under 5%, by far the lowest in the Community.

The chances of a household falling below the poverty line were over 4 times greater, on average, in the Community as a whole if the head was unemployed than if they were in work. This would seem to imply a relatively powerful incentive in most parts of the Community for people to avoid unemployment — though more in some countries, such as Belgium, Germany, Ireland, the Netherlands and the UK, where the probability was over 7 times greater in 1988, than in others, such as Denmark where it was less than twice as great. It also indicates the serious implications for their relative level of expenditure of any reductions in social benefits to the unemployed.

Chapter 7   Unemployment and labour market policy

As the characteristics of the unemployed change across the Community, labour market policies need to adapt accordingly. The scale of expenditure on these varies markedly between Member States, as does the role played by public employment services in helping the unemployed find work.

Unemployment is the major economic problem facing the Community. Since 1973, when two decades of high and relatively stable economic growth in Europe came to an end, unemployment has increased progressively, interrupted only during the period between 1985 and 1990, from an average rate of under 3% to one of 11% at the present time. In the 15 years before 1973, only Italy and Greece had experienced unemployment rates of over 5% and then only slightly over. Since then, only Luxembourg of the Community countries has consistently had rates below 5%.

Although the recent rise in unemployment is moderating and although the prospects are for little further increase in the short-term, this should in no way divert attention away from the problem. The clear lesson of the past 20 years is that no Member State has succeeded in reducing unemployment significantly and keeping it at a low level for a sustained period, except for Luxembourg. The chances of this happening in the future without a significant change in policy or without a radically different set of circumstances are remote.

A central aim of this chapter is to consider the labour market measures which are being implemented in Member States to alleviate the problem and the scale of assistance to find work being given to the unemployed. These, it should be emphasised, are only one aspect of the range of policies required to tackle unemployment effectively, though the European Council highlighted the importance of improving the use of public funds in the area.

First, however, the chapter examines the changing nature of the unemployment problem in different parts of the Community. The two major features of unemployment in the 1980s were, first, the large numbers of young people who were affected. In 1985, well over 40% of the total numbers unemployed were under 25, even though these represented only around 20% of the labour force. The second feature was the high incidence of long-term unemployment. In 1985, half of the unemployed had been out of work for a year or more.

Labour market measures in the 1980s came to be increasingly focused on these two problems. The first section below considers the present scale of the two problems and how they are tending to change over time. In so doing, it touches upon another area of concern highlighted in the White Paper and endorsed by the Council, namely, the large numbers of young people in various parts of the Community without adequate training.

The second section examines the differing methods used by the unemployed to look for work, while the third section, as noted above, considers the scale of public expenditure on labour market policies, both those of income support and more active measures aimed at increasing the chances of the unemployed of being able to find work.

Youth unemployment

The rate of unemployment among young people declined significantly in the Community during the second half of the 1980s with the high rate of new job creation over this period, the range of measures introduced to alleviate the problem and the fall in the number of those under 25.

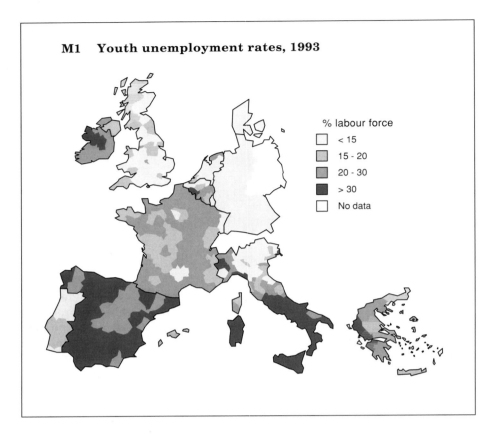

M1   Youth unemployment rates, 1993

% labour force
- < 15
- 15 - 20
- 20 - 30
- > 30
- No data

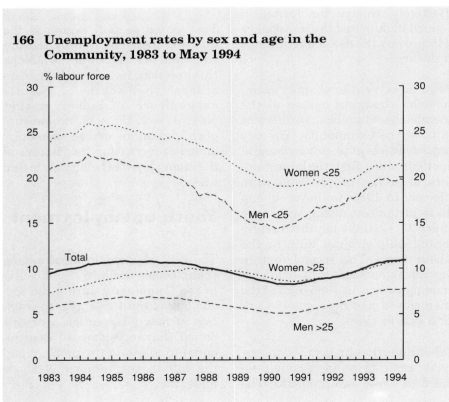

166   Unemployment rates by sex and age in the Community, 1983 to May 1994

% labour force

The youth unemployment rate fell by over 5 percentage points between 1985 and 1990, much more than the rate for those over 25 which declined by relatively little (Graph 166). Since then, the rate of youth unemployment relative to adult unemployment has changed hardly at all. However, this conceals a marked difference in the change in unemployment of young men and young women. While the rate for women under 25 has risen only slowly since 1990, the rate for young men has increased sharply — by over 5% of the labour force — and by much more than for older men or women. A gap of 5% of the labour force between the unemployment rate for young men and that for young women in 1990 — which had persisted for some years — had been reduced to one of less than 2% by May 1994.

The rate of youth unemployment in the Community as a whole, at around 21% in May 1994, therefore, remains over double the adult rate of only around 9%. The marked reduction in the youth unemployment rate relative to that of older people which occurred between 1985 and 1990 consequently came to an end with the onset of recession and the decline in employment. Since the number of young people of working age has continued to fall in the Community over this period, as noted below, the failure of the unemployment rate to come down with it emphasises the employment difficulties which they — and young men in particular — have faced.

The youth unemployment rate is significantly higher than the adult rate in all Member States, apart from Germany where it was over 2% lower in May 1994, but especially in Greece and Italy, where the youth rate was around 23% in the former case and 33% in the latter, giving a difference in relation to the adult rate of more than 4 to 1 (Graphs 167 and 168). Despite the scale of youth unemployment, in both Spain, where some 38% of the labour force under 25 was unemployed, much more than anywhere else in the Community, and Ireland, where the figure was around 27% — the third highest — the gap between youth and adult unemployment rates was less than the Community average.

Though youth unemployment remains a serious problem in many parts of the North of the Community, it is still in the South where the problem is most acute, the rate rising to 40% or more in many Spanish and Italian regions (Map 1).

Changes in youth unemployment and the labour force

The trend in youth unemployment in recent years needs to be judged in the light of the change in numbers of young people which has occurred. Over the Community as a whole, the number of young people of 15 to 24 — ie those of working age — declined by around 1% a year between 1985 and 1992 — the latest year for which data are available (at a slightly higher rate for women than for men). The decline has been most marked in Germany, where the number of young people in this age group fell by an average of around 3% a year over this period, while in the UK, it fell by over 2% a year (Graph 169). By contrast in Italy, Spain, Greece and Ireland, the number increased, though by a relatively small amount, while in France, it declined only marginally.

As a result, the proportion of working-age population (15 to 64) represented by young people of

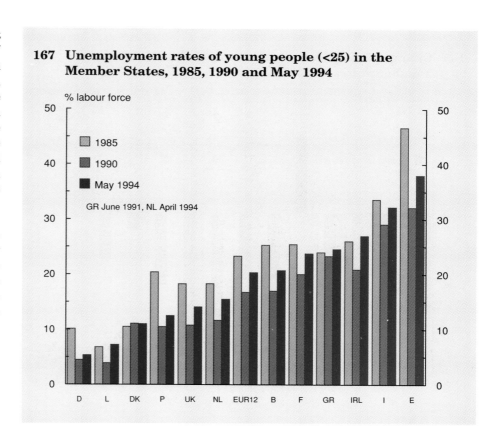

167 Unemployment rates of young people (<25) in the Member States, 1985, 1990 and May 1994

% labour force

☐ 1985
■ 1990
■ May 1994

GR June 1991, NL April 1994

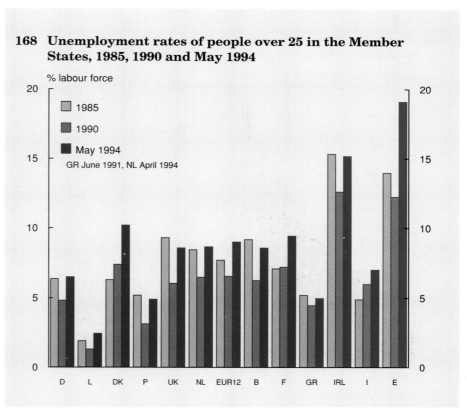

168 Unemployment rates of people over 25 in the Member States, 1985, 1990 and May 1994

% labour force

☐ 1985
■ 1990
■ May 1994

GR June 1991, NL April 1994

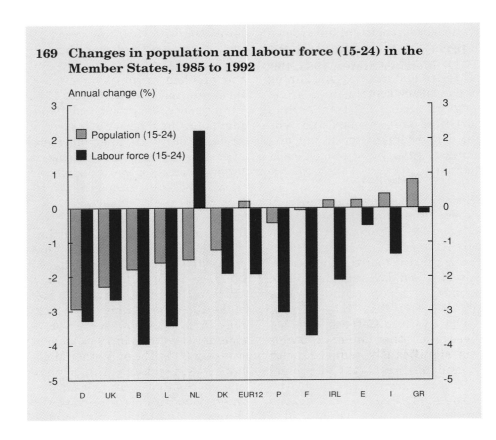

169   Changes in population and labour force (15-24) in the Member States, 1985 to 1992

Annual change (%)

Population (15-24)
Labour force (15-24)

D   UK   B   L   NL   DK   EUR12   P   F   IRL   E   I   GR

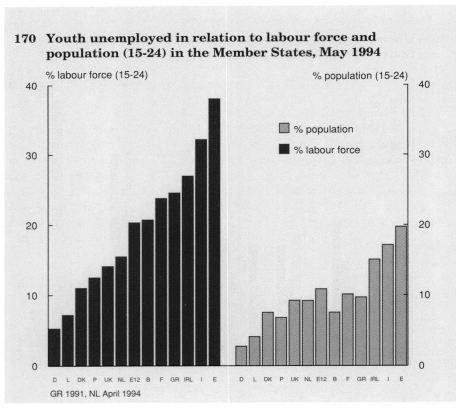

170   Youth unemployed in relation to labour force and population (15-24) in the Member States, May 1994

% labour force (15-24)   % population (15-24)

% population
% labour force

D   L   DK   P   UK   NL   E12   B   F   GR   IRL   I   E   D   L   DK   P   UK   NL   E12   B   F   GR   IRL   I   E

GR 1991, NL April 1994

under 25 fell from 23% in 1985 to 21% in 1992 over the Community as a whole. In Germany, however, it fell from 23% to 18% and in the UK, from 24% to 21%. Only in Italy was there no decline in the proportion over this period, though in Greece, Spain, Ireland and Portugal — ie the less developed countries of the Community — the reduction was less than 1 percentage point.

At the same time, rates of participation of both men and women in this age group have also tended to fall, as noted above, resulting in a reduction of some 2% a year in the numbers of people under 25 in the labour force between 1985 and 1992. The fall in participation was such as to offset the expansion in population in countries where this occurred. In Italy, the labour force under 25 declined by 10% over this period, in Portugal, by 20%, in France, by 23% and in Belgium by 24%. Only in the Netherlands, where there was a substantial growth in participation did the labour force in this age group increase (in this case, by 17% over the period).

The result of the fall in the number of young people who are economically active is a decline in the proportion of young people under 25 in the labour force. In the Community as a whole, this fell from 20% in 1985 to 16% in 1992, with all Member States showing a reduction. In Germany, the fall was from 20% to 14%, in France, from 17% to 12% and in the UK, from 24% to 19%. Even in the Netherlands, where the youth labour force increased, there was a reduction of 1 percentage point over this period.

This is not necessarily an unfavourable development if it is associated with an increasing proportion of young people staying longer in education or receiving more extensive basic training. To the extent that the fairly general decline in participation is a reflection of this, then it may mean that these people bring a higher level of skills to the workforce when they eventually enter the labour market. On the other hand, the reduction in participation may merely reflect the shortage of jobs available for young people to move into.

There is some difficulty from the data available to identify which of these two possibilities best describes what has been happening, partly because of differences between Member States in defining what is meant by education and training and, accordingly, in classifying the status of young people in the Labour Force Survey. This difficulty also extends to the figures on the number of young people counted as being in the labour force. In particular, the large variations between countries in participation rates of young people may reflect differences in the treatment of casual work by students and/or the way unemployment is defined in respect of those under 25.

These difficulties mean that both participation rates in respect of young people and rates of youth unemployment need to be treated with a good deal of caution when drawing policy conclusions.

Though it is by no means ideal, it may be better — or at least as instructive — given the problems of identifying the number of young people who are economically active, to consider unemployment of those under 25 in relation to population of this age group rather than — or as well as — in relation to the labour force. (Ideally, the

need is for a consistent breakdown between Member States of the young people who are in full-time education and training, in training or education combined with employment, in full-time and in part-time employment and who are doing none of these and are, therefore, genuinely economically inactive.)

This shows a somewhat different picture from unemployment rates as usually defined. It shows, in particular, that although Spain and Italy still had the highest levels of unemployment relative to working-age population in May 1994 — at 20% and 17%, respectively — the difference between these and other Member States was significantly reduced, with Ireland having a rate of around 15% and Greece, France, the Netherlands and the UK having rates of around 10% (Graph 170).

Moreover, whereas because of the small numbers counted as part of the labour force, youth unemployment rates in France and Belgium were above those in the Netherlands and the UK — markedly so in the case of France — in relation to population, they were at much the same level or below. Which of the two rates better reflects the problem of youth unemployment remains an open question until more detailed data are available.

Youth unemployment in relation to total unemployment

The decline in the numbers of young people is reflected in the proportion of the unemployed who are under 25. In the Community as a whole, around 32% of the total numbers out of work in May 1994 were young people, some 2 percentage points

lower than in 1990 and some 10 percentage points lower than in 1985, when the figure was 43% and the problem of youth unemployment was most acute (Graph 171). In this sense, the problem of unemployment has become less of a problem of youth unemployment over this period, though this is largely because of the decline in the number of young people in the labour force.

The importance of youth unemployment and the extent to which it has changed vary markedly between Member States. It remains most acute in Italy, where just over half of the unemployed were under 25 in May 1994. This, however, was considerably less than in 1985, when it was over 60%. The only other Member State where the figure approaches that in Italy is Greece, where some 45% of the unemployed were under 25 at the latest count — which in this case is 1991 (there are problems with Greek data after this date) — above the proportion in 1985. In Italy and Greece, therefore, the problem of unemployment is much more a problem of young people than anywhere else in the Community.

Of the other Member States, only in Ireland, where the figure was around 36% in May 1994, was the share of young unemployed in the total more than a third. Here, moreover, the proportion had increased since 1990, the only country apart from the Netherlands and Luxembourg where this was this case.

At the other extreme, those under 25 accounted for only just over 10% of the total unemployed in Germany, where the proportion had come down from almost 30% in 1985. In no other Member State apart from Denmark was the figure less than 20%.

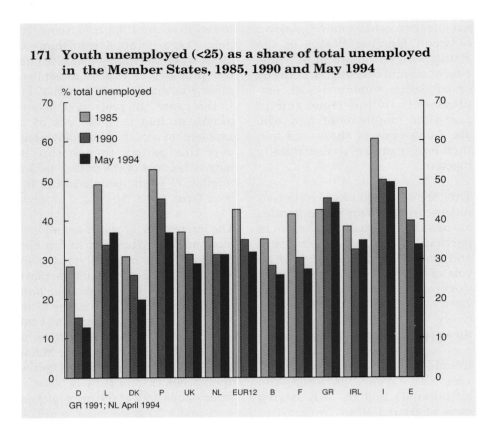

171   Youth unemployed (<25) as a share of total unemployed in the Member States, 1985, 1990 and May 1994

% total unemployed

■ 1985
■ 1990
■ May 1994

D   L   DK   P   UK   NL   EUR12   B   F   GR   IRL   I   E
GR 1991; NL April 1994

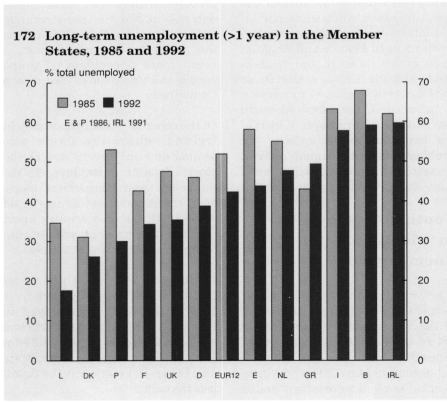

172   Long-term unemployment (>1 year) in the Member States, 1985 and 1992

% total unemployed

■ 1985   ■ 1992
E & P 1986, IRL 1991

L   DK   P   F   UK   D   EUR12   E   NL   GR   I   B   IRL

Long-term unemployment

Long-term unemployment, which rose significantly during the first half of the 1980s, seems to have become less of a problem in recent years, though it is one which remains serious. Moreover, since no data are available since 1992, when unemployment was lower than at the time of writing, it is a problem which may well have increased in 1993 and 1994.

Between 1985 and 1992, the proportion of the unemployed who had been out of work for one year or more declined from 52% to 43% (Graph 172). The reduction was particularly marked in Portugal, where the proportion of long-term unemployed was reduced from 53% to 30% over this period, and Spain, where it came down from almost 60% to 45%. This reflects the high rate of employment growth which both these countries experienced in the latter part of the 1980s.

In Greece, on the other hand, where employment grew by relatively little, the proportion of the unemployed out of work for at least a year increased (from 43% to 50%), the only Member State for which this was the case. Similarly in Ireland, where the rate of job creation was also low over this period, long-term unemployment declined only slightly.

In the other Member States, however, the extent of the reduction in the share of long-term unemployed in the total is not very closely related to the growth of employment. In the Netherlands, in particular, where the rate of job creation between 1985 and 1992 was the highest in the Community, largely because of lower hours of work, the importance of long-term unemployment declined by less than the Community average and in 1992 the proportion at just below 50% remained above the average. Similarly in Germany, where there was also a relatively high rate of job creation, long-term unemployment was also reduced by less than in other Member States.

However, as these data relate to Spring of 1992 — when the Labour Force Survey was conducted — they do not reveal what has happened during the recent recession since the main increase in unemployment in most parts of the Community occurred after the data were collected. On the experience of the previous economic cycle in the first half of the 1980s when the peak rate of long-term unemployment was not reached until 1986, some time after the recession began, the proportion of the unemployed out of work for a year or more can be expected to have risen since 1992 and still to be increasing significantly at the present time.

The proportion of the long-term unemployed who are under 25 has come down as the relative numbers of unemployed in this age group have declined. In 1992, 26% of those who had been out of work for at least a year were young people under 25 as opposed to 37% in 1985. In some countries, the decline has been much more pronounced, signifying a marked fall in the long-term rate of youth unemployment. In Luxembourg, the proportion declined to zero, while in Spain, it fell from almost 50% to under 30%, in Portugal, from just over 50% to just over 30% and in France, from over 30% to 15%. Indeed, in all Northern Member States, except for the UK and Ireland, the proportion of the long-term unemployed who were under 25 was 15% or less in 1992

and less than 10% in Germany and Denmark.

The problem of long-term unemployment in the North of the Community, therefore, seems now to have relatively little to do with young people and is predominantly a phenomenon of older age groups. In the South of the Community, in contrast, a sizable proportion of the long-term unemployed are under 25 — over 40% in Italy and just below this figure in Greece, while in Spain and Portugal, it remains around 30%. Youth unemployment and long-term unemployment are, therefore, still closely associated with each other in these parts of the Community.

Methods of job search

The methods used by the unemployed to find a job vary significantly across the Community. In particular, while public employment offices play the major role in a number of Member States, in others more informal means of searching for work seem to be more important.

As noted in Chapter 1, by no means all the unemployed, and in some parts of the Community not even most of the unemployed — especially if they are women — are registered at employment offices. Those that are not, in the great majority of cases, have no contact with the public employment services and rely on other methods to find work. However, even when people are registered at employment offices, they do not necessarily use the services provided by these offices as the main means of job search.

Nevertheless, where the proportion of the unemployed registered at employment offices is high, there is a tendency to rely on such offices to find a job. In particular, in

Germany, France and Spain where the registration rate was over 85% in 1992, the great majority of the unemployed used the public service as the main method of searching for work — over 90% in Spain and close to 90% in Germany (which in both cases means all of those registered used this as their main method), while in France, over 80% did so (Graph 173). In all three of these countries, this was almost as true of women as of men (90% of unemployed women in Spain, 84% in Germany and 78% in France).

The one exception to this general tendency is Belgium. Here despite the fact that 91% of the unemployed were registered at employment offices, only 38% of the unemployed in 1992 (with little difference between men and women) used the public employment services as their main means of finding a job.

In most countries where the registration rate is relatively low, comparatively few even of those registered use the public employment services as their main method of job search. As a result, only in the Netherlands — where the figure was 63% — in addition to the three countries listed above, did a significant majority of the unemployed rely on public employment services to find work. In the UK and Portugal, the proportion was around 30%, in Ireland under 20% and in Greece as low as 8%. This, of course, does not mean that in these countries, the public employment services were not used as one of the methods of finding work, only that they were not the main method.

In most countries, the proportion of women relying on contact with the public employment office to find a job was much the same as for men. The only exceptions were the Netherlands and Luxembourg,

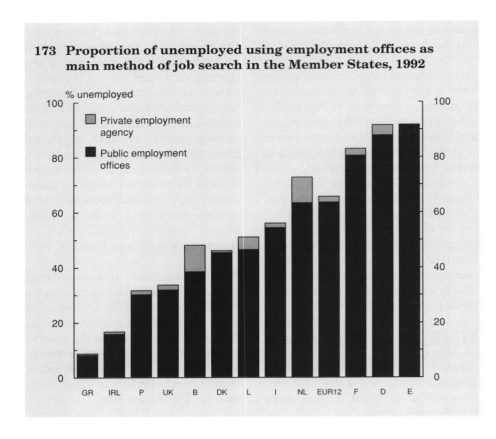

173 Proportion of unemployed using employment offices as main method of job search in the Member States, 1992

% unemployed

- Private employment agency
- Public employment offices

GR IRL P UK B DK L I NL EUR12 F D E

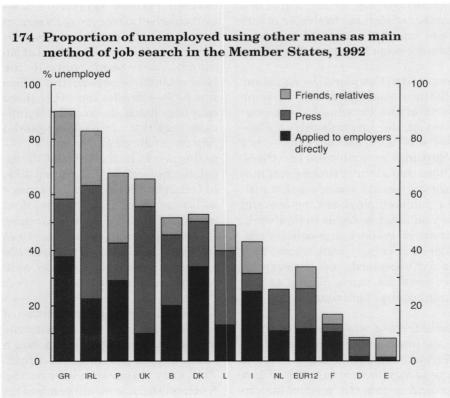

174 Proportion of unemployed using other means as main method of job search in the Member States, 1992

% unemployed

- Friends, relatives
- Press
- Applied to employers directly

GR IRL P UK B DK L I NL EUR12 F D E

where some 12% more of the men unemployed than women used this as their main method, and the UK, where 8% more of the men did so.

Only a very small proportion of the unemployed in any Member State rely primarily on private employment services to find work. In most countries, apart from Belgium and the Netherlands, where the figure was close to 10%, the proportion using these as their main method of job search was around 2% or less in 1992. Although there is a general tendency for more women than men to use private agencies — only in Denmark and Italy was the proportion of men higher than for women — the relative numbers doing so were still small. Private employment agencies, which have developed rapidly in a number of Member States, therefore, seem to cater predominantly for people who are already in employment rather than those who are unemployed.

Of the other, less formal, methods of job search, looking through newspaper advertisements or placing an advert is the most widely used across the Community as a whole. There are, however, wide variations between Member States. In the UK and Ireland, over 40% of the unemployed used newspapers as the main means of finding work, and in Belgium and Luxembourg, over 25%, whereas in Portugal and Denmark, where there was also a minority of the unemployed using employment offices, the proportion was only around 15% (Graph 174).

In all Member States, a higher proportion of women used newspapers as their main method of job search in 1992 than men — the difference being most marked in the UK and Ireland, where in each case more than half of all the women unemployed (56% in the UK) relied principally on newspapers to find work.

In countries where newspapers were not extensively used, in Portugal and Denmark as well as in Greece and Italy, applying to employers directly was the principal method of job search other than the public employment service for most of the unemployed. In Greece and Portugal, however, for a significant proportion of the unemployed, asking friends, relatives and other people was almost as important a means of finding work. In these two countries, therefore, well over half of the unemployed — 55% in Portugal and 70% in Greece — relied on asking employers or people that they knew to find a job.

Although there are some differences in the proportion of men and women using these two methods as their main means of searching for work, they are not large, nor do they vary systematically between countries.

In summary, the evidence from the 1992 LFS demonstrates clearly that there are marked variations across the Community in the way that those out of work search for employment and that, in general, less formal — and less organised — methods predominate. In only three Member States — Germany, Spain and France — do the public employment services play a dominant role, though the majority of the unemployed also use them as their main method of finding work in the Netherlands and in Italy. In the other Member States, a variety of relatively informal means are used to a greater extent than the employment services by most of the unemployed.

As noted above, however, this does not necessarily mean that the public employment services are not

used at all by most of those looking for work in these latter countries. It is possible that they were used extensively as a secondary means in many. Moreover, it is also possible that many of the unemployed in these countries took advantage of the valuable support provided by the public services in many countries, in the form of counselling and help in job applications, even if they relied on other avenues to find a job. Indeed the figures for expenditure on these per person unemployed was higher in 1992 in Belgium and the UK, for example, where a minority of the unemployed used them as the main means of job search, than in Spain or Italy where the majority did so (see below).

Although data on a fully comparable basis do not exist for earlier years (the form of the questions asked was altered in the 1992 LFS), it is apparent that the use of public employment offices has declined in importance over recent years. This is partly because of the liberalisation of regulations governing employment services in Germany and Spain. It is also, partly, however, a reflection of the significant decline in the proportion of the unemployed — as defined by the LFS — registered at employment offices, as shown in Chapter 1, which in turn in some countries reflects the tightening of rules on registration.

As a result, it may be becoming more difficult to assist the unemployed through improvements in the public employment services in many parts of the Community.

Labour market policies

Public expenditure on labour market policies aimed at improving the functioning of the market, suppor-

ting those who cannot find work or, more pro-actively, increasing their employability, amounted, in total, to around 3% of Community GDP in 1992 for the Member States taken together. Over half of this sum went on paying income support to the unemployed and another 10% on funding early retirement schemes, aimed at encouraging older people to stop working so as to increase the jobs available for younger people (Graph 175).

Under 40% of public expenditure — not much more than 1% of Community GDP — went on active measures aimed at getting more people into work. Of these, training schemes and programmes specifically intended to tackle the problem of youth unemployment accounted for around half of total spending on active measures — around $\frac{1}{2}$% of GDP altogether (not all Member States distinguish between these two items so it is difficult to separate them at the Community level) — while job subsidies, payments to the disabled and expenditure on the public employment services accounted for the remainder. Of these, the public employment services, providing advice and assistance on placement, were responsible for around 15% of total active spending (under 0.2% of GDP).

Between 1985 and 1992, public expenditure on labour market policies changed by relatively little in relation to GDP over the Community as a whole. There was, however, some increase in the share of expenditure going to active measures, which partly reflects the slightly lower level of unemployment in the later year and, therefore, a reduction in the need for income support. Expenditure on training, youth programmes and job subsidies all increased significantly relative to

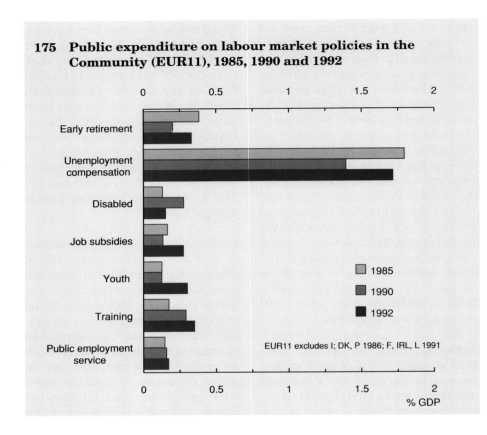

175 Public expenditure on labour market policies in the Community (EUR11), 1985, 1990 and 1992

EUR11 excludes I; DK, P 1986; F, IRL, L 1991

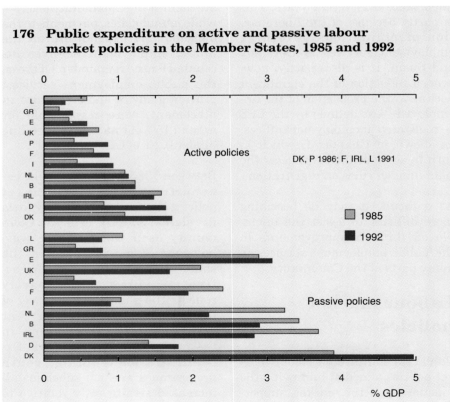

176 Public expenditure on active and passive labour market policies in the Member States, 1985 and 1992

DK, P 1986; F, IRL, L 1991

GDP over this period, though the total sums involved remained small as compared with unemployment compensation.

Expenditure in Member States

There is considerable variation in public expenditure on labour market policy across the Community. At one extreme, spending in Denmark amounted to almost 7% of GDP in 1992 (and 1993), nearly twice as high as in any other Member State (Graph 176). Around 75% of expenditure went on unemployment compensation and early retirement schemes — so-called passive measures — reflecting the generosity of such payments relative to other countries rather than the number of unemployed. Nevertheless, while only 25% of spending was devoted to active measures, the sum involved was still larger in relation to GDP than elsewhere in the Community (1.8% of GDP).

Spending on active measures was also relatively high — around 1% of GDP or more in 1992 — in Germany, because of the increase following the inclusion of the new Länder, and in Ireland, reflecting the large sums devoted to training from the Community Social Fund.

At the other extreme, public expenditure on active measures was only around ¹/₂% of GDP or less in the UK, Luxembourg, Spain and Greece, reflecting in the case of Luxembourg, the small numbers of unemployed, in Spain, the large sums spent on income support for the large numbers of unemployed, in Greece, a lack of resources and in the UK, an aversion to interventionist policies.

Spending on passive measures reflects both the numbers out of work and the scale of compensation paid. It was high in Spain and Ireland in 1992 — around 3% of GDP — because of high unemployment and in Belgium and the Netherlands — over 2% of GDP — as well as in Denmark, because of high average payments to the unemployed (a high proportion of the unemployed receiving benefits as much as a high level of benefit).

Between 1985 and 1992, expenditure on active measures increased relative to GDP in 8 of the 12 Member States, most significantly in Germany, where it doubled as a share of GDP, because of the resources devoted to tackling the substantial unemployment problem in the new Länder. In three of the other four Member States — the UK, Ireland and Luxembourg — spending on active measures was reduced relative to GDP, while in Belgium, it remained unchanged.

The distribution of public expenditure between different kinds of active measure also varies markedly across the Community. Spending on training and youth measures dominates in Italy, Portugal, France and Ireland, while job subsidies are more important in Denmark Spain and Belgium, and have also become substantial in Germany, where, as a result of the unemployment problem in the former East Germany, expenditure on both training and job subsidies in 1992 was higher relative to GDP than in any other Member State (Graph 177).

It should be emphasised, at the same time, that the distinction between youth measures and subsidies in certain cases is extremely blurred, since subsidies may be used as a means of encouraging employment of young people (for example, in Belgium, a scheme was introduced at the end of 1993 relieving employers from paying social contributions when taking on young people).

Expenditure on public employment services amounted to less than 0.2% of GDP in all countries apart from Germany and Belgium, where it was only slightly above. In the four Southern countries — Greece, Italy, Portugal and Spain — as well as Denmark, spending on the employment services accounted for only around 0.1% of GDP or less and in France and Ireland, it was not much higher. In the case of Greece, Portugal, Denmark and Ireland, the low level of spending is partly explicable by the fact that in all of these countries, as noted above, the public employment services are not the principal means used by the unemployed to find work. In Spain and France, however, they are used by a large majority of the unemployed and the low level of expenditure is, therefore, more difficult to explain.

Expenditure per unemployed person

The figures for spending in relation to GDP are difficult to interpret without taking account of the variations in the numbers of people receiving assistance between Member States. Collecting consistent information on this is not easy; moreover, other aspects such as the length of training courses are also relevant. The most straightforward approach is to adjust for the numbers unemployed, even though by no means all expenditure goes on these — most obviously, job subsidies are a

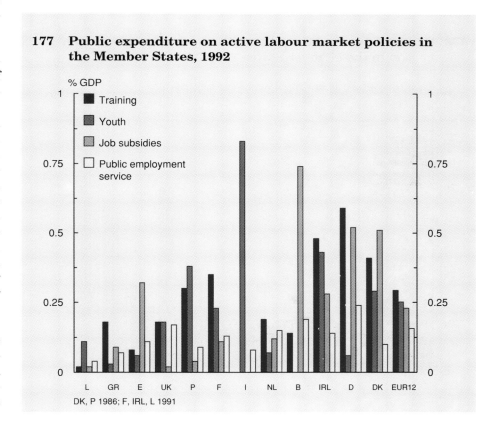

177 Public expenditure on active labour market policies in the Member States, 1992

% GDP

Training
Youth
Job subsidies
Public employment service

L GR E UK P F I NL B IRL D DK EUR12

DK, P 1986; F, IRL, L 1991

means of keeping those in work from becoming unemployed, while part of expenditure on training in a number of Member States goes to those in employment as well as the unemployed. Despite such considerations, estimates of spending per person unemployed provide a broad indication of the scale of effort devoted to labour market policies in the various Member States.

They do necessarily, however, indicate the effectiveness of this effort, which is likely to depend on other factors as well, such as the design of programmes, the efficiency with which they are targeted on those requiring support and the repercussions on other groups in the labour market who do not receive assistance (ie evidence shows that many schemes have helped the unemployed find work largely at the expense of those already in employment). These factors are not considered here, though they are crucial to an overall evaluation of policy.

In terms of this measure, there are enormous variations across the Community in the level of expenditure. So far as spending on passive measures are concerned (income support plus early retirement), the average level per person registered as unemployed (which is the appropriate indicator of unemployment to use in this context) varied from around 27,000 ECU in Luxembourg in 1992, and 18,000 ECU in Denmark and the Netherlands, to only just over 5,000 ECU in Ireland and Spain, around 3,000 ECU in Greece and 1,500 ECU in Portugal (Graph 178 — note that the figures for Italy exclude payments made to the unemployed and are, therefore, not comparable with those for other countries).

In broad terms, this variation is in line with differences in GDP per head, though the average level of expenditure in France in 1992 was below what would be expected in these terms and in the Netherlands, somewhat higher (GDP per head in ECU in France is significantly above that in the Netherlands).

Between 1985 and 1992, the average level of passive expenditure per person unemployed in the Community as a whole changed by very little in real terms (at constant GDP prices and constant exchange rates, which it should be noted gives only an approximate indication of the change in the real value of payments in terms of purchasing power). Only in France and Ireland, however, was there any significant reduction in real expenditure per person, though in the case of France, this was entirely due to a decrease in early retirement payments. At the same time, only in Spain, Germany and Belgium was there any significant increase in average spending, though for Germany, this was wholly the result of more money going on early retirement schemes, especially in the new Länder.

Average expenditure on active measures per person unemployed varies in a very similar way to that on passive measures. The level of spending in Luxembourg, Denmark and the Netherlands is much higher than the Community average, that in the Southern Member States much lower (Graph 179). In this case, however, it is Spain with its large numbers of people out of work which spends the least on active measures per person unemployed. Ireland, it should be noted, which has a much higher than average level of expenditure on active measures in terms of GDP, has a

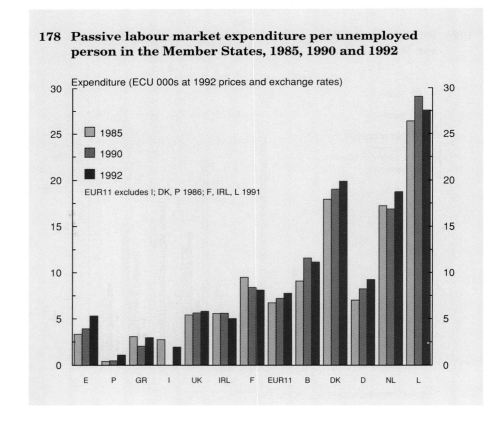

178   Passive labour market expenditure per unemployed person in the Member States, 1985, 1990 and 1992

Expenditure (ECU 000s at 1992 prices and exchange rates)

1985
1990
1992

EUR11 excludes I; DK, P 1986; F, IRL, L 1991

E   P   GR   I   UK   IRL   F   EUR11   B   DK   D   NL   L

significantly lower level in terms of the numbers unemployed.

As with passive expenditure, active spending per person unemployed varies broadly in line with GDP per head, though again the level in 1992 was lower in these terms in France and higher in the Netherlands, reflecting the greater effort devoted to active measures in the latter than the former.

Between 1985 and 1992, average spending per person unemployed increased in real terms across the Community as a whole. Indeed, all Member States showed a rise over this period with the exception of Greece, where there was a very small fall. Again the increase was particularly marked in Germany, though spending per person unemployed also doubled in real terms in Spain and Portugal, even though remaining low, largely as a result of Community funding.

Focusing on the active measures directed specifically at the unemployed (training and the public employment services) the level of spending per person in 1992 averaged 2,000 ECU across the Community as a whole — half the expenditure on total active measures — with expenditure on the public employment services averaging only around 500 ECU. Expenditure on these measures was significantly higher in Germany than in any other Member State, at around 5,500 ECU per person unemployed, and significantly lower in the Southern countries of the Community — at below 500 ECU per person in Spain, Greece and Portugal (Graph 180).

For this more narrowly defined group of active measures, the tendency for expenditure to vary with GDP per head — or the ability to

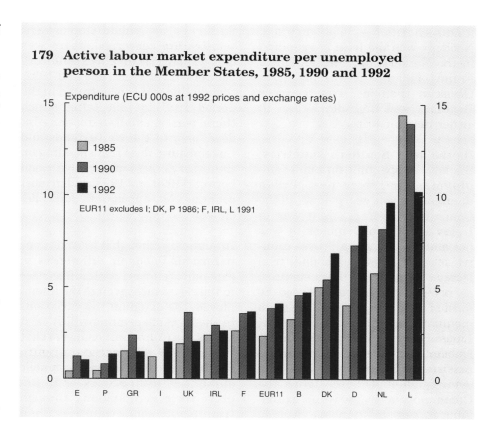

179 Active labour market expenditure per unemployed person in the Member States, 1985, 1990 and 1992

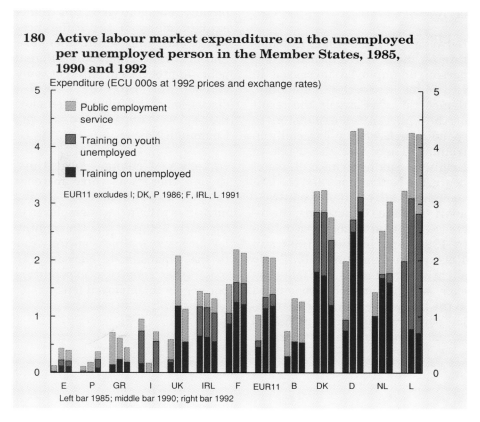

180 Active labour market expenditure on the unemployed per unemployed person in the Member States, 1985, 1990 and 1992

fund such action — is less marked. Not only was the level of spending in the Netherlands higher than in France, but also it was higher in Germany than in Luxembourg or Denmark and in Ireland than in either Belgium or the UK.

In the four Southern countries, the level of spending on public employment services per person unemployed was well below half the Community average, as it was in Ireland, while in Denmark, it was not much higher. In all these countries, apart from Spain and, to a lesser extent, Italy, these services, as noted above, were not used by most of the unemployed as the main means of finding a job. In Germany, Luxembourg and the Netherlands, by contrast, average expenditure per person unemployed was well over 1,000 ECU, over twice the Community average, while in Belgium it was slighty above average and in France and the UK, slightly below.

Between 1985 and 1992, expenditure on these active measures per person unemployed increased in real terms across the Community, though this was largely the result of the substantial expansion in spending in Germany, especially on training. There was also a rise in Belgium, Spain, France, Luxembourg, the Netherlands and the UK, though in all of these countries, apart from the Netherlands, the increase occurred in the period 1985 to 1990, and between 1990 and 1992, real expenditure fell, if only slightly in most cases. The fall, however, was particularly pronounced in the UK, where spending on training per person unemployed halved in real terms in these two years.

So far as the public employment services are concerned, there was only a small rise in real expenditure per person between 1985 and 1992, though this was concentrated in the period 1985 to 1990, after which there was a small reduction. Indeed, only in the Netherlands and Luxembourg, does real spending on these services seem to have risen between 1990 and 1992, and in most countries, it appears to have declined.

In summary, though it is sometimes hazardous to equate differences in expenditure levels with differences in the assistance given to the unemployed, the extent of the variations in the level of spending which exist across the Community suggest that the unemployed receive significantly more help from the public authorities to find work or to improve their marketability through training in some countries than others. While the scale of effort is broadly related to GDP, this cannot explain many of the differences which exist and which, therefore, appear to reflect markedly different policy approaches in different countries. (See Box for a wider discussion of differences in employment systems across the Community.)

In terms of changes over time, though there was some increase in real expenditure on active measures to help the unemployed in the early 1990s at the Community level, this was almost entirely due to the expansion in Germany. In most other countries, expenditure per person unemployed fell.

Employment systems in Member States

Member States have broadly similar employment objectives, which can be summarised as:

- to achieve employment creation on a scale sufficient to maintain low levels of unemployment

- to ensure compatibility, and to avoid mismatch, between the employment opportunities offered by firms and the needs and capacities of those who wish to work

- to ensure open access to, and continued contact with, the labour market on a lasting basis for those who wish to work

- to ensure a degree of income support for those who lose their jobs and do not quickly obtain another

- to ensure special assistance for those facing particular labour market difficulties, and risk of exclusion, because of personal or social disadvantages

- to raise the productivity and adaptability of individuals by enabling them to maximise their potential through vocational education and training

However, the complex nature of labour markets, and their central role in fulfilling social as well as economic objectives, means that there is considerable diversity between Member States in the institutional, legislative, financial and contractual arrangements that are in place.

The way employment objectives are pursued, the priorities given to different issues or concerns and the use made of different types of instruments will reflect a number of factors:

- economic and social circumstances — the level of economic development and degree of industrialisation; the openness to other economies; the level of education and age structure of the working-age population; the respective roles and importance of private and public enterprise and enterprises; the extent of collective insurance against job loss and other social risks; the treatment of the disadvantaged;

- cultural and historical traditions regarding the organisation of society and the economy — including the nature of the legal systems; the relative weight given to legal and financial instruments as ways of providing incentives; industrial relations traditions and practices, and so on.

Such differences determine, for example:

- the extent to which firms use the open labour market to remain dynamic and adjust to changes in demand as opposed to restructuring their existing workforce;

- the extent to which vocational training is integrated not only with transition from school to work, but with wider factors, such as industrial relations systems or productive systems as a whole;

- the way in which social protection systems interact with the employment creation process and the way they are funded.

Member State policies with regard to employment and unemployment are most often compared in terms of:

- their outcomes — the level of unemployment, the importance of long-term unemployment, the extent of part-time working or self-employment and so on;

- the form or content of measures — such as schemes to help the long-term unemployed or to help young people into jobs;

- the effectiveness of individual systems — such as systems of vocational training or employment placement services.

However, in order to make meaningful comparisons of the relative performance of different Member States, such outcomes or measures need to be seen, and understood, not in isolation, but within the context of individual Member State employment systems as a whole.

While Member State systems need to be understood as integrated systems, this does not mean that they are always consistent or coherent. In reality, they are often under strain, and always in transition. They are frequently buffeted by swings in attitude as well as by changes of government and prevailing political philosophies.

Acceptance of diversity between Member States does not mean either that all systems have to be judged as equally good in achieving broad common objectives. Nor does it mean that there are no grounds for taking account of wider, notably Community-wide, policy considerations.

While respecting Member State choices or preferences, therefore, it is legitimate to:

- assess the efficiency of different national systems in terms of their ability to achieve national and Community employment objectives, including the negative as well as positive effects of certain policies;

- consider whether it is possible to mix different elements from different national systems to improve overall performance or whether systems are essentially self-contained and mutually exclusive;

- encourage Member State to cooperate in policy development in order to minimise the costs and maximise the benefits of research and development on policies and measures, as well as to ensure compatibility between different national systems where they need to interact across the Community.

While diversity within the broad European tradition is long-standing and deep-rooted, the process of economic convergence within the Community may tend to encourage convergence between Member State labour market systems. Notable elements in this respect are:

- the opening up of the Internal Market, the further globalisation of markets and the break-up of public or semi-public monopolies — all of which strengthen market forces and thereby limit the possibilities, or raise the cost, for governments seeking to intervene in pursuit of employment or social objectives;

- the increasing participation of women in paid employment in the Southern Member States as their societies develop, which is increasing the demand for more varied patterns of working hours, including part-time work.

On the other hand, convergence along such lines may create divergences in policy action as Member States (and within them regions, localities, enterprises, workers) explicitly or instinctively position themselves in relation to the new economic circumstances and develop new strategies and policies (diversification, rationalisation, customisation, etc) to improve employment and/or income prospects.

The Community has an important role to play in providing a framework within which Member States can freely choose the means they use to pursue employment objectives. The Community has a particular responsibility to ensure:

- that national systems do not produce results or operate in ways which conflict with overall employment objectives elsewhere in the Community;

- that systems do not operate in ways which conflict with universally agreed standards — such as using child labour or denying trade union rights;

- that Member States do not seek to create or maintain employment within their borders either by introducing measures distorting the conditions of competition through a reduction in agreed standards, notably social standards, or by seeking to provide financial incentives outside those allowed by competition rules on State aid;

- that, just as there is free movement of capital, goods and services, there should also be effective free movement of labour between Member States — ultimately so that workers have an effective choice of environments or systems within which to work. This means, in practice, that the Community has a responsibility to contribute to improvements as regards the health and safety of workers, especially in the working environment, and has an objective of harmonising conditions in this area while maintaining improvements made.

In this respect, an appropriate balance needs to be struck between respect for Member State employment systems — within which they seek to achieve national goals — and respect for Community-wide objectives and standards as agreed in the Treaty and in various policy commitments taken through time by the Council.

Chapter 8   Where has job growth and decline occurred?

The structure of employment in the Community is changing rapidly. While many services are increasing in importance everywhere, there are significant differences in the relative numbers employed in particular activities, which makes it difficult to generalise about future areas of job creation.

Introduction

The broad sectoral shifts which have occurred in employment in the Community over the long-term are well known. As a result, service sector activities now account for some 64% of total employment and provide some 82 million jobs in the Community. Nevertheless, employment in industry remains important, being responsible for just over 30% of the total, or 39 million jobs overall, while agriculture now accounts for under 6% of employment, or around 7 million jobs.

These broad changes — driven by changes in demand as well as in technology and productivity — have been associated with growth of employment in areas as diverse as health and care provision, arts and culture, tourism, and environmental protection. These areas, which in many cases involve a complex interaction between private and public interests, have become among the most important sources of new job creation.

Moreover, with the changing interaction between family and working life, and the increasing participation of women in the labour market, a much broader range of activities are available to be undertaken on a paid rather than unpaid basis.

At the same time, the nature of work is in continuous transition — with, for example, an increasing need for inter-personal communication skills rather than physical dexterity — all under the pervasive influence of information technologies which are now an integral part of much of modern economic activity.

However, despite their importance, there is a lack of detailed, comparable, information about these changes. In particular, there is a dearth of information about the new, emerging sectors and jobs compared with the details about employment in areas of decline, such as agriculture and the iron and steel industries. Moreover, much of the data that are available comes with a delay of at least a year or two and sometimes much more.

Redressing the balance of data availability as between different sectors, and improving information about areas of employment development, remain top priorities. However, new data have recently become available which throw light on these issues, notably on changes in employment that have taken place since 1985.

This chapter exploits these new data and compares the findings with other, more aggregated, data available over a longer period, in order to present preliminary evidence on:

- the scale of employment in different activities across the Community;

- the main areas of employment growth in recent years in the Community;

- the extent to which structural differences in employment between Member States persist, or are converging, as the Community integrates;

- whether employment growth in different sectors is affected by changes in the economic climate, or whether trends persist through good years and bad;

Data on employment

The data on employment in detailed sectors of activity — NACE 2-digit — are derived from the Community Labour Force Survey and are, therefore, based on only a sample of those in employment. The figures are likely, for this reason, to give less reliable results the finer the level of disaggregation. This applies particularly to sectors in which the numbers employed are small. (More detailed and more reliable figures are available for employment in industry, but these are less up-to-date, do not cover all Member States in equal detail and, of course, leave services out of account where most of the job creation has occurred.)

For the Community as a whole, however, the margin of error is likely to be reduced since the absolute size of sample is much larger and since any errors at the Member State level may well tend to offset each other. For one major country, Italy, however, no comparable data are available at this level of detail, while for Portugal, although data exist, for a number of sectors they vary by so much from year to year that there are serious doubts about their reliability as indicators of changes over time.

In order to have a complete set of data covering the Community as a whole for 1992, however, the figures for Italy at the NACE 2-digit level have been imputed from the NACE 1-digit figures (for 11 sectors) which are available, on the basis of the average distribution of employment within NACE 1-digit sectors which applies for the rest of the Community. Although this assumption is unlikely to be valid in most cases, the error which this implies for the Community totals ought to be relatively small — and certainly smaller than most previous estimates which have been made at this level of disaggregation.

For Portugal, the 1992 data have been incorporated into the Community totals for 1992, though these should be regarded perhaps as more indicative than for the other countries.

The analysis of employment growth is, therefore, for the most part restricted to 10 Community countries.

The data used to compare the structure of employment in the Community with that in the US, Japan and the EFTA countries, are taken from the series published by OECD based on the ISIC (international standard industrial classification) division of activities into broad sectors. This has involved some estimation to adjust for breaks in the series in respect of a number of countries, especially a few Member States and the EFTA countries. Nevertheless, the figures ought to give a reasonably reliable indication of the comparative changes which occurred over the period 1970 to 1991.

- the extent to which the much-discussed shift in demand from low to high skilled jobs is actually happening;

- whether there is a marked difference between the jobs which men and women do.

The chapter presents the available evidence, first, on the relative importance of different sectors as sources of employment in 1992 and the differences which exist between Member States. Secondly, it examines the detailed structural changes in employment which took place in the Community between 1985 and 1992, looking separately at periods of high and low growth. Thirdly, it compares long-term sectoral changes in employment in the Community with those in other developed parts of the world. Fourthly, it examines the evidence on occupational changes and the changing demand for skills.

Structure of employment in the Community in 1992

While it is well known that services are now the major source of jobs in the Community, less well known, primarily because consistent data have not been available before, is the relative scale of employment in different activities within services — or even within industry — and how this compares between Member States. This section, therefore, examines the numbers of people employed in different activities in 1992 and how this varies across Member States.

At the broad sectoral level, the decline in agriculture is illustrated by the fact that it now accounts for significantly less employment in the Community as a whole than the construction sector — which employed some 7½% of the workforce in 1992. Moreover, this is true in all Member States except Greece, Ireland, Portugal and Spain, where the numbers working in each of the two sectors was about the same, at around 10% of the total (Graph 181).

At the other end of the spectrum, business services, the fastest growing activity in the Community over the past decade, now employ almost as many people — nearly 7 million in 1992 (over 5% of total employment) — as agriculture, and significantly more than mechanical and electrical engineering combined (see Table et the end of the chapter). This is true in all Member States, apart from Germany where engineering is much more important than in the rest of the Community. At the same time, employment in business services is higher in the more developed countries than in the less developed ones, accounting for over 7½% of the total numbers in work in the Netherlands in 1992, for around 6% of the total in France and the UK, but for under 3½% in Spain, Greece and Portugal.

Other, rapidly developing, services have become important providers of jobs. Over 2 million people were employed in leisure, arts and cultural activities in the Community in 1992 — as many as in the entire motor vehicle industry, and more than in the production of clothing and footwear. Travel and transport agencies employed over 1½ million people, nearly twice as many as office machinery and instrument engineering combined, while almost as many were employed in sanitary services. 4½ million people were employed in social and collective services — which does not

include education and healthcare, but includes religious organisations, employers' associations and trade unions — one million more than in the food, drink and tobacco industry. Moreover, 50% more were employed in personal services, such as hairdressing or dry cleaning, than in iron and steel production.

Differences in the structure of activity, even between countries at similar levels of economic development, emphasise both the difficulties of generalising about potential areas of job creation and the apparent influence of institutional, cultural and social factors as well as specific economic strengths and weaknesses.

Thus a prominent feature of the economic strength of Germany is the high share of employment in engineering. The proportion of the workforce employed in the mechanical and electrical engineering and motor vehicle industries was over 50% higher in Germany in 1992 than in other Member States. As a result, almost 40% of all those employed in these industries in the Community worked in Germany, excluding the new Lander, and well over 40% if these are included.

This dominance in engineering, however, also results in a relatively high share of the workforce being employed in iron and steel production and the manufacture of metal products — again over 50% more than in the rest of the Community.

By contrast, engineering industries account for only a very small proportion of employment in the less developed Member States. This is particularly the case in Greece, where only 1% of the total workforce were employed in the engineering and motor vehicle industries in 1992 as against over 6% in the rest

of the Community, and in Portugal, where they employed only 2% of the total. This compares with over 5% employed in textiles, clothing and footwear in Greece and 8½% in Portugal, both considerably higher than the figure of only just over 2% in the rest of the Community.

Within services, the importance of employment in retailing, as with clothing and footwear, seems inversely related to the level of economic development, accounting for a comparatively small proportion of jobs in Denmark and France — 7% and 8½%, respectively — as against over 10% in the rest of the Community, and over 11% in Spain, Italy and the UK. Part of the explanation for this difference — but only part — may lie in the fact that a relatively high proportion of the population are in employment in Denmark and France and, therefore, a given number of people working in retailing to service local needs will represent a smaller share of the workforce here than in Spain and Italy. In the UK, the high level of employment in this sector might be partly explained by the extensive use of part-time workers, average hours worked per person being over 10% lower than the Community average.

Nevertheless, while retailing has made a major contribution to job growth in the past, there are clearly limits on it as a source of future employment creation as economic development takes place and more efficient ways of selling spread.

Employment in other basic services, such as hotels and restaurants, also varies between countries, partly because of variations in employment rates and partly because of the comparative importance of tourism. The share in this sector was, therefore, relatively high in 1992 in

181 Distribution of employment by NACE 2-digit sector in the Member States, 1992

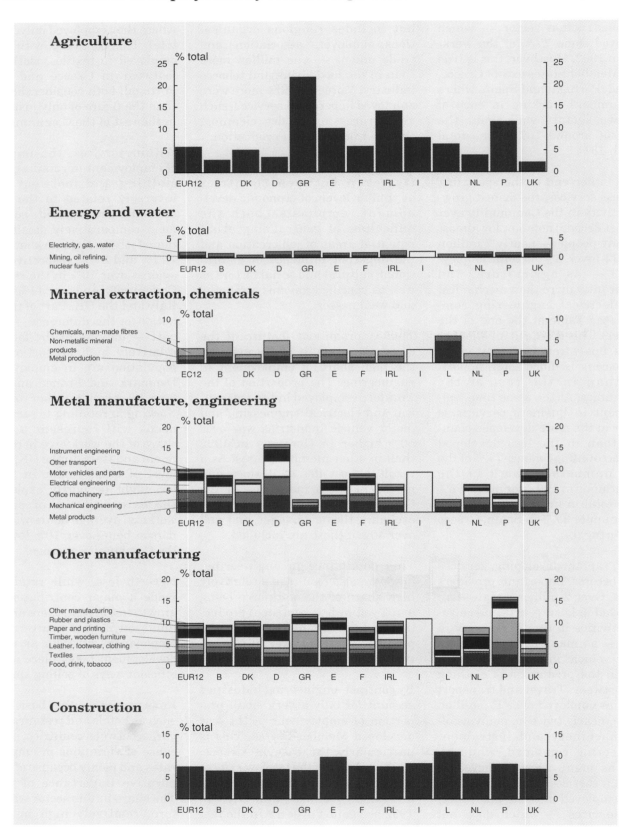

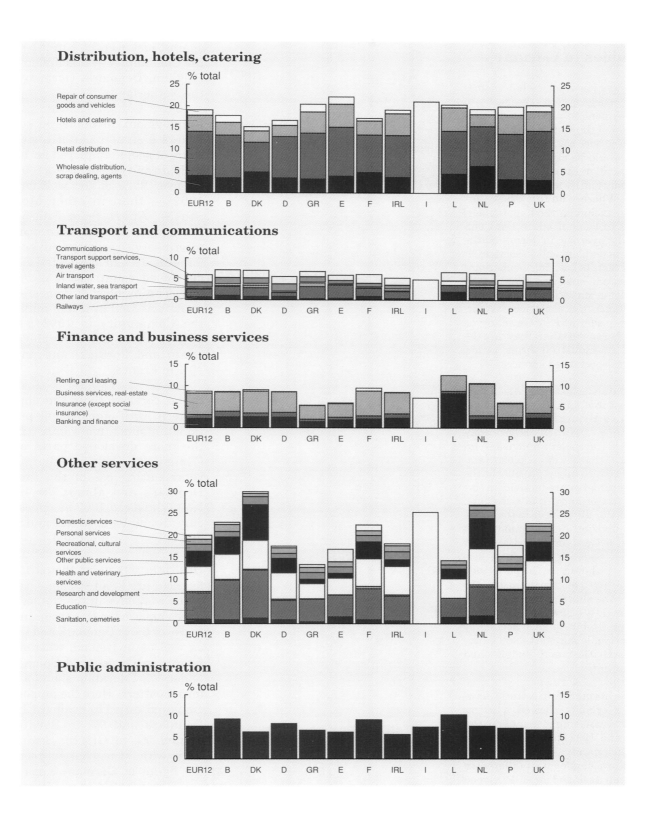

Employment in services in Germany

Germany has a somewhat anomalous position in respect of employment in services. The proportion of the workforce employed in the service sector is much lower than would be expected given the advanced nature of the German economy and its level of income per head. Whereas on this basis, Germany (excluding the new Länder) ought to be well above the Community average in terms of the share of employment in services, it is, in fact, below. It is sometimes suggested, however, that this is simply a statistical illusion and that much the same jobs are actually performed in Germany as elsewhere, but that they are located in industrial firms rather than in specialised services.

The data suggest otherwise. They suggest that, in a real sense, fewer service activities are performed in Germany than in other comparable European countries — or, at least, that fewer people are employed which might possibly be the result of higher productivity in services in Germany than elsewhere. The major differences in the sectoral division of employment between Germany and the latter are not so much in business services — where the jobs performed may be hived off from industry, but where the share of employment is only slightly below the Community average — but in such sectors as education, leisure, arts and cultural activities and hotels and restaurants.

In the former two sectors, however, Germany showed a larger expansion in employment between 1985 and 1992 than in the rest of the Community, so narrowing the structural employment differences between itself and other developed Community economies.

Spain, Greece and Ireland — 5% or more of total employment, as against just over $3\frac{1}{2}$% in the rest of the Community — and under 3% in Belgium, Denmark, Germany and the Netherlands.

Employment in domestic service follows a similar pattern with the share of people employed far higher in Spain and Portugal — accounting for over $2\frac{1}{2}$% of the workforce in 1992 — than in other Member States. Apart from Spain and Portugal, only in France does domestic service employment account for over 1%. In most of the more developed countries, it is $\frac{1}{2}$% or less. The number of domestic servants was well over one million in the Community in 1992, almost 40% of these being employed in Spain and Portugal and another 20% in France.

Social services show the opposite pattern, with employment proportionately much more important in the more developed parts of the Community than in other parts, representing 8% of the total in Denmark and almost 7% in the Netherlands in 1992 as opposed to only around 1% in Greece and Spain and only $\frac{1}{2}$% in Portugal.

Healthcare is similar, though the differences are less extreme. Over 8% of the workforce in the Netherlands were employed in this sector in 1992 and over 6% in Denmark and France as well as in Ireland, whereas the figures in Greece and Spain were under 4%. Education shows a more mixed pattern. Here the proportions employed varied from almost 11% in Denmark and 9% in Belgium to around 5% in Greece, Spain and Italy, with, somewhat surprisingly, the figure in Germany apparently being under $4\frac{1}{2}$% (see Box for a general discussion of the low employment in services in Germany).

In other service activities, apart from transport, there is also some relationship of employment to the level of economic development, but with important exceptions. In both banking and insurance, the share of employment was, not unsurprisingly, below the Community average in Greece, Spain and Portugal. However, it was also below the average in France, and above the Community average in Ireland. In leisure, arts and cultural activities, the relative numbers employed were relatively high in Denmark and the Netherlands, but most especially in the UK, and low in Belgium and Germany as well as in Portugal, while in Greece and Spain, they were around the Community average. In travel agencies, employment was relatively high in Belgium and Germany, but also in Greece, and relatively low in Spain and Portugal as well as in France.

In estate agencies, employment is also low in Spain and Portugal as well as in Greece and Ireland, but it is similarly low in Germany and Belgium. On the other hand, it is high in France and, most especially in the UK. Indeed, this country had over 300,000 people employed in this activity in 1992, as much as in the rest of the Community put together and almost as many as were employed in the whole of the air transport industry in the Community. Such differences clearly reflect institutional and market differences, as well as differences in patterns of home ownership.

Areas of job growth in recent years

Changes in employment over the period 1985 to 1992 reflect well established, long-term, structural changes which have resulted, in the

Community as in other developed parts of the world, in services accounting for the major share of total employment and agriculture and industry a progressively smaller share.

In order to compare net job creation during periods of economic recovery and periods of recession, the change is analysed first, between 1985 and 1990 when the total numbers employed in the Community as a whole grew by almost 2% a year and, secondly, between 1990 and 1992 when numbers employed remained virtually unchanged.

It should be emphasised, however, that the scale of relative rates of net job creation in these two periods varied significantly between Member States, partly reflecting differences in the timing of the economic cycle. The difference between the two periods was much

more marked, for example, in the UK, where the downturn started earlier and was more pronounced than in other countries, than in Germany or Belgium, where there was significant growth in 1991.

Most of the growth in the number of jobs between 1985 and 1990 occurred in services. Numbers employed in services went up, on average, by over $2\frac{1}{2}$% a year, while in the rest of the economy they rose by less than $\frac{1}{2}$% a year — a small increase in industry being more than offset by the decline in agriculture. However, there were large variations in the rate of change within industry and services as a whole, as well as between different parts of the Community.

In half of the Member States, services accounted for all, or more than all, of the total increase in employment between 1985 and 1990. In

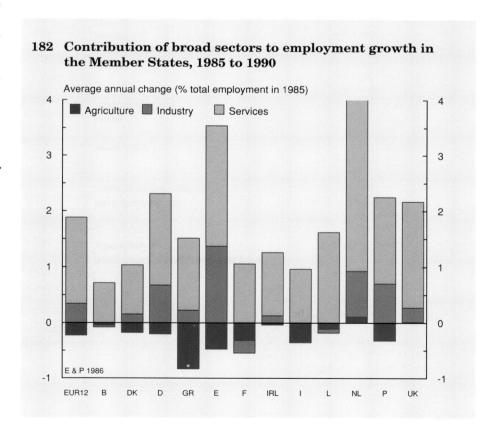

182   Contribution of broad sectors to employment growth in the Member States, 1985 to 1990

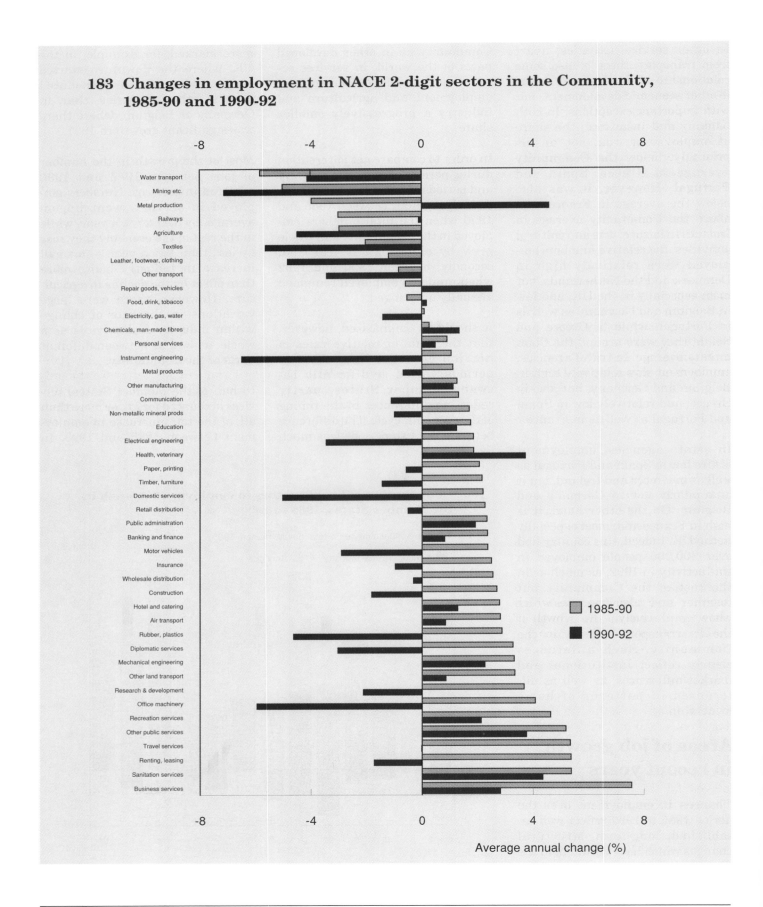

183 Changes in employment in NACE 2-digit sectors in the Community, 1985-90 and 1990-92

Average annual change (%)

1985-90
1990-92

Ireland and the UK, services were responsible for around 90% or more of net job creation, in Germany, the Netherlands and Portugal, for 80% and in Spain for 70% (Graph 182). These last two countries, were the only ones, apart from Germany, in which over 30% of the new jobs created were in industry — in Portugal, 35%, in Spain, 44%.

Over the Community as a whole, business services showed the largest rate of increase in employment between 1985 and 1990 — 7¹/₂% a year — and made the largest contribution to employment growth. On average, almost one in five new jobs were created in this sector with all Member States experiencing substantial gains. Similarly, the numbers employed in social services in sanitary services, and in the arts, leisure and cultural sector increased by around 5% a year (Graph 183).

Other service activities experiencing high employment growth over this period included travel agents and estate agents — with rates of over 5% a year on average — research and development institutes and road transport (buses, coaches and lorries) — with rates of around 3¹/₂% a year. Together, these service sectors were also the one which showed relatively high growth of employment in each of the Member States over this period, the only exception being in Greece (Graph 184).

On the other hand, the largest sector of employment decline over this period was also in the services area, namely in sea and inland water transport where the numbers employed fell by almost 6% a year between 1985 and 1990. Similarly there was a general fall in employment in railways, even in countries like Denmark, the Netherlands and

France where there was significant construction of new lines, with the decline averaging 3% a year over the Community as a whole. Numbers employed in the repair of cars and consumer goods also went down, if by much less — the decline averaging ¹/₂% a year — though falls in the more developed countries were offset by increases in Spain and Greece.

The rate of job loss in the two transport areas was comparable with that in mining, iron and steel production and agriculture, all of which showed falls of 3% a year or more over the Community as a whole during this period with few countries escaping significant job losses. Not all Member States followed this pattern, however, and in both the Netherlands and the UK, employment in agriculture went up between 1985 and 1990. Indeed, the

UK was the only country to show a rise in employment in iron and steel (which may partly reflect the massive fall which occurred in earlier years).

Other industries showing job losses over the 1985 – 1990 period of high overall employment growth were clothing and footwear — though not in Spain and Greece where employment rose considerably (by 4% and 5% a year, respectively), textiles (though not in Ireland) and the manufacture of ships and trains (though not in Greece, Ireland and the UK).

These, together with food, drink and tobacco — where the fall in numbers of jobs was far from general — however, were the only industrial sectors where the numbers employed decreased over this period. In no less than 14 out of the

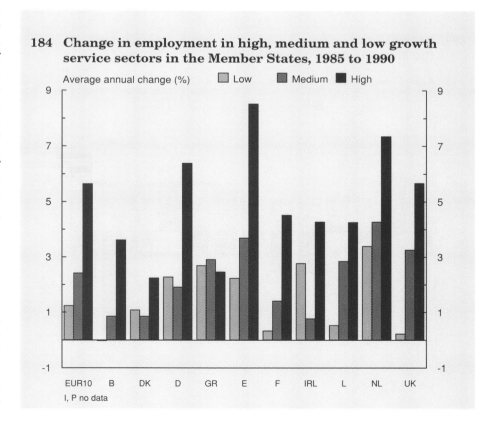

184   Change in employment in high, medium and low growth service sectors in the Member States, 1985 to 1990

Average annual change (%)   □ Low   ■ Medium   ■ High

EUR10   B   DK   D   GR   E   F   IRL   L   NL   UK

I, P no data

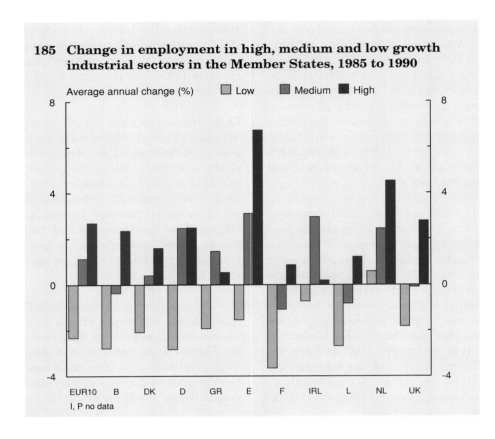

185 Change in employment in high, medium and low growth industrial sectors in the Member States, 1985 to 1990

Average annual change (%)   Low   Medium   High

EUR10   B   DK   D   GR   E   F   IRL   L   NL   UK

I, P no data

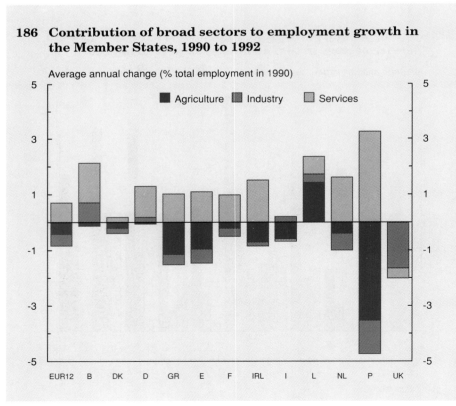

186 Contribution of broad sectors to employment growth in the Member States, 1990 to 1992

Average annual change (% total employment in 1990)

Agriculture   Industry   Services

EUR12   B   DK   D   GR   E   F   IRL   I   L   NL   P   UK

22 industrial sectors, employment increased. Indeed, the rate of net job creation in office machinery and mechanical engineering averaged 3% a year across the Community — more than in many services — and the rubber and plastics and construction industry averaged only just under this figure. Ireland was the only country which experienced a significant decline in construction employment.

Together with the motor vehicle, paper and printing and wood and timber industries — in all of which the numbers employed rose by over 2% a year between 1985 and 1990 — these 7 high employment growth industries were responsible for almost a quarter of the total increase in employment in the Community during the recovery years. Construction alone was responsible for over 10% of the increase for the Community as a whole and accounted for almost 25% of the substantial expansion in jobs which occurred in Spain, and for around 20% of the relatively small rises in employment that occurred in France and Belgium.

Greece and Ireland apart, the relative pattern of employment change across industries, as for service sectors, was broadly similar in all Member States over this period (Graph 185).

Taking together all the 14 industrial sectors where employment rose, their contribution to employment growth over this period averaged 30%. In Germany and Spain it was over 40%. Although this is clearly less than the contribution of services, it is nevertheless a significant element in job creation, the extent of which tends to be under-recognised.

1990–1992 recession period

A major change in the relative contribution of industry and services, took place, however, in the post-1990 recession. Between 1990 and 1992, while the total numbers employed remained virtually constant over the Community as a whole, employment in industry fell significantly, reinforcing the continued decline in agriculture. The two sectors together were responsible for a reduction in employment of almost 1% a year over these two years, offsetting all of the net job creation in services during the period (Graph 186).

Only Belgium, Germany, Luxembourg, Ireland and Italy showed any employment growth at all in industry over this period. Only in the first three countries was this large enough to compensate for the loss of jobs in agriculture. Only in Belgium, where the overall rate of employment growth was actually higher during these two years than it had been over the preceding five — the only country apart from Luxembourg where this was true — did the increase in industrial jobs average more than $\frac{1}{2}$% a year.

Only five of the 22 industrial sectors showed any increase in employment at all between 1990 and 1992, and two of these — iron and steel and food, drink and tobacco — were industries which had shown a loss of jobs during the growth period. All of the industrial sectors in which employment rose by over 2% a year over the preceding five years (apart from mechanical engineering where employment continued to increase) experienced substantial job losses. This was particularly so in the production of office machinery, where

the numbers employed fell sharply — by an average of 6% a year.

While most industrial sectors showed a reduction in employment between 1990 and 1992, the reversal of fortunes was most marked in what had been the high employment growth sectors between 1985 and 1990 (those with annual growth of over 2%). These sectors experienced an average decline in employment of $1\frac{1}{2}$% a year in the later period, as compared with an average growth of over $2\frac{1}{2}$% a year during the years of high economic growth. By contrast, the medium employment growth industrial sectors (all others with positive employment gains) went from an average growth of 1% a year to a fall of just under $1\frac{1}{2}$% and the declining sectors from an average reduction of $2\frac{1}{2}$% a year to one of over 3%.

In half of the 10 Member States for which comparisons over time are possible — Belgium, Germany, Spain, Ireland and, above all, Luxembourg — employment in what had been the high growth industrial sectors during 1985 to 1990 continued to increase between 1990 and 1992 (Graph 187). Only in Belgium and Luxembourg, however, did the rise average more than 1% a year, while employment in Germany grew by more over this period in the slow employment growth industries — in iron and steel, in particular — than in the high growth ones.

Among the other five Member States in which employment in high growth industries fell, the UK and the Netherlands registered a decline of over 5% a year in these sectors — more than in other industries in which over the preceding

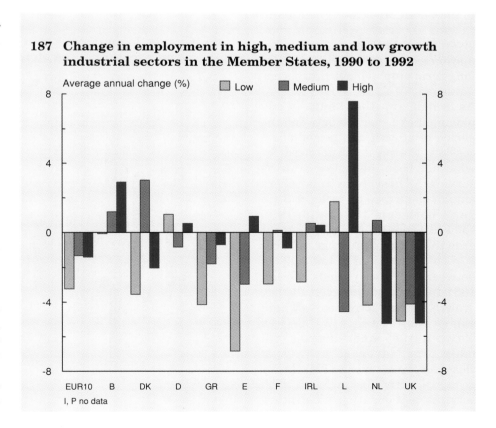

187   Change in employment in high, medium and low growth industrial sectors in the Member States, 1990 to 1992

Average annual change (%) — Low — Medium — High

EUR10   B   DK   D   GR   E   F   IRL   L   NL   UK

I, P no data

five years there had been much less of an increase in employment or a reduction.

Unlike the industrial sectors, employment in services continued to increase in the Community between 1990 and 1992. Only 9 of the 25 service activities showed a fall in employment over this period, and two of these — sea and inland waterways transport and railways — had also shown a decline during the growth period. On the other hand, three of these 9 sectors — estate agents, travel agents and research and development institutes — had been among the 8 fastest growing sectors in terms of jobs between 1985 and 1990. Moreover three more of the 9 — retail distribution, insurance and domestic services — had experienced employment growth of more than 2% a year over the preceding five years. The remaining area of service activity in which employment in the Community fell — communications — is of particular note, given the significance of the information technological revolution for long-term employment prospects.

As in industry, the change in employment experienced between the period of growth and period of recession was most pronounced for what had been the fastest growing services. Those activities where employment rose by at least 3% a year between 1985 and 1990 showed a reduction in employment growth from an average of over $5^{1}/_{2}\%$ a year to one of under $2^{1}/_{2}\%$ between the two periods (Graph 188). In contrast, however, the low growth service activities — where employment rose by 2% or less between 1985 and 1990 — still maintained average growth of close to $1^{1}/_{2}\%$ a year. This latter group of activities includes such services as education, healthcare

and personal services (where the growth in demand is likely to be relatively stable over time — unless governments choose to vary their expenditure as part of fiscal policy).

The pattern of change among different Member States shows a mixed picture. In most countries, what had been the fastest growing activities between 1985 and 1990 showed the largest fall in the rate of job creation between 1990 and 1992. However, three of the countries where services are relatively underdeveloped — Spain, Greece and Germany — experienced a continuing increase in employment in these activities on a significant scale (by $2^{1}/_{2}\%$ a year in Greece, over 3% in Germany and 4% in Spain). Such services continued to increase, however, in Belgium and France where services are already highly developed.

At the same time, in most Member States — the exceptions being Ireland, Luxembourg and the UK — there was a continuing increase in employment in what had previously been low growth services. In five Member States, the increase was $1^{1}/_{2}\%$ a year or more.

In most Member States, business services continued to be an important area of job growth between 1990 and 1992, though in the two countries where such activities had developed by most in the past, the Netherlands and the UK, employment fell. By contrast, retailing, which had been the second largest provider of jobs between 1985 and 1990, suffered a reduction in employment in half of the countries and an overall decline in all Member States taken together, presumably reflecting the slowdown in consumer spending. On the other hand, employment in public

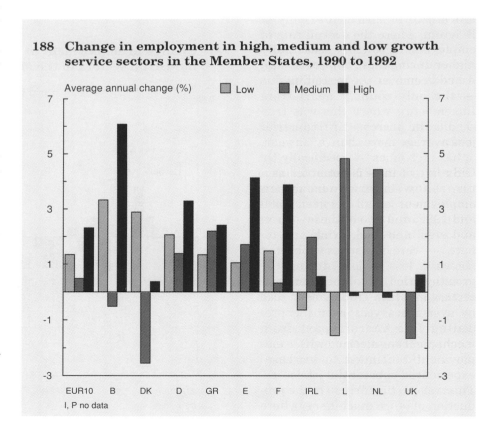

188   Change in employment in high, medium and low growth service sectors in the Member States, 1990 to 1992

administration, education, health-care and communal services — together responsible for around 30% of net job creation in the earlier period — continued to expand in most parts of the Community, with only few exceptions (public administration in Belgium, Germany and Denmark, education in Luxembourg, Ireland and the UK, communal services in Greece and Ireland).

Employment growth 1970 to 1991 in the Community and elsewhere

It is not possible to compare employment developments between the Community and other parts of the world at the same level of detail as above. However, broader sectoral data suggest that the general areas of job growth have been much the same in the Community as in the US and Japan as well as in the EFTA countries and, indeed, that the pattern of employment change is very similar in these different economies.

The most striking difference between the Community and the other economies — specifically the US and Japan — is not in terms of the sectors in which employment has risen or fallen, but in the scale of the job losses which have occurred in declining sectors.

Between 1970 and 1991, growth of employment in the Community averaged just over $1/2$% a year. This was marginally below the growth rate in EFTA countries, only slightly above half the rate in Japan and a third of the rate in the US.

All of the net addition to jobs, and more, in the Community over these

21 years was in services, which alone added over 1% a year to total employment (Graph 189). This, however, was precisely the same in the EFTA countries and Japan, where other sectors were responsible for a small decline in employment. In the US, services were an even larger contributor to the rise in employment (adding almost 2% a year to the total in work), but there was also a slight increase in employment in the rest of the economy.

Of the additional jobs created in services in the Community, half were in communal and personal services — education, healthcare and public administration as well as such jobs as hairdressing or cleaning (labelled "non-market services" in the graph). This was also the case outside the Community. In the US, they alone added almost 1% a year to total employment growth

over the period, in the EFTA countries and Japan, around $1/2$% a year, as in the Community (Graph 190).

How far the fact that a higher proportion of such jobs are performed in the public sector in the Community and the EFTA countries than in the US has contributed to the difference in employment growth is a matter of debate. In Japan, the public sector is an even less important supplier of these services than in the US, yet growth of employment was marginally lower in this area than in Europe.

Employment in private health services expanded particularly fast in the US, while jobs in personal and domestic services also grew much more than in Europe.

As well as the scale of the additional employment created in services, there are equally important

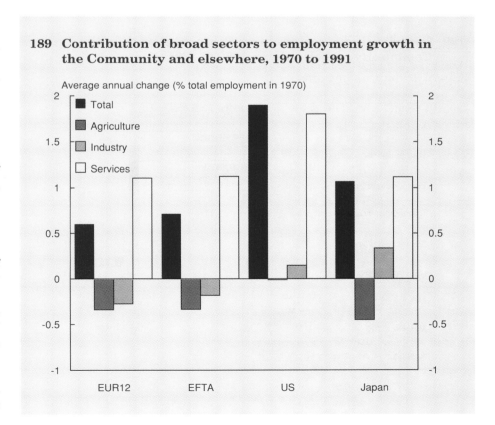

189 Contribution of broad sectors to employment growth in the Community and elsewhere, 1970 to 1991

Average annual change (% total employment in 1970)

Legend:
Total
Agriculture
Industry
Services

EUR12   EFTA   US   Japan

differences in other areas contributing to the higher rate of job creation in the US than in Europe. In particular, whereas employment in agriculture, which was already relatively low, remained broadly unchanged over the last two decades, it fell significantly and continuously in both the Community and the EFTA countries — in the former case, causing an average loss of jobs of over 400 thousand a year or well over 8 million over the 21 years as a whole. In Japan, the decline in agriculture was even more significant, equivalent to a reduction in total employment of almost $\frac{1}{2}$% a year.

In Japan, however, employment in industry expanded by almost as much as that in agriculture fell. Industrial employment also rose in the US. In the Community, however, as in the EFTA countries, employment in industry declined to

add to the jobs lost in agriculture. In these two sectors combined, therefore, the overall job loss in the Community averaged some 750 thousand a year, making a total reduction of almost 16 million between 1970 and 1991. Although there was an increase in service jobs averaging almost 1.4 million a year, which more than offset this reduction, this still left overall employment growth in the Community lower than in Japan and markedly less than in the US.

Job losses in agriculture and industry have, therefore, been a major cause of low employment creation in the Community over the past 20 years or so. The fact that such jobs were predominantly private sector ones has been responsible, in an arithmetic sense, for the observed tendency for the public sector to become the main source of net job creation. However, employment

growth in services emanating from the private sector — in financial and business services and distribution and catering, in particular — has been more significant in both the Community and the US than the growth in communal services.

Changes in sectoral growth between 1970 and 1991

Dividing the years between 1970 and 1991 into three sub-periods, 1970 to 1980, 1980 to 1985 and 1985 to 1991, provides further insight into employment growth under different economic conditions. The overall rate of job creation in the Community was negative in the period 1980 to 1985 and almost twice as high between 1985 and 1991 ($1\frac{1}{2}$% a year) as between 1970 and 1980.

The importance of communal and personal services as a source of employment growth between 1970 and 1991 was common throughout the Community. In the more developed countries, in particular, this was the main area of net job creation. In each of the three periods, moreover, communal and personal services generated much the same expansion of employment (Graph 191).

In both the US and the EFTA countries, where employment growth was more stable over the period as a whole than in the Community, there was slightly more variation in the contribution of communal and personal services to the overall rise in employment — in the US, it ranged from just over $\frac{1}{2}$% a year in the first half of the 1980s to 1% a year in the 1970s.

Financial and business services also represented a relatively consistent

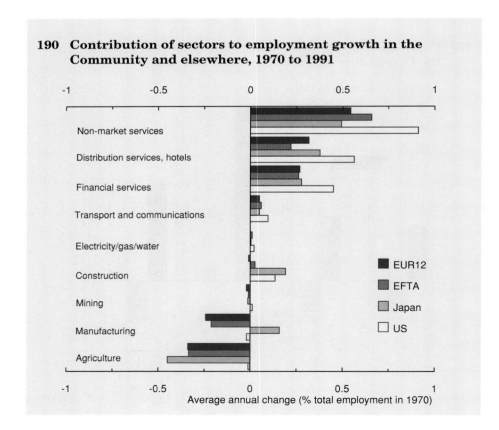

190   Contribution of sectors to employment growth in the Community and elsewhere, 1970 to 1991

Average annual change (% total employment in 1970)

EUR12
EFTA
Japan
US

191   Contribution of sectors to employment growth in the Community, EFTA, Japan and US, 1970 to 1991

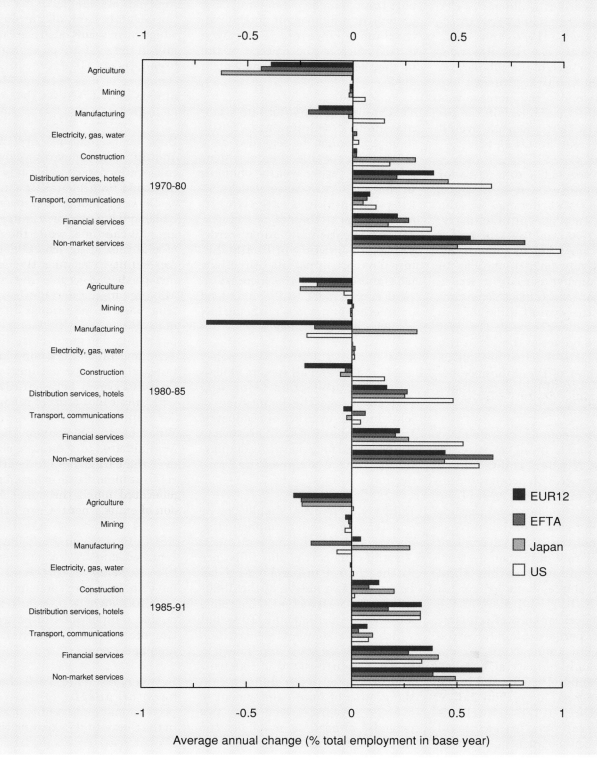

Average annual change (% total employment in base year)

source of employment creation in each of the three sub-periods in the Community. As in Japan, it was more important between 1985 and 1991 than earlier, while in the US, its main contribution to growth occurred between 1980 and 1985. Distribution and catering also generated jobs in each of the sub-periods in all of the countries, though, like financial services, the increase was larger in the Community in the period 1985 to 1991 when the overall rate of job creation was higher.

However, the major difference for the Community between the last period and the earlier ones was the change in employment in industry. Between 1985 and 1991, it was a source of employment growth, albeit relatively small, whereas in both the earlier periods it was a source of job loss. Indeed, some two-thirds of the overall difference in net job creation between the first and second halves of the 1980s can be explained by this turn-around as can over half of the difference between the second half of the 1980s and the 1970s.

This applies equally to individual Member States. In all cases — except the Netherlands, where employment growth accelerated significantly in the latter part of the 1980s, partly for statistical reasons — the major source of the increase was a higher rate of net job creation (or a lower rate of net job destruction) in industry, rather than increased employment growth in services. In Italy and the UK, the improved performance of industry in the later period explains all of the difference in employment growth (even though industrial employment still fell in the UK) and in the other countries, more than half of the difference. In the Netherlands — the only exception to this general pattern — employment in industry

also contributed significantly to the overall acceleration in job creation, but the numbers employed in services, many of them working part-time, jumped even more. (The growth in employment in the Netherlands, however, is partly a consequence of the change in the method of defining employment in 1987.)

This has implications for future employment developments. While industry cannot be regarded as a major *direct* source of employment growth in future years, changes in this sector are, nevertheless, likely to make a significant contribution to the net rate of overall job creation. In other words, although services will continue to provide most, if not all, of the new jobs, the extent of the increase in total employment will also depend on whether or not jobs are being lost elsewhere in the economy.

This implies, in turn, that policy needs to focus on all sectors of activity when attempting to identify and encourage the generation of jobs. Indeed, even within industry, there are substantial differences in the potential for generating employment between growing and declining sectors.

Industry, moreover, should not be equated solely with manufacturing, even though it is the major element. A significant part of the difference in the change in employment between the two halves of the 1980s was due to construction, which shed jobs between 1980 and 1985 but which was a source of job creation in the following six years. Indeed in Spain, the turn-round in construction accounted for a difference in the growth of total employment of over 1% a year between these two periods, almost as much as the turn-round in manufacturing.

Changing skill needs in the Community

Analyses of changes in the occupational structure of employment which have occurred in the Community in the past are possible only in broad terms. Differences in the structure of jobs between Member States cannot, as yet, be reliably identified.

Data on occupations are limited, and difficult to develop, partly because many jobs, especially those involving multiple tasks, cannot be easily categorised. Moreover, jobs which did not exist before are emerging all the time, while the nature of many existing jobs changes as production techniques alter, and as new goods and services are created. Making comparisons between countries adds an additional difficulty, not only because of problems of comparability between classification systems, but also because perceptions of particular jobs may not be the same, even between countries with similar systems of production.

What is possible given the data available is to examine changes over the period 1983 to 1991 in the relative importance of broad groups of occupations in Member States. Although these data are based on an old system of classification (ISCO 68), which has since been replaced, and are not very comparable *between* countries, they, nevertheless, give some indications of shifts *within* countries. They also enable comparisons to be made of the occupational distribution of men and women.

Between 1983 and 1991, the numbers of people classified as professional and technical workers in the Community expanded by over $2^{1}/_{2}$% a year. This compares with a growth of total employment of just over 1% a year and is significantly more than for any other broad occupational group. During the same period, employment of agricultural workers fell by some $2\frac{1}{2}$% a year, while the number of production and transport workers increased by only $\frac{1}{2}$% a year.

Professional and technical jobs, which accounted for only 15% or so of the total number of jobs in 1983 were, accordingly, responsible for around 40% of the overall rise in employment over the period. By contrast, production and transport jobs, comprising the largest single occupational group — a third of the total — accounted for under 15% of the rise.

The implied shift in occupational structure was, therefore, significant and conforms with expectations — in the sense that there was a marked growth in more skilled relative to less skilled jobs. A further dimension to the picture, however, is revealed if the period is divided into sub-periods according to the overall growth of employment — specifically, the low growth years between 1983 and 1985 and again between 1990 and 1991 and the high growth years between 1985 and 1990.

In both periods of low employment and output growth, the shift in jobs towards professional and technical workers was much more pronounced than in the high growth years. Between 1983 and 1985, the increase in numbers in this occupational group occurred at only a slightly lower rate than in the subsequent five years and accounted for 65% of all the additional jobs created in the Community. In 1991, this group was responsible for all of the increase in employment and more, the numbers expanding by almost 2% as against only a margi-

nal rise in total employment. By contrast, production and transport jobs declined in both periods (Graph 192).

Between 1985 and 1990, on the other hand, while professional and technical jobs increased at a faster rate than for other groups, the difference was much less marked. Professional and technical workers accounted for only just over 30% of the overall increase in employment in this period — about the same proportion as clerical and related jobs. Moreover, jobs for production and transport workers expanded by 1% a year over this period and were responsible for over 20% of all additional jobs created. At the same time, the employment of both sales and service workers increased at a higher rate than the total. The shift in occupational structure towards higher skilled jobs was, therefore, significantly less pronounced in the

high growth years than in the low growth years.

Much the same pattern is evident within most individual Member States. With the exception of Ireland and the Benelux countries, the relative expansion of professional and technical jobs was far larger in periods of low employment growth than between 1985 and 1990 (Graph 193). In both the two low growth periods, a substantial majority of the jobs created in Germany and France, for example, were for professional and technical workers whereas in the high growth period, they accounted for well under 40%. Similarly, employment among production and transport workers fell in most countries in both low growth periods, but increased between 1985 and 1990 in all but Denmark, France and Luxembourg — where, in each case,

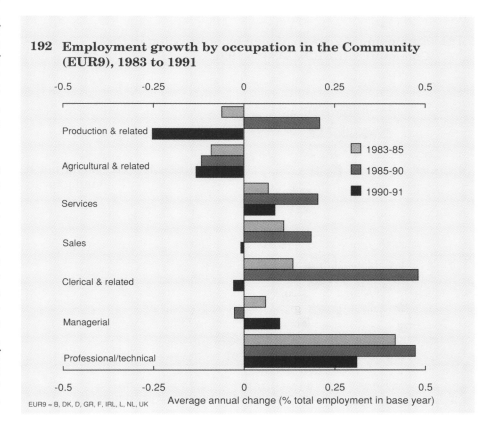

192 Employment growth by occupation in the Community (EUR9), 1983 to 1991

Legend: 1983-85, 1985-90, 1990-91

Occupations: Production & related, Agricultural & related, Services, Sales, Clerical & related, Managerial, Professional/technical

EUR9 = B, DK, D, GR, F, IRL, L, NL, UK   Average annual change (% total employment in base year)

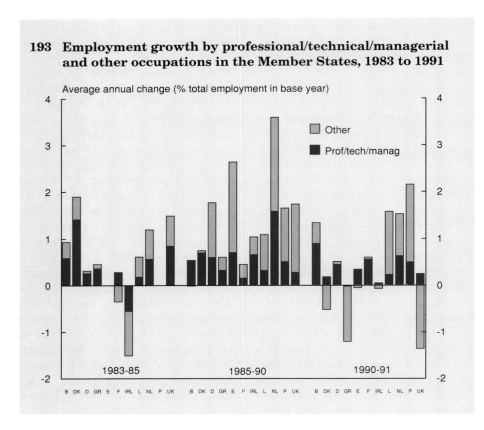

193   Employment growth by professional/technical/managerial and other occupations in the Member States, 1983 to 1991

Average annual change (% total employment in base year)

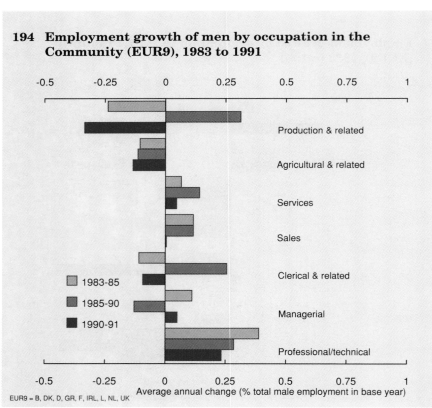

194   Employment growth of men by occupation in the Community (EUR9), 1983 to 1991

EUR9 = B, DK, D, GR, F, IRL, L, NL, UK

Average annual change (% total male employment in base year)

employment growth was much less than the Community average.

Two main points appear to emerge from this evidence. First, that in periods of low levels of economic activity, and low or no employment growth, it is the lower grade jobs which tend to be cut back and consequently the less skilled workers who most suffer job loss. By contrast, in such periods, the most highly skilled jobs are little affected and continue to expand in numbers.

Secondly, in periods of economic recovery and high rates of employment creation, lower skilled jobs account for a relatively high proportion of overall employment growth and less skilled workers benefit most. The scale of the change in the occupational structure of jobs and of the shift towards higher skilled occupations, therefore, seems to depend greatly on the economic climate and the overall rate of net job creation.

Thus, while it is the case that structural changes are likely to increase the demand for highly skilled workers in the Community in future years, the volume of lower skilled jobs is likely to be greatly affected by economic growth and the overall rate of job creation. If growth is low, then the problems faced by less skilled workers of remaining in employment, or of finding new jobs, will become more acute.

Conversely, if rates of growth similar to those attained over the period 1985 to 1990 could be achieved in the future, there may be fewer problems of mismatches between the skills demanded of workers and the jobs available on the labour market than is sometimes claimed.

This assessment should be tempered by the fact that, with the data

available, it is only possible to ana-
lyse changes in broad categories of
occupation. Within these broad
groups, the specific skills offered
and demanded may vary substantially, leaving room for greater
mismatch.

Occupational shifts for men and women

The shift towards more highly skilled jobs and the variation between
high and low growth periods is evident for both men and women,
though it is particularly pronounced for men.

In both the low growth periods,
1983 to 1985 and 1990 to 1991, professional and technical jobs
accounted for all the increase in employment of men which occurred in
the Community. In the high growth
period, between 1985 and 1990,
they accounted for under a third of
net job creation. Indeed, the increase in such jobs was less than
over the preceding two years and
less than for production and transport workers, who experienced a
significant decline in employment
in the other years (Graph 194).

This pattern is repeated in all Member States, except Belgium, where
according to LFS data, employment
of men actually declined slightly between 1985 and 1990. The most
extreme case is the UK, where employment of professional and
technical workers contributed only
just over 20% of the total jobs created for men over the high growth
period, while employment of production and transport workers was
responsible for over a third and clerical workers for almost 40%
(Graph 195).

For women, the growth in professional and technical jobs was

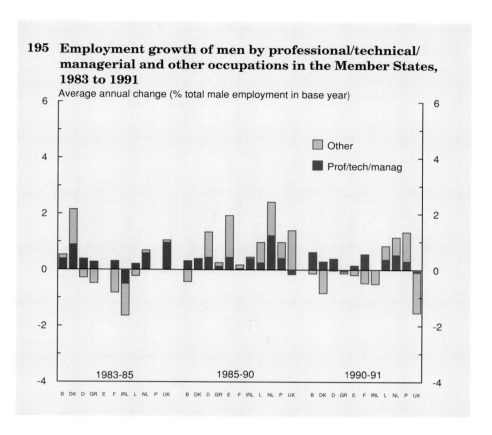

**195   Employment growth of men by professional/technical/
managerial and other occupations in the Member States,
1983 to 1991**

Average annual change (% total male employment in base year)

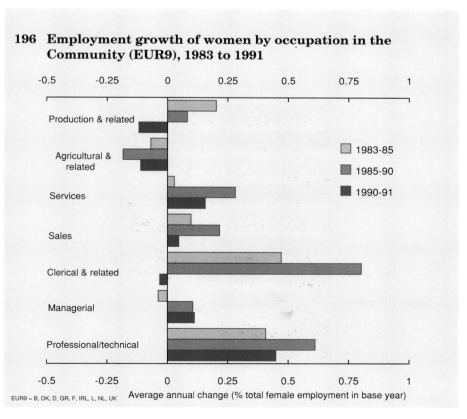

**196   Employment growth of women by occupation in the
Community (EUR9), 1983 to 1991**

EUR9 = B, DK, D, GR, F, IRL, L, NL, UK   Average annual change (% total female employment in base year)

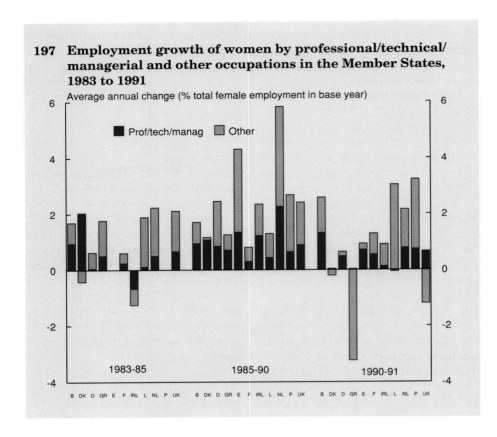

197   Employment growth of women by professional/technical/ managerial and other occupations in the Member States, 1983 to 1991

Average annual change (% total female employment in base year)

Prof/tech/manag   Other

1983-85   1985-90   1990-91

B DK D GR E F IRL L NL P UK   B DK D GR E F IRL L NL P UK   B DK D GR E F IRL L NL P UK

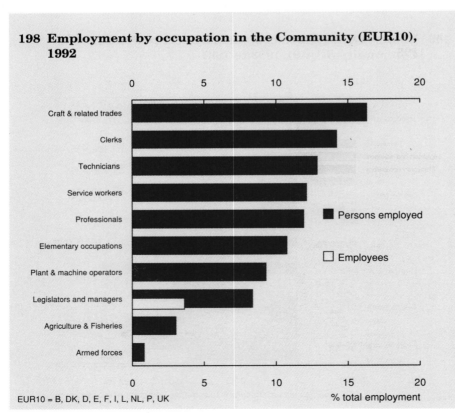

198   Employment by occupation in the Community (EUR10), 1992

Craft & related trades
Clerks
Technicians
Service workers
Professionals
Elementary occupations
Plant & machine operators
Legislators and managers
Agriculture & Fisheries
Armed forces

Persons employed

Employees

EUR10 = B, DK, D, E, F, I, L, NL, P, UK   % total employment

relatively stable over the whole period, contributing around $1/2\%$ a year to the overall increase in employment in the Community. Although such jobs accounted for a higher proportion of employment growth between 1983 and 1985 than over the succeeding five years, the difference was only small (36% as against 32%). Moreover in the earlier, lower growth period as well as in the higher growth period, clerical jobs made the largest contribution to the overall expansion in the employment of women — over 40% in both cases (Graph 196).

In 1991, however, when the employment of women rose by only $1/2\%$ in the Community and fell in the UK, Greece and Denmark, almost all of the net addition to jobs was for professional and technical workers. At the same time, employment of clerical workers — the largest area of new job creation in previous years — declined.

This decline was especially marked in the UK and Denmark, though in the latter, unlike the former, jobs for professional and technical workers were also reduced. In each case, the loss of jobs among clerical workers was responsible for a reduction of over $1/2\%$ in the total employment of women in 1991, a substantial reversal of the growth over the preceding 5 years (Graph 197). In Greece, on the other hand, where employment of women also fell in 1991, this occupational group was the only one to show any increase.

Unfortunately, the change in the system of classification, however beneficial for other purposes, means that it is not possible to examine whether the shifts in the occupational structure of employment evident in 1991 continued in 1992 when employment in the Community declined.

Occupations of men and women

The state of the data does not enable the occupational structure of the workforce to be compared reliably between Member States. Apparent substantial differences between economies with similar sectoral divisions of employment are likely to be at least partly explained by statistical inconsistencies. For the Community as a whole, however, these inconsistencies may offset one another, so that there is more chance of the apparent distribution of employment between occupations being closer to reality.

On the basis of the new international standard system of classifying occupations (ISCO 88), it is possible to see that, in 1992, 8% of those in employment were legislators or managers, more than half of them self-employed, 11% were professionals and 12% technicians. These three categories together, therefore, accounted for almost a third of the total number of people in work (Graph 198).

At the other end of the scale, 10% of those employed were in so-called elementary occupations, 3% were agricultural workers or fishermen, 9% plant or machine operators and 15½% craft and related workers. The rest were classified as clerks (13½%) or service workers (11½%).

Although the proportion of jobs classified as managerial, professional or technical was around the Community average in most Member States, the figure was only around 20% in Italy and Spain, while in France and the Netherlands it was over 40%. It is hazardous to read much into these differences until further investigation has been undertaken, or until the basic data

have been made more comparable between countries.

Cautious comparisons of the distribution of men and women between occupations in the different parts of the Community can, however, be made, since differences in classification between countries can be expected to apply to both sexes. While the absolute proportions of men and women in the various broad occupational groups may, therefore, be subject to a wide margin of error, the figures for the relative proportions are likely to be more reliable.

Over the Community as a whole, a significantly higher proportion of men than women were classified as managers or legislators in 1992 — 9½% as against 6% (Graph 199). Moreover, if the self-employed are excluded, differences in the position of men and women are relatively

similar in all Member States, except the UK, with men more than twice as likely as women to fill such jobs. In the UK, the difference between the two proportions is slightly less than two to one.

For professionals, the proportions for men and women were broadly the same in 1992. Only in Denmark, Germany and France, was the proportion of men classified to this occupational category higher than for women, while in Belgium, Spain and Italy, the figure for women was almost twice that for men. In the case of technicians, on the other hand, these three countries, together with the UK, were the only ones where the proportion of men in such jobs was higher than that of women.

Over the Community as a whole, taking these three categories of occupation together, about the same

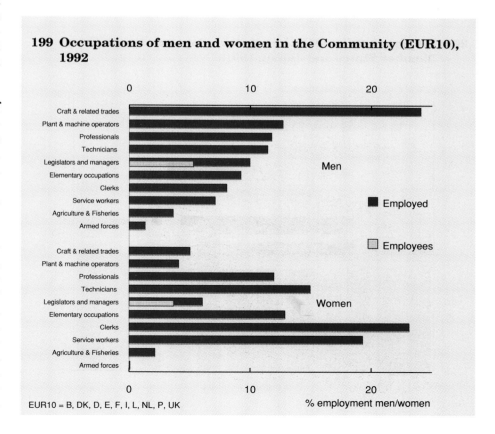

199 Occupations of men and women in the Community (EUR10), 1992

EUR10 = B, DK, D, E, F, I, L, NL, P, UK

% employment men/women

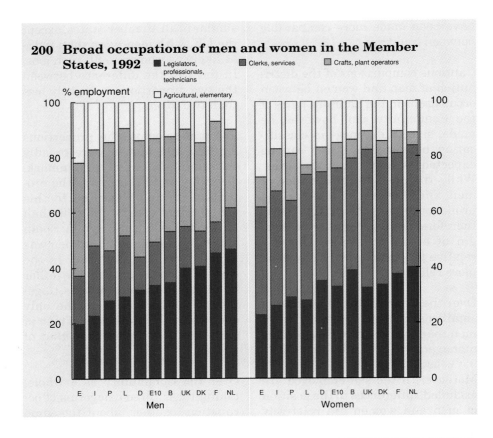

200 Broad occupations of men and women in the Member States, 1992

Legislators, professionals, technicians ■   Clerks, services ■   Crafts, plant operators □   Agricultural, elementary □

% employment

Men: E I P L D E10 B UK DK F NL

Women: E I P L D E10 B UK DK F NL

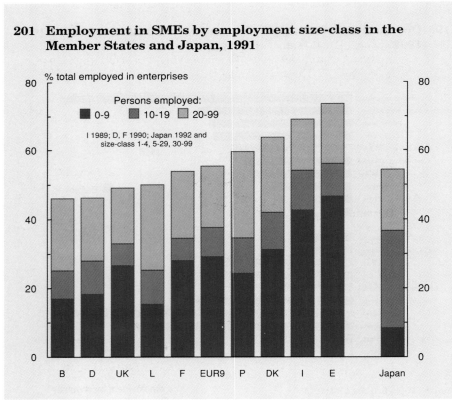

201 Employment in SMEs by employment size-class in the Member States and Japan, 1991

% total employed in enterprises

Persons employed:
0-9 ■   10-19 ■   20-99 □

I 1989; D, F 1990; Japan 1992 and size-class 1-4, 5-29, 30-99

B   D   UK   L   F   EUR9   P   DK   I   E   Japan

proportion of women as men were employed in these relatively high grade jobs in 1992 (Graph 200).

In other activities, the differences are much more pronounced. Much higher proportions of women than men were employed as clerks and service workers — on average about three times higher in all Member States — while the proportion of women in elementary jobs was also much higher throughout the Community (over 40% higher on average). The reverse is true of craft and related workers and plant or machine operators, where men predominate.

Small and medium-sized firms

Most of the people employed in the Community in the private sector work in small firms. These also account for many of the new jobs created, though the lack of reliable and consistent data makes it difficult to quantify their importance for employment growth across the Community. The evidence for one or two countries, however, suggests that they have been responsible for a significant part of the net job creation which has occurred in the private sector over the past decade. The fact that small firms account for much of the employment in the service activities in which a major part of job creation took place — distribution and catering, where they are predominant, other services and finance and business services — serves to confirm their importance.

In 1991, some 55% of those employed in enterprises in the Community (ie essentially excluding the public sector) worked in firms with less than 100 employees, almost 30% in those with under

10 employees (Graph 201). This is about the same proportion as are employed in small firms in Japan (where the data are for slightly different size-classes and for 1992 rather than 1991).

There are, however, significant differences in the importance of small firms between Member States, with the Southern countries tending to have a much higher proportion of their workforce in small firms — especially very small firms — than the Northern countries, with the exception of Denmark. Thus in Spain, 74% of those employed in enterprises in 1991 worked in firms with under 100 employees and over 46% in firms with under 10 employees, while in Italy, the proportions were only slightly lower (69% and 43%, respectively). The share of employment in small firms was also above the Community average in Portugal, where 60% of those employed in enterprises worked in firms of less than 100 employees (Moreover, this figure is likely to be an underestimate of the actual percentage since it relates solely to employees and leaves out of account the self-employed who tend to work disproportionately in small firms — see Box on the data used.)

Apart from Denmark, however, where 64% were employed in firms of less than 100, the share of employment in small firms in each of the Northern Member States for which comparable data are available was below the Community average. In Belgium and Germany, only 46% of those employed in enterprises worked in firms of less than 100 employees (17–18% in firms of less than 10), while in the UK and Luxembourg, the figure was also less than a half. (In Belgium, however, the data are confined to employees and, therefore, as with Portugal are likely to

Data on small firms

The data on which the analysis of small firms is based is derived from the European Statistical System on SMEs, first created by Eurostat in 1990 and constructed from data supplied by national statistical institutes wherever possible, but supplemented from other sources in a number of cases. The database classifies enterprises by size and NACE category. Since there are some differences in definition between countries (as regards the definition of an enterprise, for example) and only a limited degree of harmonisation is possible, there are difficulties in making direct comparisons between Member States. The analysis in the text should, therefore, be regarded as indicative only of the position in each country.

The division of enterprises between employment size-classes involves a certain amount of estimation in some cases to allow for missing figures. The latest available data have been used for each country, which are for 1991 in most cases, 1990 in others and even 1989 for Italy. The fact that the data relate to different years ought not to affect the comparisons materially since the size distribution of enterprises is unlikely to change significantly over a year or two. For the Netherlands, the lack of data for the different size classes and for a number of NACE categories do not allow this country to be included in the analysis. Since there are no data for services in Greece and Ireland, the analysis is, therefore, for 9 Member States for this sector and for 11 for manufacturing.

Total manufacturing is the sum of NACE categories (2-23)+ 3 + 4

Total services is the sum of NACE categories 6 + 7 + 8 + 9. Employment is total person engaged in enterprises classifed to the sector. For more details on the data, see *Enterprises in Europe, Third Report*, Eurostat, 1994.

For Japan, the data are taken from the *Year Book of Labour Statistics, 1992*, published by the Ministry of Labour in Japan.

Country specific notes are as follows:

Belgium: data are for employees only; size-class 0-9 includes 1-9 only.
Denmark: for NACE 7 no data available for 50-99 size-class
Germany: data are for 1990.
Greece: no data for size-class 0-9 and NACE classes 5,7,8 and 9.
France: data are for 1990.
Ireland: data are for 1990; size-class 0-9 includes 3-9 only; no data for NACE 5,6,7,8 and 9.
Italy: data are for 1989; no data for NACE 9; size-class 0-9 includes 1-9 only.
Luxembourg: data are for employees only; size-class 0-9 includes 1-9 only.
Portugal: data are for employees only; size-class 0-9 includes 1-9 only.
Japan: data are for 1992; size classes are 1-4, 5-29 and 30-99.

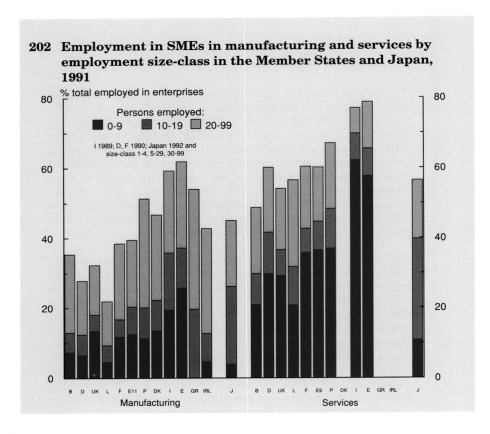

202 Employment in SMEs in manufacturing and services by employment size-class in the Member States and Japan, 1991

% total employed in enterprises

Persons employed:
■ 0-9   ■ 10-19   ■ 20-99

I 1989; D, F 1990; Japan 1992 and size-class 1-4, 5-29, 30-99

Manufacturing   Services

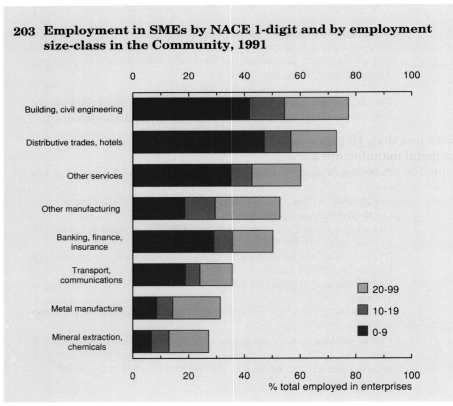

203 Employment in SMEs by NACE 1-digit and by employment size-class in the Community, 1991

Building, civil engineering
Distributive trades, hotels
Other services
Other manufacturing
Banking, finance, insurance
Transport, communications
Metal manufacture
Mineral extraction, chemicals

■ 20-99
■ 10-19
■ 0-9

% total employed in enterprises

understate the importance of small firms.)

Small firms in manufacturing and services

Small firms are much more important in the service sector in the Community than in manufacturing. In 1991, just under 40% of people employed in manufacturing worked in firms with under 100 employees in the Community as a whole (though excluding the Netherlands, for which no comparable data are available) and only 12% in firms with less than 10 (Graph 202). By contrast, 60% of those employed in service enterprises worked in firms with less than 100 employees and 36% in firms with less than 10.

The same phenomenon is also apparent in Japan, though the difference between manufacturing and services is less pronounced. Indeed in Japan, small firms are more important in manufacturing than in the Community — those with less than 100 employees accounting for 45% of employment in the sector in 1992 — and slightly less important in services — where they accounted for 56% of enterprises employment.

Given the apparent dominance of large corporations in Japan, especially in international trade, the significance of small firms in manufacturing may seem surprising. It is, however, a reflection of the prevalence of the practice on the part of large industrial concerns to subcontract substantial parts of the manufacturing process to small companies. By this means, the large concerns are able to achieve the flexibility in production and innovation which comes from small-scale operation whilst retaining the cost advantages of large-scale assembly plants as well as those of large-scale marketing and advertising — together with the long-term benefits of promoting a particular brand-name and image. This combination of flexibility in production and stability in marketing and the pursuit of a corporate strategy has proved highly successful in maintaining Japanese competitiveness on world markets, in the face of the significant cost disadvantage imposed by a strong currency.

Small firms are also important in manufacturing in a number of Community countries, predominantly in the South. In Italy, Spain, Greece and Portugal, firms with less than 100 employees accounted for over half of employment in the sector on the latest data available — in Italy and Spain for around 60%. These figures, however, do not necessarily reflect the same kind of organisation of production as in Japan — though there are some similarities in the Italian case — but more the less developed nature of manufacturing in these countries and the relative weight of industries such as clothing and footwear, where large-scale operation is not so crucial as in engineering.

By contrast, small firms are much less important in manufacturing in Northern Member States, where large firms predominate. In Germany, only 28% of those employed in manufacturing worked in firms with less than 100 employees in 1990 and in Luxembourg, only 22%, while in the UK, the proportion was less than a third.

In services, however, over half of employment in enterprises was in small firms with under 100 employees in all Member States except Belgium (where, as noted above, the figures relate only to employees

and, therefore, understate the share working in small firms). In six of the 9 countries for which data are available — the exceptions being the UK and Luxembourg as well as Belgium — the proportion was 60% or above, in two — Spain and Italy — over 75%.

Within services, small firms, as might be expected, are particularly important in distribution and catering, where those employing under 100 accounted for over 70% of total employment in the sector in the Community as a whole in 1991, with very small firms of under 10 employees accounting for almost half of the total (Graph 203). In the two major growth sectors, "other services", which in this case excludes health and education, and finance and business services, small firms are also significant employers, providing 60% of jobs in the former and 50% in the latter, with 30–35% being employed in very small firms of under 10.

Within manufacturing, in contrast, very small firms are of minor importance. Even in the other manufacturing sector, which includes clothing and footwear as well as food processing, under 20% of employment in 1991 was in firms with less than 10 employees, while in metal manufacture and engineering, the proportion was well below 10%. In the latter two sectors, large firms tend to dominate the industries concerned, 70% of employment or more being in companies with 100 or more employees.

On the other hand, even if very small firms are of minor significance, small firms of under 100 employees provided more than half the jobs in the other manufacturing sector in 1991. Nevertheless, the shift towards service activities is, therefore, in itself likely to be asso-

ciated with an expansion of employment in small firms.

Small firms are most important, however, in construction where those with under 10 employees were responsible for over 40% of employment in the Community in 1991 and those with under 100 for almost 80%.

Numbers employed in NACE 2-digit sectors in the Member States, 1992 (thousands)

1992	EUR12	B	DK	D	GR	E	F	IRL	I	L	NL	P	UK
Total employment	133347.1	3770.3	2636.6	29715.0	3680.0	12457.7	22021.4	1133.9	21015.1	164.6	6613.9	4509.1	25629.6
Agriculture	**7810.3**	**109.2**	**135.9**	**1044.0**	**804.3**	**1256.9**	**1301.5**	**158.2**	**1656,9**	**10.3**	**246.9**	**517.2**	**569.0**
Energy and water	**1877.4**	**44.2**	**21.5**	**463.6**	**50.2**	**119.4**	**253.3**	**13.6**	**288.3**	**2.3**	**58.8**	**41.5**	**520.8**
Mining, oil refining, nuclear fuels	788.4	14.6	2.5	244.6	27.7	77.1	106.1	7.0		0.0	50.6	23.4	234.9
Electricity, gas, water	1033.2	32.6	18.5	274.4	36.6	79.3	188.9	14.0		1.5	41.5	33.2	312.8
Mineral extraction, chemicals	**4826.1**	**194.5**	**55.6**	**1612.1**	**87.3**	**418.6**	**662.4**	**35.6**	**676.0**	**10.4**	**172.0**	**152.8**	**748.9**
Metal production	919.2	55.4	8.3	463.1	16.7	59.1	115.0	1.9		7.9	0.0	29.9	162.1
Non-metallic mineral products	1088.9	37.3	21.1	315.5	30.6	185.1	173.6	15.2		2.0	37.4	58.2	212.8
Chemicals, man-made fibres	1884.1	94.1	24.1	772.5	25.0	136.8	331.2	14.2			99.1	44.6	342.6
Metal manufacture, engineering	**13399.4**	**322.9**	**202.0**	**5533.3**	**111.7**	**933.6**	**1958.0**	**73.4**	**1957.8**	**5.1**	**406.7**	**190.3**	**2506.7**
Metal products	2727.2	90.4	54.9	1170.3	46.8	351.7	545.0	17.3		1.8	102.9	70.6	275.5
Mechanical engineering	2709.4	48.8	68.3	1240.9	14.4	129.1	318.3	12.0		2.1	105.3	30.9	739.4
Office machinery	405.0	15.7	0.0	75.3	0.0	15.8	71.0	8.3		0.0	0.0	0.0	218.9
Electrical engineering	2603.8	75.1	49.5	1076.8	19.2	147.5	477.6	20.5		0.0	109.5	41.9	586.3
Motor vehicles and parts	1766.8	67.9	4.7	818.5	4.6	192.3	301.9	2.5		0.0	30.4	20.2	323.9
Other transport	811.5	14.9	18.1	156.0	25.1	74.9	176.0	3.9		0.0	47.1	21.8	273.8
Instrument engineering	413.4	10.0	4.8	193.6	0.0	22.4	68.2	8.8		0.8	11.6	4.1	89.0
Other manufacturing	**13113.3**	**355.3**	**272.9**	**2852.7**	**438.2**	**1387.8**	**1947.9**	**118.6**	**2296.2**	**11.7**	**560.7**	**716.4**	**2155.1**
Food, drink, tobacco	2857.1	115.7	102.2	622.9	109.1	383.0	646.8	43.7		3.2	172.1	115.5	542.9
Textiles	1059.6	50.2	7.9	269.5	42.6	132.6	210.8	11.0		0.0	18.7	130.5	185.7
Leather, footwear, clothing	1660.3	39.0	22.3	348.9	144.5	293.4	228.2	14.0		0.0	24.3	251.7	293.9
Timber, wooden furniture	1634.7	52.0	45.9	506.9	65.6	241.2	220.6	16.2		0.8	40.5	106.6	338.4
Paper and printing	2105.6	54.2	57.5	667.9	38.6	197.6	349.1	17.4		1.9	168.1	65.1	488.2
Rubber and plastics	988.0	32.0	19.3	334.1	20,3	99.8	196.1	9.2		5.3	37.0	19.5	215.5
Other manufacturing	507.4	12.3	16.6	102.4	174	40.2	96.3	5.5		0.0	98.7	27.4	90.5
Construction	**9977.5**	**246.6**	**163.0**	**2059.0**	**245.9**	**1215.9**	**1675.8**	**85.4**	**1743.7**	**17.7**	**373.4**	**367.6**	**1783.6**
Distribution, hotels, catering	**25348.8**	**670.8**	**403.4**	**4965.5**	**752.2**	**2766.1**	**3783.5**	**221.3**	**4430.0**	**33.3**	**1227.0**	**902.4**	**5193.3**
Wholesale distribution, scrap dealing, agent	5209.6	129.6	125.5	1018.0	117.2	479.3	1035.7	40.9		7.2	395.9	146.2	796.2
Retail distribution	11103.2	367.6	178.6	2817.2	387.4	1403.0	1900.0	108.9		15.9	576.2	468.9	2879.7
Hotels and catering	4105.5	111.7	67.6	765.3	181.3	665.7	715.0	57.0		8.8	176.8	199.7	1156.5
Repair of consumer goods and vehicles	1408.3	61.8	27.3	365.0	65.5	218.2	132.8	9.9		1.1	78.2	87.5	361.0
Transport and communications	**7909.1**	**269.1**	**185.0**	**1654.0**	**250.4**	**734.5**	**1345.8**	**63.2**	**1165.1**	**11.2**	**409.1**	**219.6**	**1602.0**
Railways	761.2	40.2	21.7	253.1	13.0	57.7	196.7	4.4		3.2	31.2	23.3	116.9
Other land transport	2159.7	79.5	54.2	270.9	105.5	388.8	423.1	19.1		2.7	151.7	82.2	582.0
Inland water, sea transport	188.1	7.8	16.3	35.0	31.7	16.9	17.6	2.2		0.0	19.3	7.8	33.6
Air transport	296.8	14.5	9.8	62.9	6.4	30.5	52.0	5.1		1.7	32.1	18.3	65.3
Transport support services, travel agents & brokers	1351.9	57.0	34.3	499.2	46.0	84.4	190.5	9.3		0.0	63.2	32.3	335.8
Communication	1978.1	70.1	48.8	532.9	47.8	156.2	465.2	19.4		3.3	111.6	54.3	468.6
Finance, business services	**11618.0**	**327.5**	**240.7**	**2578.4**	**200.0**	**737.6**	**2098.9**	**102.8**	**1491.8**	**20.4**	**676.7**	**271.7**	**2871.6**
Banking and finance	2559.7	97.9	69.3	751.5	53.5	235.9	466.7	26.6		13.3	129.0	90.6	625.6
Insurance (except social insurance)	1052.5	47.9	23.1	335.6	22.2	78.0	160.3	11.3		1.0	59.1	25.7	288.4
Business services, real estate	5932.2	174.2	135.4	1459.4	120.0	403.8	1314.7	57.1		6.0	479.1	146.7	1635.9
Renting and leasing	570.8	6.6	10.6	31.9	3.9	19.9	157.2	1.6		0.0	9., 8.0	321.6	
Other services	**37041.0**	**1230.2**	**950.8**	**7754.5**	**739.9**	**2887.3**	**6959.1**	**279.7**	**5309.4**	**42.2**	**2189.,**	**1129.7**	**7569.6**
Public administration	8677.1	353.3	165.3	2473.8	246.9	785.0	2024.8	65.1	1571.7	16.,	485.8	324.6	1735.7
Sanitation, cemeteries	1167.0	34.8	32.9	273.9	15.5	192.4	196.6	7.7		2.4	113.1	2.7	295.2
Education	6855.2	335.6	284.9	1305.4	188.8	616.4	1558.0	63.4		7.1	418.9	340.3	1736.5
Research and development	369.7	7.7	4.6	86.5	4.3	10.9	112.9	3.3		0.0	28.9	10.8	99.9
Health and veterinary services	6393.6	212.3	172.1	1754.3	126.0	466.2	1357.5	72.1		7.1	517.1	193.6	1515.2
Other public services	3901.4	148.7	210.0	963.7	34.3	128.4	853.0	16.6		3.4	427.3	20.7	1095.4
Recreational, cultural services	1791.1	45.4	50.4	333.1	56.4	183.5	317.7	21.1		1.5	122.6	46.3	613.3
Personal services	1330.3	59.8	18.8	382.0	42.4	141.4	228.7	15.6		1.6	63.3	69.3	307.5
Domestic services	1108.4	19.1	11.7	121.3	24.4	362.0	293.0	5.3		0.0	10.8	119.6	141.3
Diplomatic services	123.8	13.5	010	60.4	0.0	0.0	17.1	0.6		2.3	0.0	0.0	29.9
Not stated	503.7	5.8	18.1	5.6	4.6	1.7	38.8	4.2	0.0	3.1	298.5	9.8	113.4

Note: Figures for Germany exclude the new Länder

Graphs

Graphs

Map

Sources

The main source of data used is the Statistical Office of the European Communities (Eurostat) and, in particular, the Community Labour Force Survey (LFS). This is the only source of data on employment, unemployment and related variables which is comparable and complete for all Member States. Since it is based on a survey of households and uses a common coding and methodology, it abstracts from national differences in definitions, methods of classification and administrative procedures and regulations.

Data from national sources may, therefore, differ from the figures presented in this report. This is particularly so for unemployment statistics, which in individual countries are based largely on registrations at labour offices (see Chapter 1 for a comparison of the two sources).

The LFS was carried out once every two years between 1973 and 1981 and since 1983 has been conducted annually. The results of the surveys before 1983, however, are not strictly comparable with those conducted since. Moreover, because of the sample nature of the survey, year-to year changes derived from comparing successive surveys tend to be subject to greater error than changes over longer periods of time.

The 1992 results are available for all the Member States, though at the time this report was being prepared, certain data had not been received for Ireland. In some of the graphs, therefore, no data for Ireland could be included or the data are for 1991 instead of 1992.

In a great many cases, the data presented have been specifically extracted from the LFS and, in some cases, from other databases, by statisticians at Eurostat who have given considerable help and advice in the preparation of the report.

The short-term forecasts summarised in Chapter 1 were prepared, on the same basis as those published in the Annual Economic Report, by the Directorate General for Economic and Financial Affairs, which also provided the basic data for the analysis in Chapter 3. The sources used for each of the graphs and the map are listed below. Where appropriate, a more detailed description of the data is presented in the Boxes in the relevant chapters.

Most of the data used in the preparation of *Employment in Europe* can be made available in machine-readable form in a number of standard file formats. Requests for data should indicate the graph or map for which the data are required and should be addressed to:

Commission for the European Communities
DG V/B/1
200 rue de la Loi
B-1049 Brussels

In some cases, a small fee may be charged to cover the preparation costs.

Note

Except where explicitly stated to the contrary, data for Germany presented in this report relate to the former Western part of Germany (ie the Federal Republic as it was before 3 October 1990).

Acknowledgements

Graphs and map: Alphametrics Ltd.
Page layout: Edition & Technology

Graphs

1– 2	OECD Labour Force Statistics, (1993 growth rates OECD Economic Outlook and Directorate General for Economic and Financial Affairs (DGII)); Eurostat, Harmonised unemployment statistics
3–4	Eurostat, Harmonised unemployment statistics
5	Eurostat, Harmonised unemployment statistics; National registered unemployment statistics
6	Eurostat, Community Labour Force Survey

7	Eurostat, Community Labour Force Survey; National registered unemployment statistics
8–14	Directorate General for Economic and Financial Affairs (DGII), Economic Forecasts 1994-1995
15	ILO/UN (Yearbook of Labour Statistics); Eurostat, Community Labour Force Survey"
16–18	ILO/UN (Yearbook of Labour Statistics)
19	ILO/UN (Yearbook of Labour Statistics); Eurostat, Community Labour Force Survey
20–22	ILO/UN (Yearbook of Labour Statistics)
23	ILO/UN (Yearbook of Labour Statistics); Eurostat, Community Labour Force Survey
24–26	ILO/UN (Yearbook of Labour Statistics)
27–54	ILO/UN (Yearbook of Labour Statistics); Eurostat, Community Labour Force Survey
55	Directorate General for Economic and Financial Affairs (DGII); Eurostat, Harmonised unemployment statistics; Eurostat, Community Labour Force Survey
56–88	Directorate General for Economic and Financial Affairs (DGII)
89–155	Eurostat, Community Labour Force Survey
156–162	Eurostat, Net earnings of manual workers in the manufacturing industry in the Community, 1993; Eurostat, Labour Costs, Updating 1989-1991; Directorate General for Employment, Industrial Relations and Social Affairs, MISSOC, Social Protection in the Member States
163–165	Hagenaars, de Vos, Zaidi, "Poverty statistics in the late 80s: research based on micro-data", study for Eurostat
166–171	Eurostat, Harmonised unemployment statistics
172–174	Eurostat, Community Labour Force Survey
175–177	OECD
178–180	OECD, Eurostat, National registered unemployment statistics
181–188	Eurostat, Community Labour Force Survey
189–191	OECD Labour Force Statistics, 1971-1991
192–200	Eurostat, Community Labour Force Survey
201–202	Eurostat, Enterprises in Europe, Third report, preliminary version; Ministry of Labour, Japan, Year Book of Labour Statistics, 1992
203	Eurostat, Enterprises in Europe, Third report, preliminary version

Map

M1	Eurostat, REGIO database

The following topics were analysed in previous issues of *Employment in Europe* :

Employment in Europe 1989

Employment in Europe 1990

Employment in Europe 1991

Employment in Europe 1992

Employment in Europe 1993

European Commission

Employment in Europe — 1994

Luxembourg: Office for Official Publications of the European Communities

1994 — 192 pp. — 21.0 x 29.7 cm

ISBN 92-826-8965-4

Price (excluding VAT) in Luxembourg: ECU 12

COM(94) 381

Documents

Catalogue number: CB-CO-94-418-EN-C

ISBN 92-77-80666-4

The 1994 'Employment in Europe' report is the sixth of a series which is produced annually. It aims to reach a broad readership within the Member States, covering business, trade unions and interest groups as well as governments. It covers a wide range of issues in the employment field, considering the Community as a heterogeneous whole, placing the Community into its world context and discussing the policy implications of the analysis.